d by

Global Publishing

57th Street, 4th fl

ork, NY 10022

Duswalt, Craig

RockStars: Inspirational Stories of Success by 100 of the Top Business Leaders, Athletes, Celebrities, and RockStars in the World

ISBN: 978-1-948181-67-9
eBook: 978-1-948181-68-6

Cover design and Photoshop work: Joe Potter
Interior design: Claudia Volkman
Craig Duswalt Photo : Robert John

www.CraigDuswalt.com
www.RockStarMarketingBackstage.com
www.RockYourLifeWeekend.com
www.RockYourLifeTV.com
www.RockYourLifePodcast.com
www.RockYourLifeChapters.com

DEDICATION

To Everyone — we are ALL RockStars!

Author Photo Credits

Featured Authors

Craig Duswalt — Robert John
Leigh Steinberg —N/A
Russell Hitchcock — Denise Truscello
Dean Cain — N/A
Bo Eason — Kevin Johnston
Natasha Duswalt — Val Westover
Derrick Hall — Jennifer Stewart
Ray Parker Jr. — David Ochoa
Jeffrey Finn — Jeremy Daniel Photography
Dawn Eason — Nick Onken
Garrett Gunderson — Casey McFarland Photography
Captain Charlie Plumb — Paul Mobley
RADM Paul Becker — Sherilyn Kusuda Luke
Les Brown Jr. — Veejay Arokiasomy
Craig Wayne Boyd — Justin Mayotte
Nick Lowery — N/A
Roland Williams — Roland Williams International
George Gankas — Broc Ellinger
Dr. Carol Soloway — Lori Zapata
Tim Gillette — Lori Zapata
Jacqueline Lucien — Joshua Monesson
Paul Finck — Thomas Morlock
Mary Lou Luebbe-Gearhart, Au.D. — JC Penny's
Ceola McClendon — Lance Whitfield

Contributing Authors

Robin Ahn — David Hessemer
Gale Barbe — Val Westover
Janie Becker — Karen Sinclair
Kelly Bennett — Lori Zapata
Eileen Bistrisky — Chara Berk
Christine Blosdale — Lori Zapata
Naomi Carmona-Morshead — Lisa Brook King
Toni Caruso — Janet Barnett
Laura Cipres — N/A
Natalie Clayton — Lori Zapata
Hayden Duswalt — Cornerstone Photography
Ryan Duswalt — Lori Zapata
Tyler Duswalt — Cornerstone Photography
Maryann Ehmann — Gene Ehmann
Vivian R. England — Nikkia Redd
Sandra Estok — N/A
Susie Fabrocini — Susie Speck Mayor/Mitchel Evans
Elayna Fernandez — N/A
Jay Fisgus — Forest Leo
Elle Flores — Michell Garcia
Katrina Garcia — Janet Barnett
Jason A. Gardner — Oren Goldman
Del Gerard — Val Westover
Marsha Gleit — Abbie Brewer
Raven Glover — Khaliq Glover

Ayse Gokdemir — Sengul Kurkoglu
Lisa Gold — Michael Roud
Amber Griffiths — Jessica Daniels
Stephanie Hastings — Karianne Munstedt
Annette Jacobson — Stacy Kaat
Dee Jones — N/A
Eleanor Jones — Lori Zapata
Deborah Kahler — Lori Zapata
Michelle Kavanaugh — Tricia Turpenoff
Linda Kaye — Christina Stuart
Scott A. Kent — Lori Zapata
Shannon Kent — Lori Zapata
Melody Keymer Harper — Val Westover
Leigh Koechner — Melissa Coulier
Linda Kruse – Cutter Cutshaw
Janet Kunst — Christina Stuart Photography
Janie Lidey — Val Westover
Laura Louise — Evelina Pentcheva
Pamela Malinchak — William Malinchak
Sue Mandell — Lori Zapata
Fred McGaver — Tommy Collier
Crystal Meisner — Val Westover
Andrei Mincov — Bob Garlick
Jade Molina — Brittnie Nicole Photography
Shantha Mony — Janet Barnett
Kari Murata — Christina Stuart
Lynn Murphy — Bridgette Marie Balmes
Christina Nepstad — Kitti McMeel
Rachelle Niemann — Laine Torres Photography
TK O'Geary — Lori Zapata
Ivano Ongaro — Ivano Ongaro
George Partsalidis — N/A
Roberta Perry — N/A
Cinda Roffman, C.Ht. — Jodye Alcon
Cali T. Rossen — Frank S. Aragon
Nicole Russell — Nicole Russell
Scott Schneider — Judi Grant-Johnston
Robert Sidell — Val Westover
Frank Stichter — Val Westover
Karen Strauss — Lori Zapata
Stacey Stuart — Lori Zapata
Bonnie Taub — Lana Farfan
Mellissa Tong — N/A
Carol Ann Wagner — Lori Zapata
Pat Walley — Woody Woodward Photography
Paul Wenner — Turhan Caylak
Kelly White — David Sand Photography
Jennifer Williams — Paige Donahue
Charles Woodson — Val Westover
Donald Wright — Fusaye
Lori Zapata — Lori Zapata

TABLE OF CONTENTS

INTRODUCTION

It's the end of an era.

I have produced high-energy, content-rich *RockStar Marketing BootCamps* for the past twelve years. At my first BootCamp I was blessed to have approximately 250 people in the audience. Over the years it continued to grow, and at my April 2019 event, we had more than 700 attendees.

But my last *RockStar Marketing BootCamp* will take place in October 2019.

And everyone is asking why.

Because . . .

I am a marketing coach, and I have more than 200 people in my very popular *Rock-Star Marketing MasterMind*, where I help entrepreneurs grow their business and help them with their marketing. Yet pretty much every time I'm on a coaching call, people ask my advice on how to manage their time, how to find their passion, how to get unstuck, how to stay motivated and inspired—and very little about marketing.

So it made me think.

If people aren't passionate about what they're doing, and they aren't motivated to succeed, I can teach them all the marketing "secrets" in the world, and they still won't be successful.

And that is why, in 2020 I will be introducing my new event, called *Rock Your Life Celebration Weekend*, where I'll share tools and funny and inspiring stories on how to find the balance between work and play. And help people truly enjoy their lives.

And we will continue to create RockStars!

This book marks both the end of an era, and an introduction to my new brand. I hope and pray that this book, and the 100 inspirational stories by 100 amazing people, helps you on your path to begin to Rock Your Life.

—Craig Duswalt

WHAT IS ON YOUR BUCKET LIST?

Craig Duswalt

I have two big items on my bucket list. Well, actually, three, but I'm pretty sure I won't own the Kansas City Chiefs football team anytime soon.

My wife and I started a nonprofit a few years ago called the Band Together Foundation. We put on events and concerts to raise money for other charities across the world. We have donated money and items to disaster areas in Miami, Houston, Kenya, and Mexico, just to name several.

I toured with Guns N' Roses as Axl Rose's personal assistant in the early 90s, and with the Australian pop band Air Supply in the 80s. I made a lot of friends and connections on the road, and I'm still in contact with most of them to this day.

At my BootCamps I always try to get a RockStar to interview or play a few songs at my events. I have been blessed to have the following RockStars on my stage: Eddie Money, Kevin Cronin of REO Speedwagon, Mickey Dolenz of The Monkees, Duff McKagan of Guns N' Roses, John Waite of The Babys, Ray Parker Jr., Russell Hitchcock of Air Supply, and many more. I'm blessed to be in a great situation where I can ask a RockStar for a favor, especially if it's for a good cause.

As Axl Rose's former assistant, I was the liaison between him and numerous famous people, so I got to know a ton of RockStars a little more than if I just met them in passing.

One great story involved Steven Tyler of Aerosmith . . .

On June 5, 1992, Guns N' Roses got together at a rehearsal and sound check with Lenny Kravitz, Jeff Beck, and Steven Tyler and Joe Perry from Aerosmith for a live Pay-Per-View show the next day in Paris.

I ran Axl's teleprompter when I first started with the band. We had the words to every song in the Guns N' Roses repertoire in our computer, but when the band sang a song by another band, we had to enter those words into the teleprompter so they would appear on the monitors, and Axl could sing the song.

These days, that's easy. You go on the internet, Google the name of the song, and voila, you have the words. A simple copy and paste, and you're done.

Since Axl didn't know the words to "Train Kept A-Rollin," he said to me, "Go to Steven's room and get the words to 'Train Kept A-Rollin.'"

So I grabbed a pen and a pad of paper and headed down to Steven Tyler's room, and I'm thinking to myself as I get into the elevator that this will probably be the coolest thing I will do on tour with Guns N' Roses.

I knocked on the hotel room door, and Steven Tyler, the lead singer of Aerosmith, opened the door, dressed in only a towel.

"Hey Steven, my name is Craig and I work with Axl, and we need the words to

"Train Kept A-Rollin" for tonight's show so I can put them on Axl's teleprompter."

Steven says, "Sure dude, come on in."

And I walked in. No one else was in the room, just Steven, his towel, and me.

Getting right to the job at hand, Steven said, "You ready?"

"Uh, yes. How do you want to do this? Do you have the words somewhere? I can just make a copy."

"I'll sing it to you. You ready?"

And Steven started singing his song "Train Kept A-Rollin" a cappella.

I was such an Aerosmith fan, and for the first time on tour I actually felt like one of the Guns N' Roses fans that I encountered every day. I was so entranced by listening to his amazing voice, that I forgot to continue writing after about the third word of the song.

He finished the first verse and asked, "Did you get all that?"

I looked down at the three words on my pad of paper and told him, "I'm a slow writer. I got "Train kept a . . . and then I lost you."

Now I'm thinking he's going to quickly get impatient real soon, but instead he said, "OK, here it is again."

And he started singing the song again from the beginning.

This time I frantically wrote down the words as best I could, all the time thinking that I'm getting a free concert, in a five-star hotel room, in Paris, from the lead singer of Aerosmith—and it all hit me at once. This is awesome! And how in the hell did I get here? How did all this happen?

That's my Steven Tyler story. So cool. Numerous interactions with many different RockStars was commonplace on the road. And more than twenty-five years later, I feel like I'm now ready to contact some old friends and do something very special.

So, Bucket List item #1 is that my wife and I want to put on a huge concert, similar to the Live Aid concert back in 1985 that raised a ton of money for Africa. Our concert concept is that we want to bring popular bands that have broken up in the past back together to "Band Together" for one day to help raise money for a worthy cause somewhere in the world.

I feel that we are primed to do this and that now is the right time. Our goal is to put this concert on some time in the year 2022.

The original idea came to me when Guns N' Roses parted ways in the mid 90s. I thought it would be huge if they ever got back together and that people would pay a lot of money to see that. Of course, my great idea was spoiled when Guns N' Roses recently got back together for the Not in This Lifetime Tour.

But there are still many other bands that remain broken up, and I'm sure we will add to the lineup world-famous bands that have not broken up.

Bucket List item #2 is a personal goal that I have had since I started as an actor in college at SUNY Oswego in Oswego, New York. I have been "almost famous" my entire life. I have always been the guy working with and for very famous celebrities and business leaders.

I do know that I am very successful as a speaker and as a seminar leader, and I am very thankful for that. I also know that I DO NOT EVER want to be a household name. I've seen firsthand what fame has done to people, and I have no desire for that kind of life.

But I do want to do something really cool. I tried to become a full-time working actor, and it never worked out for me. I've had some bit roles on television, and I've performed in many plays, but I've never made it big.

And now, because of a few connections I recently made, I know this is possible.

Bucket List #2 is that I want to perform a one-man show on Broadway in NYC.

I'm originally from New York, and I've been writing a one-man show featuring many of the unbelievable stories from my very interesting life. I'm not a comedian, but for some reason when I speak on stage, I make marketing a lot of fun. So, if I can make marketing funny, anything is possible. The working title of my one-man show is *Almost Famous*.

Because I have these two bucket list items, I find that it is easy to live every day with passion and hope. When you're feeling stuck, and you're not sure what you want to do with your life, choose something you've always wanted to do, put a date on it, and watch what happens to your everyday life.

All you need to do to start is ask yourself this simple question, "What is on my bucket list?"

———————————

Craig Duswalt is a keynote speaker, author, podcaster, and the creator of the brands *RockStar Marketing* and *Rock Your Life*. His background includes touring with Guns N' Roses as Axl Rose's personal assistant and Air Supply as the band's personal assistant.

After ten years on the road, Craig returned to Southern California and opened his marketing firm, Green Room Design, which was named the 2002 Santa Clarita Valley Small Business of the Year.

In 2008, Craig became a full-time keynote speaker and has been featured on hundreds of stages all across North America.

Craig is also the author of eleven books, five of which were #1 Amazon bestsellers.

Craig will launch his brand-new event, Rock Your Life Celebration Weekend, in 2020, sharing funny and inspiring stories on how to find the balance between work and play and how to leave a legacy.

www.CraigDuswalt.com

MAKING A DIFFERENCE IN THE WORLD

Leigh Steinberg

My father instilled two core values into my brothers and me at an early age: 1) treasure relationships, especially family and 2) make a positive difference in the world by helping people in need. A corollary to this was the understanding that when waiting for "who" will fix a problem and assuming that the amorphous "they"—political figures, older people, or others—will act, you could wait forever. My dad looked at me and said, "The they is you, son; you are the they." It was clear from my childhood that the metric for judging success in life would not be achieved by financial gain or fame, but by a life centered around those two core values.

When I arrived in Atlanta in 1975 with QB Steve Bartkowski, the first overall pick in the NFL draft who was also about to sign the largest rookie contract of all time with the Atlanta Falcons, it became clear that athletes were venerated celebrities in communities around the country. As we arrived at the airport, the sky was "lit up" like a movie premiere, and there was a crowd waiting to greet Steve. I then realized that athletes could be role models and trigger imitative behavior.

Throughout my career, I ask each athlete I represent to retrace their roots and give back to their high school, collegiate, and professional community by setting up charitable foundations and community-driven programs. I have represented over 120 athletes that have established scholarship funds. For example, Dallas Cowboys QB Troy Aikman endowed a full athletic scholarship at UCLA, as did Indianapolis Colts RB Edgerrin James at the University of Miami, and Giants QB Kerry Collins at Penn State.

At the professional level, I encourage athletes to set up a charitable foundation with the leading political, community, and business figures in their geographical area and sit on the foundation's advisory board. Illustrating this concept, San Diego Charger's PK Rolf Benirschke established "Kicks for Critters," which used posters and pledge cards to raise money for endangered species at the San Diego Zoo. Atlanta Falcon RB Warrick Dunn has put 170 single mothers in the first home they will ever own by making the down payment along with furnishing the house fully. Chiefs QB Patrick Mahomes established "15 and the Mahomies" to help underserved youth, and Chiefs LB Derrick Thomas established "Third and Long" to help children with reading problems. In aggregate, our clients have raised almost $1 billion for causes they are passionate about.

Athletes can permeate the perceptual screen that young people erect up against authority figures and motivate good behavior. Heavyweight boxing champion Lennox Lewis cut a PSA "Real Men Don't Hit Women" campaign that targeted domestic violence. San Francisco 49er QB Steve Young and boxing champion Oscar De La Hoya have contributed with a "Prejudice Is Foul Play" program.

I felt a responsibility to fund my own programs to tackle similar issues, so I established a series of summer camps to bring high school and middle school students from different races and ethnic groups together for leadership training. I helped resurrect the Newport Beach Film Festival as a co-title sponsor to encourage a flowering of the arts. Secretary of State Madeline Albright and I established "Adopt a Minefield" to facilitate demining in Angola and Cambodia. With the Anti-Defamation League, I funded "Steinberg Leadership," a program that trained thousands of young professionals in the fight against racism and skinheads.

We all can make a difference in a positive way, whether it is good parenting or community involvement. This is God's work!

I always have believed that by working harder or being more creative, I can solve most problems. But when my father died of cancer, things began to unravel. My family lost a home to mold, my boys experienced eyesight problems, and my marriage experienced difficulties. I felt like Gulliver in Gulliver's Travels lying on the beach, tethered down with ropes, with Lilliputians sticking forks in me. I turned to alcohol to numb the frustration. All of a sudden, I was failing in both of my dad's admonitions. Thus, I gave my sports practice to younger agents, closed my condo, and moved into sober living with two goals in mind: 1) to establish sobriety no matter what it took and 2) to be a more consistent father to my three children.

I surrendered to the reality that I was an alcoholic, joined a twelve-step program that provided a unique fellowship, and most importantly, put sobriety first. I had to work through the wreckage I had caused. Often it felt like Sophocles pushing the stone up the hill. Every time I moved the stone a few steps forward in the right direction, it proceeded to roll back. Further, I didn't have the luxury of dealing with all this privately because there had been major press coverage of my two arrests for alcohol and my bankruptcy issues.

Recovery rarely happens alone, and I had a strong reliance on a higher power along with wonderful friends and family support. The concept of proportionality and perspective was helpful. I was not a starving peasant in Sudan, nor did I have the last name Steinberg in Nazi Germany. I had luckily, through an accident of birth, received all the privileges of being born in the United States with political freedom and the highest standard of living. There was no excuse to do anything but recover. Fortunately, I was raised with optimism and resilience. Life will inevitably knock us down and push us back, but the real question is: Can we get back up with purpose and energy?

I'm now in my tenth year of continuous sobriety and have close relationships with my kids. My business is flourishing again, which is sparking conversation about a great business comeback. My real comeback is simply maintaining sobriety, being a good parent, and trying to be of service to the world.

Leigh Steinberg obtained his undergraduate and law degree from Cal, serving as student body president during his undergrad years as well as senior class president during his time in law school. He represented the number one overall pick in the NFL draft eight times, along with sixty-two first round picks, and has represented numerous MLB and NBA athletes and multiple Olympians. He has twice been a bestselling author and is credited with being the inspiration for the blockbuster film Jerry Maguire. Leigh has secured over $3 billion for his clients and directed more than $850 million to charities. He is often referred to as the country's leading sports agent.

I'M STILL STANDING

Russell Hitchcock

I was born in East Brunswick, Victoria, Australia, in 1949. We lived in the inner city between a brickworks and an iron foundry. My parents provided for my sister and I as best they could, and in spite of not having a lot of money, we always had a roof over our heads and food on the table. My childhood was uneventful except for being struck by a pickup while crossing an intersection as I walked to school. Apart from a badly bruised hip, I was fine. My mother however, being the comic that she was, told practically everyone up until the day she died that "Russell wasn't right in the head after he got hit by the truck!"

The work ethic I have today is due to my parents. They both worked, and I cannot remember either one of them ever missing a day's work. It was always instilled in us that hard work and perseverance would ultimately pay off later in life.

I attended grade school and eventually moved on to Princes Hill High School. I was an average student—I loved French and English but not much else during those years. I was too interested in having fun rather than studying. My drive to succeed in life began when I dropped out of high school at sixteen years of age. I received my exam results on a Friday, and having failed, I realized that repeating the year would be a waste of my parent's hard-earned money. I told my mother I was done, and the next day I went into the city, where I saw a sign in a small clothing store advertising for a "junior salesman." I walked in, applied, and was given the job on the spot! One of the things I've been proud of all my life is that since the age of sixteen, I have supported myself.

It wasn't until 1975, after having a number of jobs in the intervening years (I was never fired), that I found myself in the Australian production of *Jesus Christ Superstar*. On May 12th I met Graham Russell, and my life would never be the same.

We quickly became friends, realizing just how much we had in common, most of all a fanatical love for the music of the Beatles. We had both seen them live in 1964, Graham in England and me in Australia. Graham has always had great passion for the music he writes, and I've always felt I was the perfect fit to sing his songs. It wasn't long before we were performing together in coffee bars, pizza parlors, and the occasional university campus. We worked very hard to become as good as we could, and Graham, very early on, was determined to be ready when the production ended.

By the time the show ended in October 1976, we had a number one single and album in Australia, and we went on the road as Air Supply only a few days after leaving *Jesus Christ Superstar*.

We played anywhere we could—a lot of pubs that were hard-core rock 'n' roll venues and among the premier acts at the time, AC/DC, Midnight Oil, INXS, and the Angels. Needless to say, playing mostly ballads was a hard road to hoe, but in those early days, it gave us an invaluable lesson in mental toughness, perseverance, and patience.

Early in 1977 we were invited to open for Rod Stewart in Australia. When you consider that Air Supply was only three months old, it was an amazing achievement. Playing to over twenty thousand people a night was overwhelming, but it was such a great incentive for us to broaden our horizons and seek international success. We knew we had the talent and the songs and would not be denied our shot. After only a couple of shows, Rod asked us to open for him on his North American tour later that year. We were ecstatic and believed this would be our stepping-stone to international stardom. We toured with Rod from September through December, playing fifty-plus concerts in all the venues we'd only dreamed about: Madison Square Garden, The Forum in Los Angeles, Candlestick Park, and Three Rivers Stadium. It was mind-blowing!

One of the greatest gifts we received from Rod was being able to watch him every night. We would marvel not only at his talent as a singer, but also the way he handled the audiences, taking them where *he* wanted them to go. We learned so much from him about performing, production, organization, and in fact, every aspect of the business. We soaked it up, absorbing as much as we could, and by the time we arrived back in Australia in December, we thought we were going to break on a worldwide scale.

How wrong we were! Coming off the biggest tour of the year and coming home to the brutal fact that we'd basically been forgotten by the public was not only shocking to us considering what we'd achieved, but it also made us more determined to achieve the goals we had set in those very early days. Rejection can do one of two things. Either it can cause you to give up and go home, or in our case, to say to ourselves, "We have the talent, the songs, the drive, and the passion to continue," and that's exactly what we did.

We struggled through the next couple of years doing whatever we could to survive. Graham ended up in Cannes trying to sell his songs, and I was in Australia doing "jingles" for a friend who was kind enough to hire me. During this time, though, with Graham's fearless determination and incredible vision, we kept our dreams alive until 1978 when "Lost in Love" was released in Australia and once again, we had a huge hit on our hands. The song made its way to Clive Davis at Arista Records in the United States. Clive, in my opinion is the most influential person that has ever been in the recording business, and he *loved* our songs. We had seven Top Five singles back-to-back, and we were on top of the world.

Becoming successful is one thing, but maintaining it is another. We toured incessantly to support our records, playing all over the world and even in places that very few acts had been, such as South Korea, Vietnam, Thailand, Malaysia, and a host of other countries both in Asia and Latin America. We worked extremely hard (and still do) to achieve and maintain the highest level of concert performance. Graham is always looking to make the shows better and looking at the arrangements of the songs to involve the influences of the current members of the band, while of course maintaining the integrity of the songs. We want our audiences to hear what they come to hear and not some vague version of the songs they know and love.

We will never stop trying to get better, and this desire has made it possible to still be on the road after forty-two years and counting. You can always do better, be better and achieve any goal you put your heart and soul in. You must stay focused and even through adversity, rejection, and hard times stick to your beliefs and know that you will succeed and continue to do so as long as you have the passion.

Having such a brilliant writer, arranger, and prolific composer has certainly made it easier for us, but trust me, we've seen it all. We've seen the good, the bad, and the ugly in people, but we've never succumbed to the dark side of the music business. I am as excited today as I have ever been in my life about recording and performing and hopefully have some great years ahead of me.

As I frequently say to friends and fans . . . ROCK ON!

Russell Hitchcock is the lead singer of the extremely successful rock duo, Air Supply. Air Supply hits include "Lost in Love," "All Out of Love," "The One That You Love," "Sweet Dreams," "Making Love Out of Nothing At All," "Here I Am," "Even the Nights Are Better," "Every Woman in the World," "The Power of Love," "Just As I Am," and "Two Less Lonely People in the World." With seven top-five singles, Air Supply, at the time, equaled the Beatles' run of consecutive top five singles. Air Supply albums, *Lost in Love, The One That You Love, Now and Forever,* and *Greatest Hits* have sold in excess of 20 million copies. *Lost in Love* was named Song of the Year in 1980, and, with the other singles, sold more than 10 million copies. Air Supply has continued to tour around the world for more than forty years.

www.AirSupplyMusic.com

MAN OF STEEL

Dean Cain

I'm eight years old and playing in my first-ever organized basketball game. The kid guarding me is much quicker—everywhere I turn, he's already there, like an annoying gnat. Finally, I grab him by the shirt and throw him to the ground. Whistles blow and parents complain. My dad turns to my mom and says, "Maybe he should play football."

For the next fourteen years, my mettle was hammered out on the gridiron. I didn't have time or interest in drugs or other distractions, because I was too focused. Football helped me get into Princeton University, where I became an All-American and briefly made it to the NFL with the Buffalo Bills (knee injury . . . a different book). Football helped me make friends, because having 110 teammates ensures plenty of diversity and challenges and close interaction. Football helped me vent and channel frustration and aggression and anger into hard work, discipline, and ultimately, success.

I love athletics. They tell you so much about a person's character. What kind of teammate are you? How do you react to adversity? Are you coachable? How do you respond when you're tired, or sick, or injured, or under tremendous pressure? How do you react to a bad call? This is not to say that people *have* to play sports (my own son doesn't play team sports—he trains in mixed martial arts), but athletics were essential to my overall development.

I love competition. Growing up, I played every sport under the sun. Four and five sports a year, all year 'round for fifteen years. I learned how to win. I learned how to lose. I learned how to get back up after being knocked down. I learned that everyone gets knocked down. Everyone. I was voted top athlete in my high school. I was voted top athlete at my college. I lettered in three different sports at Princeton, but no sport could hold a candle to my love for football.

I love contact. In high school, my football/track coach said, "Cain, you're the only guy I know who runs FASTER when he HITS the hurdles!" In college, I ran my 40-yard-dash faster with my gear on. Running without my helmet and shoulder pads felt awkward, like a knight without his armor. Football was a great fit for me, but the road to RockStar success is never easy.

I wanted to kill my college football coach. Literally. Before my sophomore year at Princeton, the head coach was fired. Under the new regime, I tried to switch from defensive back to receiver but was quickly sent back to the defense. They never had any intention of letting me play offense. My new defensive back coach was called "Vermin." That wasn't his real name, but that's what a few of us called him. It was not a term of dearment.

As the only sophomore starting on the defense, and starting at cornerback, Vermin let me know that opposing teams would be targeting me. He let me know this every day, every practice, every meeting. He would scream at me all day long, until his voice went hoarse (which I took as a small victory). Vermin drove me and drove me and yelled at me—right in my face, EVERY SINGLE DAY. I took to staring defiantly into his beady little eyes, silent, and stone-faced. Vermin wouldn't let me drop a single ball in practice. EVER. Every pass in the air he expected me to intercept. Every tackle he expected me to make. This dude was all over me. As the season wound down, I was considering leaving Princeton and taking one of the many scholarships that had been offered to me out of high school (the Ivy League does NOT give athletic scholarships).

My dad flew to Princeton from the jungles of Brazil to catch the final game of my sophomore season. Dad had been directing a film for 6 months in the middle of the Amazon, had grown a jungle beard, and contracted malaria (he hadn't realized that yet). He didn't have time to go home to see my mother or the rest of the family in California. He had missed all my games (there was no Internet back then), and he wasn't gonna miss this last one. I talked with my tanned, skinny, and bearded dad about Vermin and all the crap he had put me through. Dad patiently gave me some sage farm-boy advice (he was raised on a farm in South Dakota). Then he told me to finish up the season and the semester, and afterward we'd discuss transferring to another school if I still wished.

We played Cornell the next day, and I faced off with their stud All-Ivy receiver. He was big and strong, and supposed to dominate me. We had a war all afternoon, and with time winding down they were driving for the winning score. They threw to the stud, but I stepped in front and picked it off for the *third* time of the day! I weaved my way through defenders and stepped out of bounds, sealing the victory! My teammates hoisted me onto their shoulders. RockStar!

I stayed at Princeton and continued to excel at defensive back. Junior year I was moved to free safety, where I really belonged. Vermin continued to ride me like a donkey, but I was getting tougher. The team had a terrible year, but I had another great season. The individual recognition felt hollow because the team hadn't won. As my senior season was about to begin, our beloved head coach suffered a heart attack and died. It was a devastating loss.

My family decided to move to Princeton for my senior season. They went to every single game, home and away. My father had just gotten his biggest break in Hollywood and was preparing to direct the film *Young Guns*. He was traveling back to Los Angeles during the week and then returning to Princeton for the weekend games. It was awesome to have their support. I was having the greatest season any defensive back had ever had in college football, and Vermin and I had made peace. I realized Vermin was like the character "Fletcher" that J. K. Simmons had won an Academy Award for playing in the film *Whiplash*. Vermin had driven me that hard to make me great. (Today we are still great friends, and Vermin continues to coach football at Princeton.)

The final game of my college career was at Princeton. Cornell again. My entire family was there. My girlfriend was there. It was the coldest game anyone could remember.

With the wind-chill factor, it was -20 Fahrenheit. My sister still complains that it permanently screwed up the circulation in her feet (they were blue, and a woman had to put them inside her fur coat). At the end of the first half, I intercept my 10th pass of the season to leave me one interception shy of the single-season NCAA record (11). In the third quarter, a pass bounces off the chest of a Cornell receiver and directly into my hands! I've tied the record! I run it back, get knocked out of bounds on our sideline, and promptly make my way over to the stands. I toss the ball to my father. He throws it back. I throw it back harder and tell him, "That's for *you!*"

That moment is still my all-time favorite sports highlight. After all the blood, sweat, tears, fights with Vermin, and separation from my family, I got to tie the NCAA record and throw that football to my dad in the stands. I was finally a friggin' RockStar! Later in the game, I intercepted another pass, and broke the NCAA record for interceptions in a single season and became a SuperRockStar! Two of those NCAA records still stand, and my dad still has his football.

Dean Cain grew up in Malibu, California, and has appeared in over 100 films, including *Out of Time,* opposite Denzel Washington, *God's Not Dead, The Broken Hearts Club, Vendetta, and Gosnell.* Dean has also starred in dozens of television productions and is perhaps best known for his role as Superman on ABC's *Lois & Clark.* He hosted and produced the long-running series *Ripley's Believe It Or Not.* Known for his incredible work ethic, Dean is currently starring in a wide array of projects, hosting the sixth season of the CW smash *Masters of Illusion,* recurring on the widely popular CBS series *Supergirl,* and can often be seen hosting *The Today Show* and *Fox and Friends.* An accomplished screenwriter, Dean has recently penned a number of screenplays which are in various stages of production. Dean's sense of service also led him to become a reserve police officer in 2018. An athlete at heart, Dean attended Princeton University and was an All-American defensive back, setting two NCAA records for interceptions. He signed with the Buffalo Bills, but a knee injury quickly ended his professional sports career before it had begun.

Twitter: @RealDeanCain

THE BEST

Bo Eason

I'm nine years old, the youngest of six kids growing up on a cattle ranch in California, and I know what I'm going to do with my life: become the best safety in the NFL. I sit down with a crayon and write out a twenty-year plan to get there, complete with a drawing of me on the football field. I carry that plan everywhere, and it's always in my mind. For the next nine years, I focus on what will get me to the NFL. I wake up every morning at 5:00 a.m. to run drills. I don't go to prom. I don't party with my friends. Before doing anything, I ask myself, "Will this get me closer to my NFL goal?" If the answer is no, I don't do it. If the answer is yes, I do it. It's easy. I don't have to make any decisions. I just follow the plan.

The hard work pays off. I'm a walk-on safety with the University of California, Davis, football team. The Houston Oilers draft me as a top pick. A few years later, I join the San Francisco 49ers. Then a career-ending knee injury kicks me out of the only life I've ever known or planned for.

I have no idea what I'm going to do. I just know that all my physical energy and focus needs to be redirected, or I'll end up in prison.

I move to New York City and study with the best acting and movement coaches I can find. I meet with Al Pacino, who tells me I need to spend more time on a stage than anyone else in the world if I want to be the best stage actor of my generation. I spend the next fifteen years acting anywhere I can get a role, starting with a children's play in Sacramento, California.

That's right—from competing against and playing with the world's best athletes, I go to acting in a kid's play. Instead of signing autographs on the field after every game, I'm standing in front of a hundred noisy kids who are so busy throwing popcorn at each other and yelling that they're not even looking at me.

But I know this is just part of the process. My mastery in the NFL doesn't mean I can walk into any acting job anywhere and be great. I need another long-term plan, one that focuses on acting, movement, writing plays. My football skills do not transfer to acting. But my ability to focus, practice, rehearse, and keep my plan in mind at all times does.

I get on every stage I can. I rehearse constantly. I'm as focused as I've ever been. Eventually, I write and stage a one-person autobiographical play called Runt of the Litter. I train with Larry Moss and Jean-Louis Rodrigue, world-renowned movement and performance coaches, who help me bring more action and energy to the play. I perform the play off-Broadway and in more than fifty cities across the country. The New York Times refers to it as "one of the most powerful plays in the last decade."

Eventually I begin to notice that people come up to me after the show and ask me to perform Runt for their executive board or their sales staff or their entire company. My reaction is always the same: Hell, no! This is a play, not a corporate educational tool.

One day an executive tells me he wants to fly me, my wife, Dawn, and our kids to Hawaii and have me perform the play at his company's annual corporate retreat. I'm about to refuse when he names a price that literally has my jaw dropping. That's when the light goes on in my head: this isn't just a play. This is an entire life toolkit. I can keep performing my play at auditoriums all over the country—or I can step up onto a bigger stage, literally, and impact thousands of people at a time. Change their lives. Help them figure out how to tell their own life stories. Show them how to be the best.

It's an easy decision.

Now I work with people and corporations all over the world through my company, the Bo Eason Experience. I work with groups ranging from five or six people to auditoriums full of thousands. In weekend and weeklong workshops, I train them to step up into positions of leadership, no matter what their role in life. I show people how to tap the power of their personal story and become effective, persuasive communicators.

Day after day, I'm obsessed with helping people realize their own capacity for greatness. It's all I truly care about. I don't care if they're a financial advisor, Green Beret, doctor, lawyer, firefighter, athlete, stay-at-home parent, whatever. I only care that the people I work with take themselves seriously, commit to a course of action, and focus on becoming the best.

Bo Eason. Former NFL All-Pro. Actor. Playwright. Motivational Speaker. Leadership Trainer. Author. Bo Eason started his career in the NFL as a top pick for the Houston Oilers. Continuing on with the San Francisco 49ers, during his five-year career Bo competed beside and against some of the greatest players of his generation. After his football career ended, he branched out into acting and wrote a one-man play called Runt of the Litter that went to Broadway. Now, as a speaker and leadership coach, he trains some of the most successful people in the world—athletes, artists, entrepreneurs, C-suite execs—on how to communicate for maximum impact and success. His book, *There's No Plan B for Your A-Game: Be the Best in the World at What You Do*, will be published in September 2019 by St. Martin's Press.

www.BoEason.com

WIN/WIN

Natasha Duswalt

Driving home one day from school with my mother at the young age of seven years old, I witnessed a bullying situation that was hard to comprehend. When we pulled up to the melee, I started to shake at the sight of what was happening before my eyes.

A much younger boy was being tugged and pulled off his bike and was being pummeled by four much larger boys. The younger boy was covered in lipstick and baking flour. At first glance at the grisly sight, it looked like he was bleeding under all of the flour. As we got closer, it was clear that it was crimson red lipstick, but the effect was the same: devastating, poetic, and sinister. The red lipstick under the flour gave him a clownlike look with tears streaking his checks to break up the image. There are some images you can't un-see—this was one of them.

Suddenly my mom did something I did not expect. She slammed on the brakes, pulled over, and stormed out of the car. The older boys looked terrified. With her thick, European accent mixed with the many languages she had mastered, she yelled for them to stop. The bullies looked confused and terrified all at the same time. The boy being bullied was grateful and humbled. The range of emotions that day coming from everyone at the scene was nothing short of astounding.

I sat there and took it all in. I felt the emotional overload, and I could not help but feel every emotion playing out at that moment. I saw the compassion my mother felt for the boy being bullied. I felt the shame and humiliation of the boy being targeted and beaten. I felt the confusion and embarrassment of the bullies who stood there ashamed. The realization of what they had done struck them with my mother's powerful voice.

I realized at that moment that I would someday become like the woman I so greatly looked up to—my mom. It all happened so fast, but the message was loud and clear. I saw kindness, grace, and compassion beyond measure. I saw the boys melt into a reality that they regretted.

Growing up from that day forth, I knew that everyone mattered, that we all deserved to be treated with respect. It was very clear that not everyone can always stand up for themselves and that we need to be there for others.

It is said that a strong woman stands up for herself. It is also said that a stronger woman stands up for those who cannot stand up for themselves. There are many people who need others to help them find their voice. When you are a parent, it is your voice that stands for your children. When you are leading any group of people, you are taking on the role of looking for what is best for that group or team.

In any arena there are people who will take on the responsibility of speaking for others.

Women today are doing so much that sometimes we are missing out on our true superpower. Perhaps our true superpower is our unending compassion. Perhaps there are instincts that we are wired with that make us want to nurture and protect those that need a voice.

The success of my life and business has been directly tied to the principles I saw set forth by my mom on that fateful fall day. My business representing talent has been a mirror of that day. I have had to stand up for others as far back as I can remember. My core values have been shaped by my willingness to stand up for others even when it is not easy.

My life's choice to represent others in the entertainment industry comes with its own challenges. My intention has always been to be the safe place that models and talent could come to and find someone who is on their team, someone that will stand up for them from start to finish with every project we book.

Prior to opening a modeling agency, I was always the one who would speak for the other models when it came to negotiations for a booking. Realizing that everything hinged on the success of others was the fuel I needed to generate a business consistently booking for over twenty years. My goal has always been to create win/win partnerships.

My journey was not the typical path—the "go to college, get a degree" route. I was thrust into life with nothing but my ability to work hard and stand strong. Sometimes we need someone to stand in the space to give others the time to grow into their own. When we stand up for others, we are also showing the next generation what it looks like to be courageous in our daily life.

For my personal success, I hope that my life has had an impact on those that may or may not know that I have been there for them behind the scenes. I also hope that someday my kids can look back and see where I stood up for someone else and carry that forth in their own lives.

Natasha Duswalt is an author, speaker, and the president and founder of Peak Models & Talent in Los Angeles. As an international model, Natasha has had the rare opportunity to travel all over the world, including New York, Miami, Hong Kong, Japan, Taiwan, Mexico and several other locations working with top designers and companies. Natasha has been featured on numerous television shows including Baywatch and Growing Pains, as well as the hit movie The Doors by Oliver Stone. She was also hired as an ESPN spokesmodel and has appeared on numerous television commercials.

Peak Models & Talent has been touted as one of Los Angeles' top agencies, booking with numerous Fortune 500 companies.

Natasha, a proud cancer survivor, currently lives in Los Angeles with her husband, Craig Duswalt, and their three boys.

For speaking inquiries, please email Natasha@craigduswalt.com
or Natasha@peakmodels.com.

www.peakmodels.com

Workforce Reduction into Lemonade

Derrick Hall

It can be an absolute challenge to feel like a RockStar with your employees when they know economic conditions have forced the organization to analyze the necessity of eliminating all full-time positions. This was the setting in 2008, when Arizona was experiencing one of its worst economic downturns in decades. With over 350 full-time staff members at the time, I realized the fiscally responsible action was to assess all levels and determine which jobs could be combined and which could ultimately be eliminated.

This was a daunting task for a team president who prided himself on the award-winning culture that had been created. Each and every one of my employees was like a member of my own family to me, as well as to my wife, Amy. After weeks of consultant engagement and internal interviews, it had been decided that forty positions could be abolished—the largest workplace reduction in the history of our organization.

With such a sensitive topic and people's livelihoods being at stake, this information was kept confidential between just a few of my key executives. This made it perhaps even worse. There were few I could talk to in order to fully process the accuracy of our findings. The nonstop questions kept ringing in my head—"Was this totally necessary?" "What if the economy recovers tomorrow?" "Should we enforce furloughs instead?" "Am I identifying the proper individuals?" There were sleepless nights and hour-long tearful conversations each night at home with my better half. I could not look close friends in the eyes leading up to the reduction, knowing that I was sending them out the door in need of new jobs.

The Friday came when it was time to take action, and we did so in a very respectful and dignified fashion, giving these innocent and hardworking loyalists a way to exit with their heads held high and enough to make ends meet while they searched for their next career moves. We eliminated jobs across the board, not just at the lower or entry levels. There were managers, directors, senior directors, and even vice presidents from my leadership team who all fell victim to this swift and appropriate plan. It was the most difficult day in my professional career.

When the dust settled days later and those who survived realized and trusted there would be no further cuts or waves, what could have been an extremely negative time for this franchise became one of hope and belief in its leaders. The feedback was in direct contrast to how I had envisioned the outcome. Our staff actually respected the decisions we made and were confident that they had been made objectively and without favoritism. I was also told on several occasions that the employees could tell how deeply moved and saddened I was by the process.

The Arizona Diamondbacks culture was actually strengthened during these days that

I had deemed so dark. Remaining employees thanked me for having faith in their abilities and made promises to make us proud. A tight-knit group got even closer, and the overall mission was in focus sharper than ever before.

Those few who joined me in the miserable task of eliminating positions and negatively impacting some lives were now considered RockStars by the staff for analyzing the entire organization thoroughly enough and without bias, and making decisions that all could universally get behind and never question.

In our positions, we will be forced to make choices that will not always be favorable or popular. But if we remain fair, consistent, and honest, our integrity will always stay intact, and our fiduciary responsibilities will forever be fulfilled.

Considered by many to be among the leaders of the game, Arizona Diamondbacks president and CEO **Derrick Hall** has turned the D-backs into a model franchise within the sports industry and throughout the business world during his ten years at the helm of the club. Hall focuses the organization's efforts in five areas he has called the "Circle of Success"—fan experience, performance, community, culture, and financial efficiency— each of which has seen tremendous success during his tenure.

The D-backs were recently named the No. 1 franchise in baseball and No. 6 in all of sports by ESPN the Magazine based on eight categories on and off the field. Among his most significant accomplishments during his tenure as president and CEO has been the opening of Salt River Fields at Talking Stick, the D-backs' Spring Training home in Scottsdale; hosting the 2011 Major League All-Star Game at Chase Field for the first time ever; two division titles in 2007 and 2011; an NLCS appearance and hiring of Hall of Fame manager Tony La Russa as Chief Baseball Officer to oversee the team's baseball operations; the positioning of the D-backs as one of the largest philanthropic entities in the Valley, having recently surpassed $40 million in charitable giving since the team's inception in 1998, including more than $4 million last season; and the creation of a corporate culture that led Yahoo! to deem the club as "the best workplace in sports."

www.dbacks.com

A High School Break

Ray Parker Jr.

One big jump in my career came when I was seventeen years old. It was just a few weeks before my eighteenth birthday. I was in college studying to be an architect so I could work for one of the big three in Detroit. It was my father's dream to have me work at Ford Motor Company, as he did. My dad worked at Ford for forty-eight years as a crane operator. His big dream for me was to have a white-collar job instead of a blue-collar job like his. I was attending Lawrence Tech College in the drafting department. I was bored out of my mind and well aware that this was probably not the right path for me. But it was my father's dream, and he had been saving money for my college education for years before I was born. I had already established myself as a working musician by this time and was enjoying it. I had been recording with many major artists like Marvin Gaye, Smokey Robinson, Honey Comb, the Spinners, and the Temptations.

Music for My Mind was my favorite album at the time. I had an eight-track tape player in my car, and it was the only album I listened to. One day I got a call from someone claiming to be Stevie Wonder! I knew it had to be one of my friends, so I hung up the phone. This person called back, and I hung up again. He then called back, and I added a few four-letter words before hanging up again. The next time he called, he asked me to listen. He played the beginning track to "Superstition"!

I finally understood that I had been hanging up on Stevie Wonder, so I apologized and listened. He said that he'd heard about me and wanted to know if I would be interested in going on tour with him and the Rolling Stones for several months, as well as work on his new album, *Talking Book*, and do some recordings with Crosby, Stills, Nash & Young!

This was certainly a great opportunity, and I really wanted to go. I told him of my situation with my father and said that I would have to get back to him. I then had the big sit-down conversation with my dad, telling him that this was his dream, not mine, and that I really wanted to go on tour. He explained how he wanted me to graduate college and be the first one in the family to do so. I had little interest. I was really frustrated with school anyway.

I had just finished a three-week-long drawing for class. I felt I had done a great job on the test, but I received a failing grade on a Friday evening. I sat up all weekend trying to figure out what was wrong. Because of the weekend I couldn't confront the teacher until Monday. When I did, she told me that my drawing was really impressive and the work was well done. She failed me because the arrows I used on the Ford car were GM specs, not Ford specs. For example, Ford arrows flared at the end and GM's didn't, even though the size was a slight difference. She explained to me that that's how things work at the Big 3.

I wanted out!

After talking with my father for quite some time, listening to what he had to say as well as letting him know that I was totally unhappy in school, he agreed to let me go on tour! I can't imagine where my life would be now if I'd stayed in school and took that path. This was a major turn to the left, and I've been happy ever since.

American guitarist, songwriter, producer and recording artist, **Ray Parker Jr.** is best known for writing and performing the theme song to the motion picture *Ghostbusters*, for his solo hits, and performing with his band Raydio as well as with the late Barry White. Now, Parker enjoys spending time with his family while continuing his love and passion for music. He regularly performs in various concerts throughout the world.

www.RayParkerJr.com

A Babysitter and a Firefighter

Jeffrey Finn

Ignorance is bliss. Right? Especially when you're freshly graduated from college and actually believe you can achieve anything—personally and professionally.

At twenty-two years old, I didn't just subscribe to this philosophy—I expected success without question. Was it arrogance? No. It was wide-eyed optimism. And, in hindsight, perhaps a little ignorance. Because at twenty-two, and lacking any "real-life" experience, you don't—and can't—have any clue how high the mountains are that you are going to climb.

Having graduated college with a major in psychology and a minor in English, I always thought I would be some sort of therapist. Verbal communication and interpersonal connections were skills I prided myself on, and I enjoyed the prospect of bringing that approach to a future vocation.

And while theater had always been my passion, I had no interested in acting. Whether it was a deep level of stage fright, or just knowing I didn't have the talent to perform onstage, being an actor was completely unappealing.

But in my early twenties, I discovered a career path that I had never encountered: that of a Broadway producer. A job where I could combine artistic passion and vision with business acumen seemed too good to be true. And best of all—the producer was the person in charge. Of everything. All of the boxes were checked, and I knew exactly what I wanted to do with my career.

Which proves the concept that "ignorance is bliss." I didn't know enough to ask how the heck someone becomes a Broadway producer without having a trust fund (which I certainly did not have) or a patron with the financial means to "write a check" that funds a show.

The truth is that timing is everything. I was lucky to be offered jobs out of college with industry leaders from Broadway and presenters working on "the road" on nationally touring shows, and many of these people remain mentors to me today. Fortunately, Broadway is both a global brand and a very small community, so my network expanded quickly, and I began speaking with investors, agents, actors, managers, directors, and designers. Producing, like any entrepreneurial job, is about networking, hustling, and maintaining great relationships and a trustworthy professional reputation.

Perhaps this is the best moment to explain what a Broadway producer does. Short answer: everything that happens behind the scenes of a Broadway show. You're responsible for securing the rights to produce a play or musical (and this often can involve underlying rights from source material—i.e., a book or movie), hiring and engaging a creative team (director; choreographer; designers for sets, lighting, sound, projections, costumes); overseeing casting and budgeting; finding investors and raising money; securing a venue; coordinating advertising, public relations, and house operations; and on, and on, and on. . . . A good producer needs to have a finger on the pulse of every aspect of the business and the creative world of a show. But frankly, when people ask me what I do as a Broadway producer, I always have the same simple response: "I'm a babysitter and a firefighter." And that's really all you need to know.

At twenty-three years old, I was growing a business of producing small cabaret shows in New York City based on the songbook catalogues of Cole Porter, Rodgers & Hart, Irving Berlin, and other iconic songwriters. Each show featured top Broadway talent. My simple philosophy was to only work with the best—the material, the onstage talent, and the creative team—and, in doing so, it would metabolically create the right combination for success.

In those early days, one of the most important industry relationships I cultivated was with the theater programming staff at the Kennedy Center. My work had been noticed, and in the summer of 1994 I was asked to produce a twelve-week series of these songbook shows in the Eisenhower Theater at the Kennedy Center, which I titled *Broadway Songbooks*. The shows each happily received rave reviews and a positive audience response.

Following the success of *Broadway Songbooks* at the Kennedy Center, I spent the next year cold-calling presenters around the country to book the US tours, citing the reviews and leaning on the prestige of the launch in D.C. From 1996 through 1999, the shows toured around the country (plus a few new *Broadway Songbooks* titles that I launched each new season). And by 1999, I had forged new relationships with theaters across the country as I began producing national tours of full-scale musical revivals, which continued for many years in a new hybrid partnership between a New York producer and Broadway touring venues.

During the ongoing US tours, one of my top priorities was to continue producing shows at the Kennedy Center. During the early 2000s there was a lack of quality touring plays in the market. I was able to seize this opportunity and deepen my relationship with the Center by producing one show each season for several years. The Kennedy Center felt like home.

The first of these plays was a revival of *On Golden Pond* in 2004, starring James Earl Jones and Leslie Uggams. The show was a hit in D.C., had the momentum to interest investors, and an offer to transfer to a Broadway theater from the Shubert Organization. *On Golden Pond* became my first of many future shows on Broadway and London, my first of five Tony® nominations, and other accolades.

As I look back at my career from the beginning, it all makes perfect sense. That doesn't mean it makes sense in the present moment, and usually it doesn't. But hindsight is 20/20.

In early 2016, so many years since I produced my first show at the Kennedy Center, I received a call from the Center's programming team inquiring if I could bring one of my current Broadway plays there. And while that wasn't possible, the conversations we had were ongoing; and ultimately resulted in my appointment in a newly defined position—as the Kennedy Center's vice president of Theater Producing and Programming. There was no doubt in my mind that I deeply desired to grab this opportunity and fulfill the hope I had in my early twenties of creating, producing, and programming theater at our nation's cultural performing arts center.

At the risk of sounding preachy, I do believe we can manifest the things we want in life. It's never easy, because anything with high reward takes a high amount of risk, failure, and strife. Success is ultimately a combination of drive, determination, tireless passion, and luck. But sometimes, ignorance is the exact bliss that allows you to scale the mountain and make your dreams become your reality.

Jeffrey Finn is a five-time Tony nominated Broadway Producer and recipient of The Robert Whitehead Award for Outstanding Achievement in Commercial Theater Producing. At the Kennedy Center, he is the vice president of Theater Producing and Programming, a position created with a mission to produce, curate, commission, and present all theater at The Kennedy Center, including programming and presenting the Broadway touring shows.

Jeffrey's Broadway producing credits include *Ain't Too Proud—The Life and Times of the Temptations; Sunday in the Park with George* starring Jake Gyllenhaal; *Hughie* starring Forest Whitaker; *An Act of God* starring Jim Parsons and Sean Hayes; *The Elephant Man* starring Bradley Cooper; *The Realistic Joneses* starring Toni Collette and Michael C. Hall; *I'll Eat You Last* starring Bette Midler; *Dead Accounts* starring KatieHolmes and Norbert Leo Butz; Kathie Lee Gifford's *Scandalous; Seminar* starring AlanRickman and then Jeff Goldblum; Green Day's *American Idiot; A View from the Bridge* starring Scarlett Johansson and Liev Schreiber; *Blithe Spirit* starring Angela Lansbury; *Oleanna* starring Bill Pullman and Julia Stiles; and *On Golden Pond* starring James Earl Jones and Leslie Uggams. Off-Broadway: *Game Show*. Regional Productions: *An Act of God* and *Seminar*: Ahmanson Theatre, *Poor Behavior* and *Oleanna*: Mark Taper Forum, *Saving Aimee*: 5th Avenue Theatre, *The Subject Was Roses*: Kennedy Center. National Tours: *The Music of Andrew Lloyd Webber; On Golden Pond*; The Who's *Tommy; Tell Me on a Sunday; Promises, Promises; Company; Chess;* and *BroadwaySongbooks* concert tours.

In 1992, Jeffrey Finn Productions launched Hot On Broadway to address the need for premium customized entertainment in the corporate arena. Offering entertainment with stars from current Broadway productions, Hot On Broadway has garnered an impressive corporate list of Fortune 500s including General Motors, Pepsi, Harrah's, Ritz Carlton Hotels, Disney, H & R Block, Toyota, Prudential, and Bayer.

www.JeffreyFinnProductions.com

GAL WITH A CLIPBOARD

Dawn Eason

I begin modeling and acting when I'm twelve. If it had been up to me, I would have started at age five, but my mother is the exact opposite of a stage mom. She holds me back for years, telling me that I need to be older, much older, before plunging into that world. But I am so impatient! After I finally convince her to take me to auditions, she drives me into the city from our suburb for months on end, audition after audition, rejection after rejection.

A stage manager finally tells me that if I really want to do this, I need to hone my craft. I need to take acting lessons, voice lessons, and learn how to work with photographers and directors. She tells me that this process—learning the craft, practicing for the love of it—will make all the difference. So I do as she says, and I practice until I get my first agent.

But by the time I'm sixteen, I have a secret: after all the work, all the practice, all the hours and weeks and months and years, I don't love it. I don't even like it. I built my young life around this dream, but it turns out to be the wrong dream.

Acting is so hard. I'm emotionally sensitive and leaning into all the pain and struggle of a character upsets me deeply. Even when I start getting great parts, I don't feel empowered in my abilities. It starts to affect my confidence.

But I can't tell anyone. This is what I've wanted for so long! This is what my mother gave up her time for. This is what I've been working tirelessly at for years, while other girls my age are having their middle-school fun.

And isn't this the dream? Doesn't everyone want this? My friends are so jealous.

You get to be famous. You can make so much money. You live such a glamorous life.

In 1990 I land a part on a new show called Hull High, billed as the TV version of Fame. I arrive on set, and the assistant director comes over to sign me in. He gives me the schedule for the day, tells me where to be and when, and says he'll be back to take me to hair and makeup in ten minutes. He is in charge, and everyone knows it.

As he walks away, I think, *I want to be the guy with the clipboard!*

But that thought is dangerous, and in the same moment, I think, I can't tell anyone that. I'm not supposed to be the guy with the clipboard.

Later that day, when I finally get on set, I convince the director to let me yell "Action!" I get a huge rush from it, like nothing I've experienced before, and it scares me so much that I don't tell a soul. I put all those dangerous ideas out of my head.

Seven years later, I go to Australia to film Roar with Heath Ledger. During the auditions, I ask so many questions about how the show is going to run that the producer, Sean Cassidy, sees the dangerous idea buried so deep inside me. He calls a mutual friend, a scriptwriter, and tells him that I'm not an actress—I'm a producer. He sees straight through me, and all my hopes come rushing back.

When I marry Bo a year later, I get my big chance to become the producer I'd secretly wanted to be. He finishes writing his play Runt of the Litter, and I step right in. I find someone to type the script, I show up to every rehearsal, I run the lights, I even engineer the sound for the play. I tell Bo, "You have to tell this story!" And he does. As it goes on tour all over the country, I get to put on a production. I get to entertain and create an amazing experience for the audience. I have creative control, I work with incredibly talented people, and I create a safe environment in which Bo can perform at his best. And I don't have to spend a second on stage.

In time, I do the same for people all over the country. When Bo and I launch our first live event, Personal Story Power Event, I create the same safe environment and amazing experiences for entrepreneurs, leaders, and professionals who want to learn how to tell their personal story in a powerful, authentic way.

These days, Bo is always telling audiences that I'm like a grizzly bear. I've been fighting for his dream, for our dream, for the past eighteen years, and now we fight together for other people's dreams. My ability to connect deeply with people, to understand what they need in each moment to deliver their best, is a core part of how I fight on their behalf.

Twenty-eight years ago, I was a sixteen-year-old actress on a set in Hollywood, living the wrong dream. Today, far more than being just a gal with a clipboard, I am a producer, living the dream I was made for, helping people get their story, their message, out to audiences all over the world.

Dawn Eason began as an actress and was well known for her recurring role on television's Melrose Place. Her career as a producer began in 2001 with Runt of the Litter, which was named one of the top off-Broadway plays of 2002. Along with producing the play's national tour, Dawn is currently producing the feature film of Runt of the Litter with Frank Darabont (writer/director of The Shawshank Redemption and The Green Mile). As managing partner of The Bo Eason Experience, Dawn runs operations for the company's ten live events, manages Bo Eason's speaking commitments, and helps develop and present digital and print material to create the superior quality of experience that the company's coaching and workshop clients have come to expect. Prior to their marriage in 1998, Bo and Dawn formed a dynamic partnership whose mission has evolved into helping others tap the power of their personal story and become effective, persuasive communicators. Dawn and Bo live in Southern California and have three children, Eloise, Axel, and Lyla Bo.

www.Bo Eason.com

FULL CIRCLE

Garrett Gunderson

I remember the first line of my college business textbook: "The purpose of business is to make a profit."

I thought to myself, *Really? Is that it?*

This perspective is limited and influenced people to chase money at the cost of their dreams and ironically, at the cost of their fortune.

The responsibility of a business is to be profitable, but the purpose of the business is the vision of where you're going and the difference that makes for you and others. It determines what you do, why you do it, and whether certain things are worthy of your time. Purpose adds focus and meaning to the actions we take each day. It takes us beyond the minutia of the day-to-day. When our purpose is greater than our problems, we find ways to be resourceful and solve those problems. With a lack of purpose, we lose energy or our problems feel insurmountable.

My business purpose started when I was a teenager. I created my first business, Garrett Gunderson's Car Care, at fifteen years old. I took third in the Rural Young Entrepreneur of the Year six months later and then won the Rural Young Entrepreneur of the Year the following year. I won the Governor's Young Entrepreneur of the Year for the State of Utah, and eventually at age seventeen, I was the SBA Young Entrepreneur of the Year for thirty years. These experiences changed my life, my perspective, and how I operate today.

Rural Young Entrepreneur Search and Governor's Honors Academy changed the trajectory of my life because what I thought was possible was now much bigger than what I found in my town of East Carbon, Utah—a place where there's not a lot of possibilities or a lot of vision. I met senators, scientists, inventors, philanthropists, and bright students that expanded what was possible for me.

One conversation, one person, one moment can make a permanent imprint on the mind of our youth. Thankfully, my teacher Teri Tubbs and my parents supported me in applying for and being able to attend these programs. This was a catalyst for me to create a life and business of opportunity and purpose. Seeing past trading time for money or the only purpose of a business being to make a profit, I have found how to make purpose profitable and therefore my life more meaningful.

This has now come full circle for me.

Recently, I returned to Governor's Honors Academy to speak. As I was about to take the stage and present to the top fifty students in the state of Utah, I thought back to what it was like when I was in their place—I felt afraid. Ironically, one of the attendees from a neighboring county where I grew up wasn't going to attend even though he was selected because he was afraid too. As a sixteen-year-old, traveling three and a half hours each way to a new city with high performing students is intimidating. This was my chance to reach and impact him and the other students.

I spoke to them about the rarest commodity in the world: vision.

We are bombarded with busyness and activity in the world. We have plenty of effort, and we have plenty of labor. The limiting belief is that hard work will create success. Hard work with the wrong philosophy leads to limited results at best, and hard work with the wrong vision will lead to bankruptcy. Hard work without vision is like a treadmill where there is no wealth at the end of the rainbow. When a person lacks vision, it's common for them to sacrifice the things in their life that they love and enjoy in the name of one day someday.

When I finished sharing, the young adults asked amazing and insightful questions. A wonderful buzz of energy filled the room. It's exciting to think about the opportunity they have to create value with their own compelling visions.

Part of my business purpose is now liberating one million people to be economically independent—to build a life they love and create a legacy that will last. My business purpose and social mission now intersect. I give 1 percent of all my revenue to support these programs with both time and money. I hosted the latest Rural Young Entrepreneurship program by funding it and being on the panel.

Through this partnership I can teach young people to see beyond the small town or small thinking while I invest time and money to be part of the process that was instrumental in my own life and success.

Garrett Gunderson is called a "financial genius" in entrepreneurial circles, but he wasn't born with a silver spoon. In fact, Garrett's blue-collar roots are what make him so passionate about helping entrepreneurs build economic independence.

Garrett's approach to personal finance is firmly rooted in this history. His company, Wealth Factory, helps self-made business owners and entrepreneurs who understand hard work buthaven't been given the proper financial tools to build lasting wealth.

www.wealthfactory.com

FORGIVING THE UNFORGIVABLE

Captain Charlie Plumb

I was really angry. Angry at my government for sending me to Vietnam, angry at myself for getting shot down, angry at my God for not sending a miracle angel to rescue my copilot and me when our supersonic F-4 Phantom was blown out of the sky by a surface-to-air missile. And perhaps, most of all I was angry with the enemy for the torture and brutality; the unbelievable physical pain they had brought to my body in clear violation of the Geneva Convention. I lay on the filthy prison floor and bled . . . and wept.

I had no idea, in that moment of misery and pain, the sweeping significance and indelible impact that experience was to have on the rest of my life. In fact, I was convinced that the most value this window of time could ever be would be a period of my life I could someday FORGET! It would take months of anguish to teach me a life-saving lesson. And even today, having had many years to reflect on the value of my POW experience, I'm still learning . . . and growing from being a prisoner of war for nearly six years in North Vietnam.

In some ways, my psychological response seemed to follow Kubler-Ross's model in her book *Death and Dying*. I can track her stages pretty clearly in my personal experience.

I began the first stage of denial having flown that world-class jet fighter through the skies of Vietnam for seventy-four successful combat missions, with only five days left of my tour of duty . . . I thought I was bulletproof. I couldn't believe the enemy had a gun big enough to shoot down Charlie Plumb. (The pain of the first bayonet stab in the back of my thigh quickly brought me out of that fantasy and into the next stage of *Death and Dying*.)

Kubler-Ross's second stage, anger, is where I dwelt the longest (and perhaps learned the most). It would take me years to finally understand and appreciate all this. At the time I really wanted to kill something . . . or someone. And I felt totally justified in that feeling. After all, by any intelligent analysis, I was the quintessential victim of circumstances beyond my control; twenty-four years old with a new wife back home, graduate of the Naval Academy with a great future ahead of me, I thought I had clearly been victimized by the fickle finger of fate.

But my simple formula for the most impactful lessons of life is this: L = PT. In order to really Learn something new, it takes a certain amount of Pain multiplied by a certain amount of Time. And for me this lesson took a considerable amount of physical and mental pain for about three months. That's how long it took for me to move on to the next stage. Kubler-Ross calls it acceptance. For me the psychological tool to implement acceptance is forgiveness.

An engineer by education, I tried to reason this through with a set of facts leading to a conclusion. My professors called it QED, from the Latin *quod erat demonstrandum*, or "thus it has been demonstrated." First, I started to consider the consequences of my anger. It became pretty clear to me that no matter how much rage I could muster, I wasn't going to affect the outcome of the war (which had been, as a military guy, my primary mission). In fact, my personal wrath seemed to actually encourage and delight my captors. And, in harboring all this vitriol I was eating myself up—from the inside out! Assuming I still had the choice, it just didn't seem very profitable to harbor all these negative feelings.

So I found a new definition for anger. Using our secret prison-communication system, a fellow POW passed me this Mark Twain quote: "Anger is an acid that can do more harm to the vessel in which it is stored than to anything on which it is poured."

It took him several minutes to tap out that message through our mutual prison wall using our cumbersome code, but when I deciphered the final words and understood the meaning, I realized that I was that vessel. But even understanding that, the next question was to be the most daunting: If I can't pour the acid onto something, how on earth do I get rid of it? How do get the poison out of the vessel . . . my body? How do I change my attitude? How do I ignore the atrocities perpetrated on my fellow fighter pilots and me?

After much soul searching I found a simple tool. Simple to say but difficult to implement: unconditional forgiveness. It worked in the prison, and it works for me today. I heartily recommend it.

I had learned a lot about forgiveness from my mother. As a devout Christian, she practiced it daily. I tried to as well. But my POW experience taught me it's more than a kind, Christian thing to do—it's vital for self-preservation in life-threatening trauma and in the rigors of our daily life.

And it isn't just forgiving our enemies; sometimes it's forgiving our loved ones, and sometimes even ourselves. This, in turn gives us permission to step forward, take control, and move on with our lives. I'm convinced that we can imprison ourselves with blame, guilt, and self-doubt to the point that we are paralyzed. And those mental prison walls can be more restrictive than the ones of stone and steel that I was behind in the Vietnam prison camps. We can set ourselves free from those self-imposed chains when we implement unconditional forgiveness.

So the act of forgiveness can actually be a selfish one. (And I believe it's OK to be selfish once in a while.) In my experience, if you can maintain a forgiving heart, you can sustain a healthy heart.

So forgive the unforgivable . . . for the good of others, but mostly for yourself.

Charlie Plumb completed thirty-one years in the US Navy, retiring with the rank of captain. Since returning home, more than five thousand audiences in nearly every industry have been spellbound as Captain Plumb draws parallels between his POW experience and the challenges of everyday life. One of the most sought-after motivational speakers of his time, his presentations are as he is: sincere, straightforward, and humorous. In addition to delivering renowned keynote presentations, he proficiently creates and executes seminar workshops, safety stand-downs, and sessions for continuing education credits. To learn more about the speaker and the man, please visit his website.

www.CharliePlumb.com

"Teamwork, Tone, Tenacity" Triumphs Over Stage IV Cancer

RADM Paul Becker

On December 23, 2014, I was diagnosed with Stage IV bone marrow cancer. There is no Stage V. A large tumor was eating up my right femur. The blood results for this disease, known as Multiple Myeloma (MM), were off the charts in the worst direction. After a detailed radioactive scan, I asked the doctor, "Can you tell me where else the cancer is?"

She replied, "It would be easier to tell you where it isn't."

I can't remember the last time I was speechless . . . I'll never forget this one. My wife, Kim, and I braced ourselves for what would be a sporty holiday season and 2015.

I was fifty-three when I was stunned by this unexpected, unwanted, and uncertain disease. At the time I was a US Navy Rear Admiral serving as the Director of Intelligence for the Joint Chiefs of Staff in the Pentagon. Considered healthy and fit with no family cancer history, I spent the better part of the previous decade serving afloat and ashore in southwestern Asia during periods of crisis and combat. Throughout this time I witnessed illness and injury. The military's ethos regarding illness and injury was reinforced many times over: Be sympathetic but also stoic about absorbing fellow service members' tough, sometimes tragic news. It was the cultural norm that when a service member's personal difficulties appeared to be at their worst, the victims quickly blew through Dr. Elizabeth Kubler Ross's famous seven stages of grief: acknowledging 1) shock, then bypassing 2) denial, 3) anger, 4) bargaining, 5) guilt, 6) depression, and proceeding directly to 7) acceptance. Military mission success and lives often depended on service members addressing grief in this fashion. This background was an essential element of how I would mentally and physically prepare for a great battle ahead.

I'm a man of Faith: practicing my religion afloat and ashore. I'm devoted to Family: wife, parents, brothers, friends, and dogs. I'm a man of Fitness: a marathoner and Cross-Fit regular (or at least I was). I knew Faith, Family, and Fitness would be part of what would help me triumph over adversity; they always had. But this time I knew I'd need something more. I needed a framework that I could reflect upon quietly, that I could declare aloud, that I could physically demonstrate during dire circumstances. I needed something short, memorable, and actionable. I needed something that I'd previously developed, applied, and succeeded with in peace, crisis, and combat. I needed something that would impact, invigorate, inspire. I needed "Teamwork, Tone, Tenacity."

Why "Teamwork, Tone, Tenacity"? When I reflect on three decades of service, I often think of leaders I worked for who weren't just good—they were great. Because of their philosophies, personalities, and practices, they inspired our organizations to meet our mission in the toughest of circumstances while maintaining high morale to boot. This provided the practical example and framework I'd need for the tough circumstances ahead. But why in an ocean of descriptors, adjectives, and narratives was it worth focusing on just three? Because "Teamwork, Tone, Tenacity" form a superior set of mutually reinforcing behaviors aimed at meeting mission and maintaining morale. They also happen to fit together well in a short, actionable, memorable phrase. This inspirational maxim would be immediately retrievable during months of debilitating high-dose chemotherapy, strength-draining stem-cell replacement, and two life-threatening cardiac events.

A few specifics on each of "The Three Ts."

Teamwork: Begins by building trust. One of the most important tasks for building a team is building relationships. Because the result of strong relationships is trust, the by-product of trust is loyalty, and loyalty to the team is the essence of organizational morale, whether wearing camouflage, a business suit, or medical scrubs. Immediately upon diagnosis I embarked upon an accelerated program of building relationships with a network of medical professionals involved in my care and other cancer patents/survivors, building trust by engaging with them on all aspects MM. This partnership in turn helped develop a mutual loyalty with these caregivers and colleagues by advocating their positive efforts and results to those in our hospital and beyond in the greater military and medical communities. After months of intense professional and personal interaction, we became a Team, completely invested with each other toward a common goal of triumphing over MM.

Tone: There are a lot of dimensions to tone, but when I reflect upon the military leaders who demonstrated it best, I recall their bright attitudes which caused a chain reaction of positive thoughts, events, and outcomes. I esteem their genuineness and integrity, taking the time to help others, never complaining or showing fatigue, always consistent in their actions. Good tone is also maintaining advantage over any crisis by remaining cool and unruffled despite chaotic circumstances. No matter the level of discomfort at the time, when dealing with family and friends, I tried to be as cool and positive as possible with a smile. Even my first comments under medical duress were usually in the fashion of Apollo 13 astronaut, Jim Lovell, who calmly exclaimed in crisis, "Houston, we have a problem." Now that's Tone!

Tenacity: I agree with Thomas Edison: Genius is 1 percent inspiration and 99 percent perspiration. There's no substitute for hard work in understanding all aspects of an issue, being involved and visible to teammates, setting standards, and applying sustained effort to strive for a solution. The most tenacious leaders I've seen in the military placed the burden of overcoming the most difficult circumstances on their own backs ahead of their personal comfort and ambition. Succinctly, they just tried harder, and they demonstrated an indomitable spirit while serving our nation. Pick any Medal of Honor awardee from any conflict, and I'll guarantee the one characteristic they have in common is Tenacity.

To sum it up, I consistently relied upon the inspirational framework of "Teamwork, Tone, Tenacity" to overcome the Unexpected, Unwanted, and Uncertainty and triumph over cancer. I am now, thank God, two years into a stable remission. MM is still an incurable malignancy, but it is treatable, and my way ahead is regular low-dose maintenance chemotherapy treatments. Considering all the potential outcomes, this is a great place to be. I hope my actions in this personal crisis serve as an example to others that "Teamwork, Tone, Tenacity" can be applied against any type of adversity, especially when the stakes are extremely high. Teamwork, Tone, Tenacity: They rocked my life and are allowing me to help others . . . and that is truly the best revenge against cancer!

Rear Admiral Paul Becker, USN (Ret.), is a highly decorated veteran who served around the globe in peace, crisis, and combat as a Naval Intelligence Officer. Upon retirement in 2016, he founded The Becker T3 Group LLC, a consultancy focused on improving organizations' bottom line by applying leadership's core tenets of "Teamwork, Tone, Tenacity." He is a dynamic keynote speaker whose articles and interviews have been widely published. A Stage IV Bone Marrow cancer survivor, he regularly inspires health care professional and patient audiences by sharing firsthand lessons for overcoming adversity.

www.TheBeckerT3Group.com

High Hopes for Your Future

Les Brown Jr.

The little seven-year-old boy wanders through the seminar, walking past the round tables as if they were bouncy balls that were on sale at the local supermarket. He is completely oblivious to the speaker in the front of the room. As the executives and entrepreneurs listen to the orator (who happens to be the wandering child's parent) describe the keys to rock star status, there is only one person in the room that has mastered those keys more than the star on the stage. The seven-year-old is holding the key to becoming a rock star in his heart. He does not have to unlearn misery, because all of the people he encounters go out of their way to encourage him. He is not stressed by competition or the emerging fiscal cliff because this little wobbly, laughing, wondering, playful little star is fully present. He's not reminiscing about stories of an ancient Great Depression. This motivational superstar did not tune into the Constant Negative News (CNN) the way too many of us find entertaining. No, this baby, this kid, this youth is becoming the new-age seminar superstar.

He effortlessly holds the key to stardom in his hand, as if it were a priceless smartphone in the pocket of a teenager. The father in the front of the room, with the cordless microphone gripped as if it were his only hope in life, can captivate every single person in the audience but his own child. His child, this seven-year-old boy does not have to take notes or pretend like he is interested. For this child has within him, as do all children, a secret download of awareness. A download that is virus-proof, a download that can prevent us all from crashing our lives into a sea of complacency. For this child has discovered and will go on to teach the world the power of high hopes.

Picture this little rascal, skipping from the back of the room to the front of the room, but this time he had a look of purpose on his face. In a high-pitched voice that is far too mature to come from such a cute package, the little boy tugs at his father's coattails and shocks the audience by saying, "Give me the mic."

In that moment, the child had an idea to share, yet his dad saw him as a mere distraction with nothing truly to offer such a distinguished crowd. The audience laughs and pleads to the presenter to let his offspring take the microphone and share his key to achieving rock star success. After all, are there any experts on the planet more qualified than those amongst us that have imaginary friends? Or those of us who find the dirt fascinating, or who can be totally engulfed in joy by a bouncing balloon? Well, unfortunately this child never got the opportunity to speak that afternoon. He had to wait twenty-one more years before the world would hear the message he concocted as a child. I am a man now, and below is the only key to being a rock star that I know works all the time.

Connect to the INNER NET, the software inside you that is closer than your sight. Upload your life to the INNER NET. Not the internet—what I mean is that when you pull your gifts out to share them with the world, go inside yourself first and grab hold of all the substance of your total being. The key to happiness is the INNER NET. It is what connects fathers and son, wives and husbands, friends and allies. The internal program that was installed at birth in order for us to be able to locate our utopia at all times is the INNER NET. There will come a time when you might find yourself wandering through life, ignoring all of the activities around you that are affecting you whether you know it or not. If you ever get disconnected from your happiness, to the point that you might have forgotten the last time you truly had a tearful laugh.

If you ever misplace your joyful skip as you move forward in your job or in your business, forget about internet marketers; they are important, but they can't save you. You need to become an INNER NET marketer. Start refreshing your happiness by doing an INNER NET launch to get out all of those gifts, dreams, ideas, inventions, books, poems, curriculums, business plans, nonprofit organizations, widgets, apps, television shows, and branding opportunities out of your net and into this world. I pray that you don't wait twenty-one years to log on. No matter who stands in your way or whose shadow you must come out of in order to truly connect, the INNER NET is the key to happiness that makes the internet possible. The INNER NET will move your life so fast that 4g speeds will not be able to keep up with your progress. Once you connect to your INNER NET, you won't be overwhelmed by your inbox when you awaken in the morning. Your inbox will stay full, and you will love it because you recognize that every opportunity that has ever come your way has been as a result of this key.

The strong signal to infinite intelligence so you can handle the abundance of laughter, joy, bliss, love, courage, passion, peace and pleasure that is surely on its way to you will only come from inside you." Can you hear me now? If so, I just have one final question. Are you connected?

Step 1—Connect to the INNER NET through INNER NET marketing. That means we must pull out all of our inner abilities, no matter how strange, misunderstood, or underdeveloped they may be. Pull them out and launch them to the world!

Step 2—Once you connect to your INNER NET, make sure you upload everything you've got. If for some reason you do crash, it would be a crime to take those gifts and talents with you, so UPLOAD EVERYTHING! Leave no file behind.

Step 3—After completing Steps 1 and 2, I would like you to log on to your family's destiny and figure out an original process for fulfilling it using your unique skill sets and voice. Remember, the INNER NET can keep your family together even when it appears that you are far apart.

In order to be a true rock star, you don't need a fancy car (even though they are nice). You won't even need a fancy house or a smartphone (even though they are convenient). All you need in order to unlock the key to being a rock star is your INNER NET connection.

Mark Twain said, "Twenty years from now you will be more disappointed by the things that you didn't do than by the ones you did do. So, throw off the bowlines. Sail away from the safe harbor. Catch the trade winds in your sails. Explore. Dream. Discover." I know he was talking about exploring and discovering your INNER NET rock star. Find out more about how we can work together and get a free download from my rock star father Les Brown and me by texting Time to 26786 so you can receive a priceless gift.

Les Brown Jr. is the international bestselling author of Harvard Effect and co-Emmy winner for Outstanding Creative Achievement in Interactive Media in the area of Social TV Experience.

Known as one of the top five speakers under the age of forty in America, Les Brown Jr. has helped his family business generate over $100 million in sales with a weekly reach of over two million people online in the area of personal growth and business development. In the words of Bob Proctor, "I saw Les Brown Jr. speak when he was about fifteen years old, and he had the audience eating out of the palm of his hand."

www.LesBrownJr.com

TIDBITS

Craig Wayne Boyd

A wise man named Bob Speir once told me: "Life is made up of all these tidbits. What you do with them, and how you use them is what dictates the rest of your life, so concentrate on the small things." For me, those "tidbits" always had something to do with music. Whether I was singing in my church choir, school plays, listening to the radio, or completely devoting myself to learning the instruments I picked up at garage sales, it was always around. As the son of a honky-tonk player and with a mother who raised me to sing the gospel, I was constantly conflicted on which genre of music I fell into. One day the pastor of my church explained to me that you can't always preach to the choir and told me to go where I was led.

I wasn't sure what all of that meant until I was twenty-three. My father and I traveled to Nashville, where I was fortunate enough to meet a very prominent person in the music publishing scene. He told me I was on the right track but that I had to be present to win. He asked if I was willing to move to the Music City. I said yes, surprising myself with no hesitation. On the way home I looked up and said, "God, is this what I'm really supposed to do?" After all, I'd just built a new house, I was married, and I had a stable six-figure income. Did this make sense? The answer came to me like a two-by-four across the forehead when I pulled back up to my house in Dallas and found a note from my then-wife. She had left me for good and specifically asked me to never try and find her.

After moving to Nashville, it seemed as if I were on my way to fulfilling my dream. I was writing with some great songwriters, performing in writers' rounds, and formed the trio Southland with musicians Cole Lee and Levi Sims. A year later I landed a publishing deal with EMI, one of the most renowned publishing companies in the world. For three years, life was good. The trio was getting positive attention, we had labels interested in us, and we were playing packed venues. But if there's one thing the music industry will teach you, it's don't hold your breath. Before I knew it, my trio had broken up, I had lost my publishing deal, and my close friend and former band mate Levi had passed away from cystic fibrosis. I was back to square one, grieving the loss of my friend, and trying to figure out how to pick up the pieces.

After much contemplation, I decided to pursue a solo career. I was introduced to a new independent label, and we recorded another album. The single from that album was a direct reflection of my journey so far, aptly titled "I Ain't No Quitter." The single reached the top 30s on the Music Row Charts, defying the precedent at the time that if you weren't on a major label, it was nearly impossible to get a song played. I'd been playing nearly 250 dates a year, including a radio tour. When I returned from one of my tours, I saw movers pulling furniture out of my independent label's office. My immediate thought was Awesome! We're getting new furniture! But the reality was that the company had lost its funding. Even with my single still moving up the charts, I was headed back to square one once again. No label, no money to pay band members, and back to the drawing board. It was 2012, strike three.

I'm not sure if it was my stupidity or my "stick-to-itiveness" that kept me going. By now, I was a new father to my first son, Jaxon. It wasn't just about me anymore, and I had the pressing responsibility to be successful. I started over again, and for two years I played as many gigs as I could on the road. I picked up jobs working construction while also writing and performing as often as possible. One day in particular I was working on a job site when a label executive came into the house we were building. He looked at me and asked, "Aren't you Craig Wayne Boyd? What are you doing here?" I told him I had a son to support now and needed to pick up some extra work. I've never been ashamed of who I am. Hard work has never been beneath me, but in that moment I felt defeated.

With quitting on my mind, I opened up my computer to find an email from a producer of the NBC TV show *The Voice* asking if I would be interested in auditioning for Season 7. I thought it was spam. Turns out, it wasn't. After debating whether or not I wanted to be in a televised singing competition, I felt this opportunity must have crossed my path for a reason. With no official home, I spent the weeks leading up to my audition packing my things, moving them into storage, sleeping on any sofa available, and mentally preparing myself for what was to come.

On the flight from BNA to LAX, I decided this was not going to be a competition against other artists; it was my battle against myself. Those that watched Season 7 of NBC's *The Voice* know the outcome, but to touch briefly on the finale, I remember being on the stage with the last four contestants. I was the only member left from Team Blake, and the other three were from Team Adam. We huddled together on the stage in front of a live audience as the results slowly dwindled our numbers from four to two. I watched Damien walk off first, then Chris, and then there were two. Once again would my hopes be dashed? I'd never set out to win the show; I had come to prove to myself that I could stand with the best and was worthy of being there. Now here I was, in the final moments suddenly realizing I wanted it so badly.

Carson Daly called my name, and I was crowned Season 7 winner of *The Voice*! As I held that trophy in my hand, confetti falling all around me, and tears streaming down my cheeks, I thought back to Bob Speir and his wise words. I thank the good Lord every day for my "tidbits" and for blessing me with some serious "stick-to-itiveness" to make this music dream a reality on one heck of a reality show ride.

Born with a collapsed lung, no one was sure he would breathe let alone sing. **Craig Wayne Boyd** came into this world determined to beat the odds, and that is what he has proven to do time and time again. He grew up in Mesquite, Texas, to a Pentecostal, gospel-singing mama and a banjo-picking, bluegrass-playing daddy. But it was his grandma with a heart after Johnny Cash that opened the floodgates to all things country. These are the "ingredients" that make up CWB's style of music.

Boyd moved to Nashville after going through a "lost my wife, lost my dog, lost my truck" real-life kind of country song. He spent ten years writing, recording, and touring with much success, but winning Season 7 of NBC's *The Voice* blessed him with that "overnight success." Since then he has been able to share the stage with Rascal Flatts, Lynard Skynard, Travis Tritt, The Marshall Tucker Band, Randy Houser, and many more. His most recent album, *Top Shelf,* is available on iTunes and Amazon Music.

www.CraigWayneBoyd.com

LETTING GO—A LIFE PhD FROM MISTAKES UNIVERSITY

Nick Lowery

In 1990 I had my best scoring year in the NFL—hell, I led the NFL in scoring and received not only the NFL All Pro team but Pro Football Weekly's "Golden Toe" award as the best kicker OR punter in the NFL! Can't get much better than that! The second-most field goals in a season in NFL history, the Kansas City Chiefs record for points in a season, twenty-four field goals in a row into the playoffs . . . really good stuff—especially after following my worst season ever. Even though I was already the most accurate kicker in NFL history at the time, I had been humiliated in one intense, dark, insane, very cold, muddy, and very public fifteen-minute span of time the year before on a muddy, frigid field in the old Cleveland Stadium.

That taught me once again that we must always cherish the hunger for greatness, the urgency, the humility to love the awkward, uneven process of hard work that is at its core. As I look back, I used that profoundly painful event—three missed field goals right at the end of the game and in overtime, to re-learn what I already knew deep in my bones: that it's all about pulling out the stops, devoting yourself to and totally trusting your preparation as the only way to allow yourself to find a new level. I made a conscious decision to let go of both the expectations and judgments of others, and many of my own as well. I gave back to myself that simple power to be the best I could be, to be content to focus only on perfecting God's beautiful gifts to me. That's all we can ever do! Find that peace to bring all our energy, all our focus, all our discipline and passion to our own four-by-three-yard-square office between the hash marks on the field. For me, that lonely Persian Rug shaped, Magic Carpet ride to complete fear and totally insane life-giving risk.

I knew that the standards and goals I had set for my performance exceeded the expectations of others, and that was enough. How sad to live a life where not only do we never taste the best we can be, but we live based on the standards, judgments, and expectations of others. In essence, we are living someone else's life! To me, it's only the conversation with ourselves and God's purpose waiting to be awakened and set on fire that is where the Light truly lives.

We all have and will have defeats and losses. We all will make a thousand mistakes along the way. I say, make a million mistakes—try so many times that the fear of mistakes becomes the brilliant enlightenment and confirmation that making unlimited mistakes is giving you permission to be YOURSELF.

The New England Patriots were undefeated through the entire season and into the

Super Bowl a few years ago, yet in the end they ended with a crushing loss that interrupted and destroyed their dream of a perfect season. That year may be more painful than many less-outstanding ones because sometimes in the midst of great effort and extraordinary achievement, failure still rears its head. But Failure is merely Greatness and Wisdom in disguise.

We all have bad, even horrible, games. We will all miss our own field goals, sometimes even the potential game-winners. We fall short of our own expectations, but at least they are our own! How much better to focus our expectations on superb preparation? How about not worrying about the outcome? The great players stay focused on the work at hand and find a way to remain alert yet relaxed as the process of their own form of Field Goal and scoring points unfolds. They find peace knowing they have done the good work to be ready for the chaos of life and the game—and they trust that preparation as they enter the fire because that practice was likely as hard or harder than the game itself.

The media tries to bully a player's attention away from the right things, and turn a Tom Brady, Drew Brees, Aaron Rodgers, Cam Newton and RG3 into Hall of Famers in one season—or even seven games . . . or they trash them into complete failures just as fast! All NFL greats like Tom Brady, Brett Favre, Johnny Unitas, and Joe Montana have tasted defeat. Some knuckle-head will always criticize our performance. Think about it! The better we are, the more people are watching . . . the more visible and interesting we are . . . and the more expectations and people to please . . . or to ignore.

So how can we focus when so many cameras become a collective mirror that blocks the sense of space, distance, and context we all prefer? If we spend our minutes, hours, or days worrying about the expectations of others, we miss out on what is happening now! And being present in THIS MOMENT, my friends, is the essence of living and winning! Those moments of being fully, calmly, charismatically alive to ourselves and others; alive to each breath we take; each pair of eyes we connect with—equally alive to the unique energy, spirit, and story that people bring to us. A moment of truth is not just an apex moment; it is also a present-ness truly full when it is about little details, small surprises, and miracles of our whole world, not just us!

The narcissistic hero athlete kicker in us (speaking from experience!) sometimes takes much too long to learn. The universe is unlimited and infinite in value. It's our choice to invest in the currency of success and not that of defeat. More than the traditional idea of success, I am talking—no, I am singing—about a tactile feeling far beyond any naive notions of intuition. It's that feeling that takes place in our heart's epicenter, where instead of seeing ourselves as impostors and saboteurs in our own defeats and reaffirmed failures, we brand ourselves legitimate and worthy and loved. And that, my friends, is victory!

Nick Lowery transcends any category: Hall of Famer, Ivy League scholar, presidential aide, author and poet, teacher, philanthropist. The Kansas City Chiefs Hall of Famer was the most accurate kicker in NFL history. Nick's story is about persistence that leads to Focus, Passion, and Purpose. Nick won the NFL Man of the Year Award for both the Kansas City Chiefs and the New York Jets. A Harvard and Dartmouth graduate, he is the winner of the NFL Player's humanitarian award, the Byron Whizzer White Award. For information about Nick's speaking or community work, contact Nick at Nick@Loweryspeaks.com.

www.nicklowery.org

Teamwork Is Life—The Rest Is Just Details

Roland Williams, NFL Super Bowl Champion

Growing up in the 19th Ward in Rochester, New York, I was constantly surrounded by negativity. Poverty, gangs, drugs, violence, teenage pregnancy, and abuses of the body and spirit were commonplace. I look back with awe at my ability to make it out and gratitude for those who helped me. I am so thankful for the abundance of teamwork at home, at school, and in my neighborhood, helping me think differently, speak differently, and do what it took to transcend my toxic surroundings.

My introduction to football came through my father, a large and athletic man who worked for decades as a correctional officer at a juvenile detention center in Rochester. He loved the game and especially enjoyed watching his beloved Dallas Cowboys and Tony "Touchdown" Dorsett dominate opposing teams. Dad taught me that I had to work hard if I wanted to go far in football, stay committed, and not let anyone push me around. I listened to my dad, and it worked. By my senior year in high school, I became one of the nation's top student-athletes and earned a full athletic scholarship to Syracuse University. I am so grateful for all my dad, my teammates, and the teamwork taught me about believing in myself and never giving up on my dreams.

While in college, I worked hard to take academics as seriously as football. Graduating early with a BA in Speech Communications and a minor in Management from the Whitman School of Management was a big deal to my family and me. On the field, I was fortunate enough to be playing with some of the most talented players in college football history. I'm so grateful for the talented teachers, teammates, and spirit of teamwork that pushed me to do what was necessary get to the next level.

Drafted in the fourth round by the St. Louis Rams, I came into the NFL with a big chip on my shoulder. I was determined to prove to the football world that I should have been a first-round pick. I worked really hard. I learned from coaches and any veteran that wanted to take some time to teach me. Despite our team having a dismal four win and twelve loss season, I started making a name for myself with the Rams. I became a starter and won the team's Rookie of the Year award. I'm grateful for the teamwork and teammates and even the adversity and humility that gave me the extra motivation to succeed my first year in the NFL.

My second year in the NFL, things got even better. I caught seven touchdown passes and was known around the league as the best blocking tight end in the NFL. To add to the fun, I played alongside of some of the greatest players to wear a football helmet. Our offense became known as "the greatest show on turf," and went on to win the Rams' only Super Bowl title in franchise history. I'll never forget the amazing feeling of holding the Vince Lombardi Super Bowl trophy for the first time. I'm was so grateful for how far talented teammates and a commitment to teamwork had gotten me.

At the Rams' ring ceremony, Head Coach Dick Vermeil said something profound to us that I will never forget. He said, "The Vince Lombardi trophy only weighs 7.5 pounds, but it takes an entire organization to lift it." He was so right. Sometimes people only pay attention to those on the field or on stage and forget about those behind the scenes. I'm grateful for all the strength and conditioning coaches, trainers, doctors, surgeons, nutritionists, agents, friends, skeptics, and other off-the-field teammates that were key to my football success.

My career ended abruptly in 2006 after suffering a career-ending knee injury, but before then I was fortunate enough to also play for three seasons with the Raiders and one with the Buccaneers. While I was with the Raiders, we won an AFC Championship in 2004. Both experiences were amazing lessons in teamwork, resiliency, and how to come out better on the other side.

Syracuse University. Eight years in the NFL. Multiple divisional championships. A conference championship. A Super Bowl. Rams. Raiders. Bucs. Teamwork.

In life after football, I haven't gotten far away from teamwork or the game at all. I jumped into sports broadcasting as an in-game and studio analyst for ESPN, CBS, and NBC. I started a mentoring program in my hometown that teaches urban teens in poverty the comprehensive benefits of teamwork. I consult, speak, and train organizations interested in extraordinary production and team cohesion in fiercely competitive environments.

I coached my son's youth football teams. As I write this, I'm forty-four years young and my oldest sons, Trustin and Justice, are both playing in high school and middle school football respectively. I'm so grateful for the lessons of teamwork my sons now get to learn through the game that has taught me so much.

So now, after forty-plus years of living teamwork firsthand around some of the most successful athletes, business leaders, and organizations in the world, my contribution to this book is a simple reminder of one of the most critical truths I've learned during my journey: Teamwork is life. The rest is just details.

Please take time to think of every teammate helping you win at home and in your professional life—and be grateful. Understand what makes a great teammate. Teamwork is the greatest gift ever given to humankind. Use it more often and watch your world expand.

Roland Williams was born and raised in Rochester, NY. He is a graduate of Syracuse University, where he excelled in the classroom and on the football field. Roland played eight years in the National Football League, winning a Super Bowl with the St. Louis Rams, and received wide recognition for his philanthropic activities. Roland is currently a teamwork expert, entrepreneur, and philanthropist. One of his businesses was recently featured on ABC's Shark Tank, and his groundbreaking Champion Academy Extreme Mentoring & Empowerment Initiative is transforming the lives of urban teens in poverty. Roland has three sons and resides in Los Angeles.

www.RolandWilliams.com

Professional Golf on Hold

George Gankas

My father was a pretty good golfer, and in the summer of my senior year of high school, he took me out to play with him. After the round he told me that I was a terrible golfer. I probably was, but then he said that I would never beat him, and that was all the motivation I needed.

I'm a pretty competitive guy, so within a year, I beat him. My motivation was originally to score better than my dad. After that, I just got addicted to it. When I started playing seriously, my mechanics were bad because I didn't have a coach, so I started reading a bunch of golf books. That's when I started getting more of an understanding of the golf swing, and that became my focus.

At eighteen years old, I wanted to be a professional golfer and make the PGA tour. I started focusing on all the different types of golf swings—why does this one work? Why can't I do it this way or this way? I started reading books and magazines, and I watched videos tapes in my VCR.

I originally thought I was going to college to wrestle, but that changed as I had to make a decision of where I wanted to go to school. I wasn't good enough at golf yet to go to a Division 1 School, so I went to a junior college and made the team. The next year I made the team again, and I was voted the Most Valuable Player. After that, I decided to try out for the Cal State Northridge golf team. I not only made the team, but I also received a scholarship.

While trying to qualify for the PGA Tour, I worked as a caddie at the famed Sherwood Country Club. While caddying, I gave golf tips to some of the members at the club. Word started to spread that I actually knew what I was talking about.

All of a sudden people started asking me to teach them outside the course. Then while I was playing, I was like screw it, I'll just start teaching, because so many people were asking me. Then a good buddy named J.T. Kohut who played golf at UCLA asked me to help him. He was my roommate at the time, and I helped him for free. He had a bunch of buddies who were like, dude, who's your coach? Next thing I knew, it just spread.

I decided to rent a golf stall at Westlake Golf Course in Westlake Village, California, and start giving golf lessons. I charged $80 an hour, and within a week I had two to five clients a day. So I was a caddie, I was giving lessons, and I was trying to play enough golf because my goal was still to make the PGA Tour.

Then world famous volleyball player Gabrielle Reese started taking golf lessons from me. I met her at Sherwood, and we went out and played a round. She saw that I was a good player, so she asked, "Hey why don't you just help me?" So I helped her.

I soon realized that I was better at coaching and understanding the golf swing, and I knew how to get people to play better golf. I kept getting more clients, so I had to make a decision. "Do I want to keep giving lessons, or do I want to focus my efforts on making the PGA Tour?"

I got so consumed with teaching, because I started making money for the first time in my life. It became a different type of addiction. I really enjoyed making money.

Plus, I always felt like I was the best teacher in the world. I felt like I knew more than anybody. I didn't, but I felt like I did. That gave me confidence to keep making people believe in what I did.

I decided to focus on being the best golf technician in the world and on how to get more speed with a golf swing. I became known for my unique and powerful golf swing. If you believe in your heart that you're the best, then you will be successful, and I had a thriving business giving golf lessons.

I quickly became very popular with the top junior golfers in the area. Every day there would be five to ten kids at a time hanging out watching me give a lesson to their friends. It became a small community of junior golfers that all wanted to be the best. I worked with Tristen Gretzky, Zack Amadi, Jake Marek, Spenser Soosman, Brad Dalke, Ryan Duswalt, Sean Crocker, Seldon Doyle, and the former #1 Junior in the world, Akshay Bhatia, among others. And my top junior golfer so far is a kid named Matthew Wolff.

My schedule got so packed that I was able to charge more per lesson and get it. I went from $80 an hour to $100, then to $120. I opened an Instagram account called George Gankas Golf. I would film my golfer's swings and put them on my page. It became sort of a competition among all the juniors of who was going to be featured on my Instagram page every day. My Instagram account currently has more than 167,000 followers and continues to grow every day.

My juniors were becoming so successful I had a huge waiting list. And because my Instagram account went viral, I was contacted by a few professional golfers on the PGA Tour. I have worked with Sung Kang, Danny Lee, Darren Clarke, Padraig Harrington, Adam Scott, Matt Every, Johnny Ruiz, and many others.

So, because I had to squeeze in professional golfers, and because there were some great potential junior golfers on my waiting list, I decided that I would see who the serious golfers were and continued to raise my prices. I went from $200, to $250, to $350-plus an hour, and they all decided to stay with me.

A few years ago, one of my star students, Matthew Wolff, went to college at Oklahoma State. And just recently he won the 2019 Individual NCAA Championship as a sophomore. After his sophomore year, Matthew left college and became a professional golfer on the PGA Tour. In only his third tournament as a pro, Matthew won his first PGA Event at the 3M Tournament in Blaine, Minnesota. His rapid rise to fame is pretty unique, and I have no doubt in my mind that Matthew will be one of the greatest golfers to ever play the game.

People ask me all the time now about how it feels to work with players on the PGA Tour and now have a player that has won on the PGA Tour. I say this: "It's just as exciting for me when a junior golfer does well in a local tournament as it is when Matthew Wolff wins on the PGA Tour."

I still have a dream. I'm forty-eight years old now, and my new goal is to play on the Champions Tour—a professional golf tour for players fifty years old and older. If I make it, great. If not, I still have one of the best jobs in the world.

George Gankas graduated from Cal. State Northridge with a Bachelor's Degree in Psychology. He played professional golf on the Mini Tour. George caddied at Sherwood Country Club, and then started giving golf lessons at Moorpark Country Club and Westlake Golf Course. He started teaching some of the best amateur and junior golfers in the country, and his popular Instagram account helped get him noticed by professional golfers. George has worked with numerous professional golfers including Sung Kang, Adam Scott, Padraiq Harrington, Danny Lee, and Matthew Wolff, just to name a few.

www.GeorgeGankas.golf

ONE KEY TO VICTORY

Dr. Carol Soloway

What's the one trait that enables us to overcome disappointment when things didn't go as planned; disillusionment when everything you believed in—like marriage—turned out to be an illusion; or devastation when you didn't think you could go on?

I traveled across the United States last year and asked one hundred powerful women to define success. Their responses were similar: persistence, courage, fearlessness, tenacity. There was one thread that was consistent: they all had a quality which I describe as unshakable drive.

Unshakable drive is what allows us to overcome obstacles on our way to success. I remember how easy marriage and motherhood were: all I had to do was cook like Julia Child, have the patience of Mother Teresa with our three sons, and be a sex goddess like Marilyn Monroe! It was easy—until my husband said he wasn't happy. Everything I believed in became just a mirage.

I was disillusioned, but my husband promised to provide for the children while they were living with me; therefore, if my children were taken care of, everything would be fine, or so I thought. One Sunday night my three sons came home from a visit with their dad and told me about his fabulous house, pool, and even a puppy. And they were going to live with their dad!

The night they left, I walked from empty room to empty room. I passed the dining room and thought, No more family dinners, no more holidays. I walked into the family room, sat down in that big white chair, and stared at the clock: 11:15. The tentacles of the past grabbed me, and all my failures flooded in. Devastated, I thought about giving up, ending it.

But I remembered a wedding. The bride was beautiful, the groom was handsome, and when they said, "I do," doves flew overhead. A few years later, they had a baby, and then, they got a divorce and the father got custody. Several months after that, I saw the father and his daughter—at the funeral of that beautiful bride, the beautiful bride who took her own life. I thought of the little girl's sad face, and I couldn't do that to my children. I couldn't give up.

Les Brown says, "You have greatness in you," and I had to rediscover my greatness, my unshakable drive. I had to let go of the past in order to create something new—a new canvas. Speaking of creating canvases, during WWII, Picasso couldn't get canvases since they were being used for berths on the ships; therefore, he painted over his old canvases. We have to be willing to paint over our old masterpieces. Eliezer Wiesel, the Nobel prize author of Night, said, "Even in the darkest life there is light."

Even when we don't think we can go on, we have to find our light, our greatness. We can either be a victim of our history or victors of our new story. I was going to be the victor of my new story. Since I'd just graduated from chiropractic college, I decided to become an entrepreneur and start a chiropractic practice. I walked into the bank to get a business loan, but all I had was a mortgaged house and a Datsun Maxima. Nothing was in my name—except a $10,000 student loan! There was no way I could get a loan.

But I had unshakable drive. I invested in myself and sold the only thing I owned—my home—and netted enough for four months' operating expenses. Forty percent of businesses fail in the first year, and I only had four months!

After months of networking, even sleeping in the office some nights, my chiropractic practice was successful. My patients included Marie Osmond, the New York City Rockettes when they toured in Orange County, and Lisa Nichols of *The Secret*. I was even a paid expert on *Judge Judy*.

I had a fabulous house overlooking the ocean, but it was a house, not a home. I had money, but no meaning. My success was like Teflon; it just slipped away. But my failure—my inability to hold on to my children—clung to me like Velcro. My shame plagued me for twenty years.

Then everything changed. I was diagnosed with melanoma. I lost a piece of my leg, then a piece of my arm, and I thought about the twenty years I'd wasted due to my shame. I thought about other women who allowed someone else to decide whether they were pretty enough, sexy enough, enough. Nora Ephron said, "Marriages come and go, but divorce lasts forever."

I decided to do something. As a former English teacher, I thought about stories. Stories are how we learn, connect, and remember. So I wrote *Sex Happens*—as gut-wrenching as *Eat, Pray, Love*, as titillating as *Fifty Shades of Gray*—about a mother's struggle to regain custody of her children, a struggle that almost costs her her life. It became an Amazon #1 bestseller, and I was asked to keynote at numerous fundraisers. Therefore, when I heard about Child Rescue, an organization that rescues and rehabilitates children who are trafficked, I decided to write *Gracie's Gone* and give 25 percent of the proceeds to that organization.

Gracie's Gone takes the reader into the home and hearts of a blended family when their beautiful six-year-old Gracie is abducted. It also became a bestseller, and it's being agented for a book-to-movie proposal. If—or rather, *when*—it becomes a movie, then Child Rescue's motto, "Every child deserves a childhood," will become a reality.

Making a difference in the world is true victory, and it's only possible when we have unshakable drive—when we embrace our successes like Velcro and let our failures slip off us like Teflon. As Winston Churchill said, "Success is the ability to go from failure to failure with equal enthusiasm." Then, and only then, we'll walk gently through life and leave deep footprints.

Dr. Carol Soloway writes contemporary fiction set in Orange County, California. After decades of writing medical legal reports, Dr. Soloway picked up her pen and decided to write stories about a young woman who discovers her resilience. Soloway explores marriage, motherhood, and sex—and what we'll do for each.

In *Sex Happens*, her first bestselling novel, the main character faces a custody battle so poisonous it threatens to become murderous. In *Gracie's Gone*, her recently published novel, the blended family is thrust into a nightmare when their six-year-old daughter is abducted.

www.carolsoloway.com

I'M GONNA BE SOMEBODY

Tim Gillette

It's been such a long time, I think I should write this down. Sorry, this is not Foreplay/ Long Time, but the story did start in Boston. I had just decided Here I Go Again, growing my hair long. It was a Slow and Easy process, but it had its downside. One time in a bar in Boston, someone pointed at me and said, "That Dude Looks Like a Lady."

This whole thing started because I had told myself I'm Gonna be Somebody someday, believing I could break the chains. I told friends and family, "You can bet I will." Soon I would get caught in a trap, Free Fallin' out into nothing. I thought I was Running Down a Dream. If only I could get a guitar teacher like the Eagles' Don Felder. But you might end up at the Hotel California, trying to check out but unable to leave.

After years of being told that you look like one famous person or another, it becomes hard to find your own identity. You get trapped in the world you got placed in by other people. Like being told you look like Dave Grohl; It's Times Like These that you Come as You Are and Go with the Flo, and are All Apologies, hoping the world looks up to you and thinks There Goes My Hero.

So you change your hairstyle, and now they say you look like a taller Tommy Shaw. Not with a mask like Mr. Roboto, but a Man in the Wilderness, just Rockin' in Paradise like a Renegade with Too Much Time on My Hands. You are just a Blue-Collar Man, but you keep Fooling Yourself while looking at your Crystal Ball, wanting to create The Best of Times, all while hoping you do not run into those Girls With Guns.

You get all wrapped up in trying to be somebody, feeling you failed, taking time off to work serving coffee. Your sarcastic view on life can only make you look like some know-it-all who plays a doctor from New Jersey with a motorcycle, popping pills, being rude with no friends. It's like you are a British actor with an American accent and a strange name, Dr. House.

You walk into the airport one day and meet a wonderful TSA agent who grabs you by the arm and says, "Tom Petty!" and you start wishing now that you are Learning to Fly, Running Down a Dream. You feel like Even the Losers get lucky some time. But knowing you're late for your flight, you tell him You Wreck Me. You want to say You Don't Know How It Feels to Be Me. It's not like you have a group of Heartbreakers just ready to play a gig. You look him in the eye and ask your friend Stevie to help you tell him to Stop Draggin' My Heart Around.

But this guy is a real fan. He's not just chasing you because you just had your Last Dance with Mary Jane before getting in line. You're just another Face in the Crowd, and you want to turn to the American Girl behind you and say, "Here Comes My Girl." But she'll just be Jammin' Me and saying, "Don't Come Around Here No More."

At this point my mind goes to work and I'm thinking, Yer So Bad. But I Need to Know how big a fan this TSA guy really is. Can I string him along Into the Great Wide Open? Hey, I'm in an airport, after all, maybe we get a bunch of Wilburys: Roy, George, Jeff, and Bob. We Handle Him with Care and turn him Inside Out while taking him to the End of the Line.

But back to the problem of always being someone else. Really, I want to be somebody all by myself. If the tables were turned, I'd say, hey, Don't Do Me Like That. I know It's Good to Be King, but it's Time to Move On. If I took this too far the wrong way, I might end up living like a Refugee.

This is where it stopped. I was not born in Gainesville, Florida, in 1950; I was not influenced by Elvis; Don Felder didn't teach me guitar; I'm not a British actor playing a doctor in New Jersey; I was never friends with Kurt Cobain. I did meet Tommy Shaw a few years ago, and he was nice enough to make me look like a Rock Star in our picture together.

Yes, I was once told I looked like a lady with my long hair, but, no, it was not me that Steven Tyler saw in Boston when he came up with the idea for that song. Rumor has it that it was Vince Neil, another great rocker, who had the idea first.

For years, I was stuck in the world of being someone else, like so many others who try to be the next [fill in the blank]. For me, the journey started with wanting to be the Number One me. The thing that helps me most now is working with my clients to help them find the same thing for themselves. And it all started when the TSA agent at Los Angeles airport really thought I was Tom Petty.

This was where I found me. The movie Rockstar shows how having to live a life being someone else is the fastest way to get lost. You can run down your own dream, stop free-falling into nothing, and stop letting the world wreck you. You don't have to dance with Mary Jane or play with things to enjoy the life you have when you are a Number One you.

I am proud to say I'm not Tom Petty; I am Tim Gillette. I love writing and helping other entrepreneurs with a Simple Easy Marketing Plan online. Thank you, Zig Ziglar, for telling me to be a Number One me. I knew I could do it and, finally, I am somebody . . .

Tim Gillette is the creator of Simple Easy Marketing and Branding, a blog, video, and online content creation system that is designed to get sales results. He is an award-winning blogger, bestselling author, and highly sought-after speaker who brings entertaining, educational, and empowering content to corporate and entrepreneur events across America. He also hosts the top blog and video conference, Blog and Video Con, held in Dallas every May and November. Tim resides in Dallas with his wife, Gwynne, and cat, Sefu, and he has three grown children.

www.NotTomPetty.com

THE LETTERS W AND M

Jacqueline Lucien

Not knowing is like missing a piece of a puzzle. When I discover what I don't know, then understand, the answer makes me soar. And I feel Wow!

Early on, I created art, drew pictures, and wrote poetry. Words fascinated me, even in different languages. My mother spoke Spanish; my brother practiced French. I studied Spanish and learned about the culture of Spain. As a result, I became curious about my history. I had a vague sense of my ancestors' home, although I did not know anyone on the vast African continent where they resided. Nor did I have any idea of the language they spoke. I was on a quest.

Often school left me with more questions than answers. In my forties, I attended a church where scholars taught me how to read hieroglyphics—my initiation to a language using symbols that were not like the alphabet I knew. The significant difference, my grandson Giovanni profoundly said, is that "Kemetians used pictures of everyday things to create words." Many of the images were familiar, but I did not know their significance or how to use them. That was the question.

Studying history and traveling increased my curiosity. I visited Kemet and made the first connection to the Roman alphabet and the ancient glyphs, and also English and Egyptian words. At that time, I did not know the significance of my discovery, or where it would take me. But clearly, I knew it was huge.

After retiring, I studied graphic design at UCLA. I experienced an aha moment when the instructor said that the Egyptians used the same process to create their ancient glyphs as we would use to create logos. We both observed our environment, determined the essence of the targeted object from which we created a symbol to be universally understood. You could see it and know its message without saying a word.

Delving deeper into history, I found that the Romans studied in Egypt for five hundred years. They learned how to read the glyphs. I began to see that they maintained the essence of the glyphs from which they developed the Roman alphabet and the resulting words. That spirit of the glyphs is apparent even in the words we use today. But that meaning has been disconnected. As a result, we learn that the alphabet is only phonetic, implying it has no other purpose than sound.

As I studied Egyptian and English words and the meaning of the glyphs became increasingly apparent, I found connections and clues from words in the derivative family of languages such as French, Spanish, German, and even Chinese. I drew upon my childhood exposure to language and look forward to connecting with scholars that know African languages. The connections are there also.

Grateful for this opportunity, I will explore two letters. My focus is the letter "W," for which I have an affinity. We share insatiable curiosity. To personify this glyph, I named it Wingy. Let us follow this innocent, curious, chick until it becomes mature and develops wisdom. Then I will provide the meaning of the letter "M."

W/U IS FOR WECHAK / QUAIL CHICK

The essence of the chick is wakefulness, curiosity, and higher consciousness. Aware, it has been a witness since the beginning of time. It corresponds to the burgeoning development of a child known to ask questions relentlessly: who, what, where, how, and why.

The consciousness of the chick as the letter "W" is present in Egyptian and English. A brief story illustrates how it showed up in words. In the beginning was the word and the word became flesh. Able to communicate, the chick asked the primordial question: "What came first, me as the chick or me as the egg?" The answer is yet to come. Thus, this ancient question established the quail chick as the personification of curiosity and inquiry since time immemorial. Do you still wonder which came first?

It is fascinating that the pronoun "I" is a person and chick, showing that consciousness is with and beyond the body. The word wired is the person and the quail chick together. The more I understand the essence of the glyphs, the more I understand the formation of English and Egyptian words.

As the chick's awareness increases, the Kemetic word to illustrate this evolution is a wise elder with a walking stick who remains curious.

M IS FOR MULAK / OWL

Have you ever wondered about the word wisdom? Well, the glyph M is an owl considered to be wise with its penetrating ability to see. As a glyph, it represents another level of mastery and acuity.

The relationship between the quail chick and the owl are like the child and the elder or mother—thus, the chick's journey from childhood to adulthood and or maturity.

The quail chick inquired, "Is my spirit in every word that has a letter W/U?"

The elder replied, "Ask and see if you have the patience, discernment, and wisdom to find your answer. By asking, you demonstrated who you are. Know yourself. Remember who you are."

The chick graciously responded, "I am in the world, here since the beginning of time. I am the word made flesh, the personification of consciousness. I witnessed nature, then created words. Because I am curious, I ask questions; I seek until I find answers. I am words, the tools used for the evolution of humankind. Wherever wonder and awe exist, I am—even in the water (primeval water) the womb from which I emerged. Through my dedication to conscious evolution, I reached maturity and developed "WisdoM."

A preeminent expert on the relationship between ancient hieroglyphics and the development of the alphabet, **Jacqueline Lucien** has committed her life to teaching people how to use the secret of the letters to unleash creativity and power. Successfully bridging past and present with her Lucien's Solution, retired therapist Lucien is known as the "Secret Finder." She is also the author of The Authorities, co-author of the bestseller Fight for Your Dreams, and author of the upcoming book, 26 Letters: The Secret to Words Revealed. A student of history, traveler, and graphic artist, Lucien began her journey of linguistical discovery while visiting Egypt.

www.considerthistoday.com

THE MAVERICK MINDSET: WHAT SET ME FREE!

Paul Finck

I grew up in a "challenged" family. Addiction, psychosis, and infidelity was the backstory to lies, miscommunication, and disruptive life decisions. After thirty-five years of mental abuse on both sides, my parents finally divorced. Strength of character, personal responsibility, values, and trust were not concepts discussed in my household, let alone demonstrated. I had no role models for what a successful relationship looked like. I had no parent who was capable of guiding me to make effective life decisions—they weren't able to make them for themselves. I had no "Rich Dad" to show me the path to business or financial success. So HOW the heck did I end up becoming Paul Finck, The Maverick Millionaire®? The answer came from the set of mindsets I developed over decades of searching . . . experimenting . . . testing out what worked and what didn't that I now collectively call The Maverick Mindset.

In this journey out of chaos and confusion, I recognized thoughts that were not working for me. It was time to throw them out. The hardest part in this process was that these were the thoughts taught to me by my parents. In that moment, I had to acknowledge that my parents had no clue. Their advice was based on a lifetime of fears, anxieties, and regrets. In following their advice, I would be buying into the same . . . and in turn would be destined to get the same challenged results. It took me nearly thirty years of my life to recognize that I could not rely on their advice any longer; I had to learn about life (and create my destiny) on my own.

This was an overwhelming, scary, and daunting task. To accomplish this, I would have to write "The Rule Book" from scratch. This book would be my rules to live by. Every time I would be unsure or in doubt, "The Rule Book" would be my guide. At first, this concept wasn't formed in any deliberate sense. Initially I was changing one thought here and another idea there. I would create ideas for a habit I liked, and then structure it as a rule to live by. For example, my parents had a terrible relationship. To prevent the same from happening in my life, I started with a basic question: What would I want in a relationship? Affection! From this, I devised a "rule" of behavior that would create more affection in my personal relationship. I called it the "Two Foot Rule." Whenever my wife and I are within two feet of one another, we would kiss, showing our affection and love for one another. With this one simple rule, even in the craziest and busiest of times, we stayed connected to each other.

My new rule book began to take form. Over the years, I kept adding to the "rule book," establishing the foundation for the life I wanted. I added rules like "When something scares me, move forward faster" and "When I hesitate, immediately jump forward." I realized step-by-step that I was ultimately in charge. I could be who I wanted to be regardless of circumstance, regardless of my upbringing, regardless of my past!

Unfortunately, my "ultimate me" wasn't that great. I was still limited by my imagination of what I thought was possible. My "ultimate me" was doing OK financially in an OK business with OK relationships. It was better than what I had seen growing up, so I figured it was GOOD—or good enough. Then life happened!

Over the course of six years, I got married and became dad to six children— THREE SETS OF TWINS! The first set were my nieces that my wife and I took in at birth. The second set occurred via in vitro fertilization (IVF). The third set of twins, born just fourteen months later, was a surprise! My family size had changed dramatically—and with it my drive to create a greater "ultimate me." The old level of play had to shift to serve a greater purpose. It was time to create a new, more powerful productive version of me.

I began to look for mantras to follow, mentors to emulate, and models of behavior to adopt. I looked to identify the chitchat in my head that represented ineffective concepts that would pull me away from my goals. Thoughts like "That is too much for me to accomplish"; "I don't think that is able to be done by me"; "He could do it, but I couldn't possibly" were profound thoughts in my head that needed to be rewritten. I began to recognize that I could shift—I could change who I was—I could change how I was showing up . . . one rewrite at a time.

So what set me free? This new set of mindsets centered around the following concept: Your background doesn't define you. Your circumstance doesn't define you. Your past doesn't define you.

YOU DEFINE YOU.
YOU get to DECIDE
who you are and how you show up.
YOU get to CHOOSE.
YOU are the ruler of your destiny.

Once you acknowledge this truth and take 100 percent responsibility for your destiny in light of it, anything—EVERYTHING—is possible! I refer to this set of mindsets collectively as The Maverick Mindset. (Download your FREE summation of my maverick mindset today called The Maverick Manifesto. Simply go to www.TheMaverickManifesto.com).

I realized I could be greater than I had imagined. I decided at that moment that there was no limit to where I could go or what I could accomplish. From that singular thought, I went on to establish a multimillion dollar real estate portfolio, became an international speaker, bestselling author multiple times over, developed multiple million-dollar companies, and now consult companies on a worldwide basis, all while raising six amazing children with my soul mate and enjoying a great lifestyle traveling all over the world with my family. Define the YOU you want to be and DECIDE to be that person TODAY!

Paul Finck, The Maverick Millionaire® is one of the foremost authorities in business and personal development today. Paul speaks to entrepreneurs, organizations, and companies of all sizes, empowering them with his energizing message and assisting them with direct answers to the toughest challenges in order to get the results they are looking for in life and business. When you are looking for the strategic plan to get out of your own way, design your future, build great teams, and double your income in the next twelve months, you want to listen to Paul Finck.

www.paulfinck.com

Rock Your Ears and Rock Your Life— The Importance of Treating Any Hearing Loss Early

Dr. Mary Lou Luebbe-Gearhart, Au.D.

Music to my ears, and the meaning and purpose of my life, comes from the following comments made by my patients who say things like "You've given me back my life"; "You've made me whole again"; "You've saved my marriage"; "You've relieved my Tinnitus and ringing in my ears"; "You've removed stress, embarrassment, and frustration from my life." "I can understand speech clearly, and have a satisfying conversation in a noisy restaurant." My grandchildren know I love them because I can understand their words clearer, and I don't ignore or miss the cute things they're saying."

"You've removed the pain and blocked feeling in my ears." "You've reconnected me with my family and friends. They're happier too." "I feel younger because I can hear well again." "I don't have to ask others to repeat or raise their voice anymore." "My golf game is better because I can hear when I hit the ball and recognize the 'sweet spot.' " "They thought I was losing my memory and acquiring dementia, but it was really my undiagnosed, untreated hearing loss." "I told everyone I had selective hearing, but now I realize it was my inability to hear high-frequency consonants like s, f, th." "I don't have to turn up the TV volume so loud and run my family AND DOG out of the room so I can hear."

"I can hear and enjoy MUSIC again!" "I thought the birds had stopped singing and the sounds of Nature at night had ceased because I couldn't hear them." "I heard my daughter's wedding vows." "I got promoted at work and am making the money I should because I seem 'smarter' and am more productive. Now that you've helped me hear well, I can actually understand directions easily, enjoy my job, get along with my co-workers. They used to make fun of me because I would give the wrong answers and misunderstand what they were saying."

"I've changed my WILL twice since I can hear what my niece and nephew are really saying about me." "I'm a safer, better driver because I can hear, and I can enjoy a fun conversation with the others in my car." "I've gone back to church." "Now that I can hear better, I do the things I enjoy and am more physically active and healthier. Oh yes, I've lost fifty pounds, my blood pressure is lower, and my doctor has taken me off all my medications. We're both thrilled. Thanks for giving me a new lease on life."

It is not easy being a doctor of audiology, going to college for thirteen years and still requiring continuing education to stay innovative and at the forefront of my profession. Nor is it easy to own and operate a private audiology and hearing technology practice that employs other dedicated doctors of audiology and hearing aid specialists with an experienced, knowledgeable, and dedicated support staff.

Daily I risk my life, health, feelings, reputation, and investments to educate, reassure, evaluate properly, diagnose, and determine proper treatment and/or the need for referral. I must diplomatically mediate with families, convince people they're worth helping and deserve a life without the myriad of health issues, relationship struggles, and "cognitive burden" associated with a hearing loss. Sometimes hearing test results that used to be considered within the "clinically normal" range cause "processing" problems, such as trying to understand speech when there is noise or music in the background. We receive many testimonials from those patients too.

I empathize and understand that most people go through unnecessary, many times "self-inflicted," stress and reduced quality of life because of misinformation, misdiagnosis, and the procrastination of living in denial. That can impact and destroy even the closest relationships over time.

Why did I choose to become a doctor of audiology? When I was just three years old, I watched my amazing father, an electronics and industry "pioneer," totally change the life of a soldier returning from WWII with a noised-induced hearing loss. I asked my Daddy, "Why is that big man CRYING?" He answered, "He's a brave soldier who lost his hearing. Now, with hearing aids, he can understand speech again, and that's what JOY LOOKS LIKE!" Dad continued, "You'll bring comfort and joy to people, too, honey." My destiny was determined, and I felt spiritually "dedicated" right then.

There are about 48 million people in the USA with untreated hearing loss and or Tinnitus (head noise). That's about 1 in 6. And it's not just because of aging, although two-thirds of people seventy or older have hearing loss and would really benefit from proper treatment. Did you know, for example, that being diabetic doubles the likelihood you'll develop a hearing loss because the glucose levels affect heart and blood innervation in the ear? We all know that dangerous decibel levels from music at live concerts can create permanent hearing loss. Today's earbuds are even more dangerous because they have less distortion, so users tend to turn them up louder!

Remember, hearing loss is a progressive and degenerative condition. So be a Rock Star yourself and help someone hear well again. Memory loss, isolation, and a higher risk of falling occur with increasing hearing loss. Reread the testimonials from my patients. They sought help. They're my Rock Stars!

Dr. Mary Lou Luebbe-Gearhart is recognized as one of America's most experienced and trusted hearing experts. She is a board-certified doctor of audiology and has been the second-generation president of Luebbe Hearing Services since 1973. Her passion for helping people hear what they've been missing has taken her around the world, using state-of-the-art hearing aid technology to transform their lives. She is a founding member of the Audigy Group, a charter member of the Women Presidents Organization (WPO), and serves on the board of trustees for People-To-People International.

www.HearOhio.com

SUCCESS IS WITHIN YOUR REACH

Ceola McClendon

"It takes work to be successful. If you do your job, God will do his job."

My entire life I have been interested in God's plan of salvation and living a good life. I always thought everyone should have whatever their heart's desire. However, when I arrived in Los Angeles from Detroit, Michigan, I quickly found out better. Growing up, I observed my parents working hard from sunset to sundown while my brother worked hard to help raise me. I have always had a good life, and my perception of that lifestyle was working hard, eating good food, and living in a house. My parents and brother set an example for me. I chose to follow in their footsteps and began to work at six years old. I was driven to work hard and never give up if I wanted to receive a better life. I developed an insatiable desire to learn more about God and my spiritual walk, helping people stay healthy, and becoming a successful entrepreneur.

Six is a significant number in my life, because that's also when I accepted Christ as my personal Savior and Lord began to work in his vineyard. I studied the Word of God and always attended church with my parents and my brother. God in his infinite wisdom called me to the ministry when I was twenty years old. I kept ignoring his call and putting it off until a later date, but finally I acknowledged his voice and answered his call upon my life. To better equip and prepare for my Christian journey, I enrolled in religious studies and ministry courses at Crenshaw Christian Center School for three years as well as various other Christian schools. In 2014 I became an ordained minister by Crenshaw Christian Center to minister the Word of God—truly a blessing.

Before I became a minister, I was working for a successful real estate and construction company, where I took the state board and received both licenses. I was determined to be successful so I could share my knowledge to help others. My goals were to help people become happy homeowners and invest in real estate years before the market rate and cost became unimaginable. I have attempted to help people by loaning people loan to purchase homes and rebuilding their credit. Nevertheless, very few people would listen.

I truly believe there is enough money in this world for everyone to eliminate the need to be poor, homeless, or live without three meals a day. I always try to help others live a better life.

There are far too many people in this world who are selfish and unwilling to share with others their God-given gifts and talents to help other people succeed. If you know something that will help other people become prosperous, why not share it and help someone live the life God has intended for everyone, not just 1 percent of the population?

Lastly, I believe that it is important to take good care of your temple (i.e., your body) and live a healthy, wealthy life without abusing it.

My grandmother was highly favored and lived a healthy, wholesome, and blessed life for 115 years. My mom lived to be 101 and was never ill. You can live a successful, beautiful, happy, and blessed life if you believe in God and watch what you say and eat. The Bible says, "Life and death is in the power of your tongue," so watch what you say.

We have not because we ask not. I would never tell anyone that they have enough, because my dreams may not be your dreams. However, no matter how old you get, God will give you your heart desires. Live the blessed life.

Ceola McClendon spent a large portion of her youth in Motown, Detroit, Michigan. She has resided in Los Angeles, California, since 1962. Evangelist McClendon has been a successful entrepreneur for many years and holds active real estate, B1 contractor, and child development licenses. Her thriving real estate business, Citywide Realty and Investment Company, has been in operation in California for over thirty years.

McClendon spends a great deal of time providing ministry to the sick in the hospital, lovingly visiting with seniors, shut-ins, and individuals in nursing and convalescent homes, and providing a healing ministry to the sick. Evangelist McClendon is very happy when she can help her family and other people.

citymac@sbcglobal.net

No Safety in Numbers

Robin Ahn

My heart was pounding like a jackhammer. I was sure my necktie was strangling me. My palms were clammy, and it was definitely a million degrees in that conference room. I was terrified I was making a wrong choice and then would have to face everyone, hearing "I told you so" forever. My parents' voices kept playing over and over in my head. My mom's voice: "It sounds too risky, Robin. Why don't you just do what everyone else does? There's safety in numbers." Then my dad's voice: "The smartest decision is usually the safest one, son." I was about to make a life-changing decision.

My parents were the traditional Korean immigrants, believing there was "safety in numbers." I grew up hearing that I should go after the American Dream and do what everyone else was doing: "Be an accountant, doctor or lawyer. It's the smartest path because it's safe. You will always find a job that pays well." So the good Korean boy that I was, I did exactly what they told me to do. I became an accountant—talk about safety in numbers!

All my life, I watched my parents struggle by doing what most people did and taking the safety in numbers. Things were always tight. My mother worked two jobs, and my father was gone about nine months out of the year working for the U.S. government. Eating out was rare. We never went on vacations. My parents did a great job, especially for recent immigrants. Although I was proud of my parents, I watched them living to work, instead of working to live. I wanted more out of life, for myself, my parents, and for my sister.

In seventh grade, I went back to school after winter break and was forced to endure the stories of all my classmates' vacations. I, of course, had stayed home with my little sister, watching TV during the break, just like I did every break. Seventh grade was different. I had had it. I told my mom that night that I was going to be a millionaire and go anywhere I wanted to go whenever I wanted to. She laughed and told me, "Of course, Robin, of course."

The summer after college graduation, in the middle of the economic downturn, my friends all traveled to different corners of the earth, but I kept hearing my parents' voices telling me to make the safe choice, so I stayed here where it was safe, putting numbers in columns and counting beans. Total job security.

Wow. Was I miserable!

I was done. I needed to capture that seventh-grade passion.

So, on that day in the conference room, I decided there's no safety in numbers. I didn't make the popular choice. I didn't take the safe path. I did what most people wouldn't do. I chose to take a risk. I left my safe job that guaranteed paying me a salary and accepted a job with a Fortune 500 company that only paid a commission. And I took a chance doing a job I had never done before: sales.

My decision changed my life forever. I soon had doubled my income and was making six figures. I had been promoted several times and was making even more money with stock options. I was traveling and rebuilding the sales culture in different offices, even being promoted above thirty-year employees. Sure, the money was great, but that's not what changed my life.

What changed my life was that I was willing to take risks. Did I still get afraid taking risks? Of course, I think everyone does. The difference is that I'm still willing to take risks, despite being afraid.

In November 2001 after the World Trade Center attack, my wife and I were pregnant with our first child. I had had enough of the corporate life and being just a number, so I decided it was time to open my own business. Family, friends, and co-workers told me that I was making a big mistake, that I should wait until the economy improved, because no one knew what was going to happen and the economy could get worse. Despite all of this, I took a risk and left my company and opened my own business.

I was rewarded once again. My first year in business, I made more money than I ever made with the company I had just left. Like before, making more money was great. But what changed my life again was that I'm doing the type of work I want to do. I work when I want to work. I work with whom I want to work with. And I can earn as much as I want to earn. Since then I've never looked back.

I love reading about successful figures in business, people like Steve Jobs and Warren Buffet. I finally understood what all the successful people I read about meant when they said, "To be successful, you have to be willing to take risks." There's no safety in numbers. Don't do what everyone does. Don't play it safe. You will be afraid, but only the few earn the rewards and riches that come from being courageous enough to take the risks, despite being afraid.

Robin Ahn is a keynote speaker, business coach, author, entrepreneur, and co-creator of the brand Become A SuperHero In Your Business. Robin has a remarkable way of helping entrepreneurs and organizations identify weaknesses, shift their focus to their strengths, and inspire self confidence in themselves. He brings laughter, fun, and real-world actionable advice.

Robin has worked with the some of the most admired brands, including Tony Robbins, Richard Branson, Red Bull, Idealab.com, Stamps.com, Sony Ericsson, Science Applications International Corporation (SAIC), Paramount Pictures, Walt Disney Company, Twentieth Century Fox, Fox Sports, Sony Pictures Entertainment, and Venture Capitalists.

www.robinanderikaahn.com

An Empty Nester's Journey

Gale Barbe

I remember that day so clearly. The summer before my daughter's senior year of high school, I took her to have her senior pictures taken. As she posed, I saw her growing up with each flash of pictures being taken. It was all I could do to hold back the tears as I didn't want my daughter to see me cry. Then it hit me like a ton of bricks. Not only was I going to be an empty-nester in a year, I was also going to turn fifty years old. Now what? I'm not ready for this change in my life. Who am I now? My daughter is about to leave the nest to discover who she is as she goes off to college. It was all about taking care of her for the last eighteen years and being involved with all aspects of her life.

I lost my identity when I became a stay-at-home mom. How is my identity going to change? I'm going to be a half a century old, and I don't know who I am or what my purpose is. Nobody told me how to handle this. I felt all alone and depressed. I had low self-esteem, and I was grieving my younger years and wanted them back. I wanted a do over! Even though my daughter was going to a university close to home, it was still a big change.

I was not happy with who I was or how I felt. I needed to make some changes. But how? Where should I start? I needed a plan to get myself together. Here is what I came up with. I call it guidelines for becoming a happy empty-nester. If you are facing an empty nest, know that you're not alone, and there is help out there to get you through this season of life.

1. Learn to have fun again. Go out and try new things
2. Rekindle your relationship with your spouse.
3. Get together with friends and catch up over dinner.
4. Take care of yourself with healthier cooking and eating.
5. Start exercising regularly, even if it is just walking.
6. Volunteer. You will feel better as a person.
7. Take a class. Keep learning new things.
8. Pamper yourself. Treat yourself to a pedicure and manicure.
9. Practice the art of gratitude and keep a gratitude journal.
10. Find a hobby.

I took some classes that taught me how to change my mindset, how to eliminate limiting beliefs, and helped boost my self-esteem. Then I decided to get certified in these classes so I could help others. I also joined a mastermind to help me learn to communicate with others as well as exchange ideas. Four years of college went by, and then my daughter moved across the country to Boston. She was continuing her education to become a registered nurse in an accelerated program, planning to return home in fifteen months. I thought I had gone through the sadness of her leaving home, but this was different. She was going to be really far away, and I think it was just as hard for her as it was for me. The last four years were more about taking care of my physical and emotional self, but none of it prepared me for this. I continued to take classes and attend the mastermind group to figure out what I could do to help other empty nesters. I saw a need to start a community of women who needed support, one where they could do fun things together while enjoying life to the fullest. This to me is being a true and real Rock Star empty nester!

After fifteen months, my daughter was about to move back home when my mother unexpectedly had a heart attack and passed away. During that time my daughter was offered a job to stay in Boston and help care for a friend's daughter. She decided to take the job and not move back home to California. Within a couple of months, she passed her exam to become an RN, and she started to date someone. When I heard that, I realized she wouldn't be coming home. I felt she was gone for good. Yes, we could visit each other, but it wouldn't be the same.

After just over a year of dating, my daughter got engaged, and she got married in the summer of 2019. Now I was a real empty nester! It's been a struggle to stay positive. Don't get me wrong, I am very happy for her. My son-in-law is a wonderful, loving, and caring Christian man. I just want to be closer than across the whole country from each other. I will welcome them when they come to visit, but then I will have to say goodbye again.

It's been a bumpy ride dealing with all my feelings. Despite that, I've come to realize that the one thing that filled the void in my heart and stayed with me throughout all of this was hope! It helped me to have faith that everything would work out.

The season of life that I have gone through in the past eight years was not only a season of lasts, but a season of firsts. It's exciting to see my daughter and son-in-law starting their lives together. The one thing I know for sure is that nothing could separate my daughter from my love or the love and presence of God. He still holds her in the palm of his hand even though she has let go of mine. I can hold on to that forever. And after our daughter's wedding, my husband and I are going on another little honeymoon ourselves! While there, we will find a little chapel where we can renew our vows to each other.

"Your child's life will be filled with fresh experiences. It's good if yours is as well."
Dr. Margaret Rutherford

———————————

Gale Barbe is a dedicated mother and housewife. Since her daughter graduated from high school, Gale has struggled as an empty nester and has been on a journey to improve her physical and emotional health. Part of that journey has been getting certified as a master practitioner of NLP (Neuro Linguistic Programming), hypnotherapy, time techniques, EFT (Emotional Freedom Techniques), success coaching, and Reiki practitioner. She is passionate about helping others with their health and happiness by using these tools and other natural and holistic practices.

www.galebarbe.com

Cancer Lancers

Janie Becker, the Encourager

Have you heard words similar to "You have a mass; we need to test further," or after strenuous testing, "You have cancer"? Curing the cancer mindset can be daunting . . . more so than the cancer diagnosis' initial impact. Most of us know someone in our family, network, neighborhood, or workspace who is battling cancer. Do you feel a loss for what to say or how to help? I have gathered a toolbox of healing methods and techniques you may find helpful for yourself and others to have handy.

Twenty-seven years of volunteering to raise awareness and funds to help other people through the cancer journey with the American Cancer Society (ACS) Relay for Life (RFL) events in Whittier, Lakewood, Long Beach, Anaheim, and combined cities gave me a strong understanding of how "it takes a village" to raise a child or support a cancer patient as a caregiver or for yourself; it surely does. I've found many essential oils helpful to support myself and others in their cancer treatment and recovery.

Cancer is a "disease caused by an uncontrolled division of abnormal cells in a part of the body." Every member of the local Cancer Support Group demonstrates courage in their journey through the mystery of symptoms, showing up to different tests and treatments, doctor appointments, listening to people who want to help and have suggestions or "know someone," and enduring stages of subsequent testing and potential health issues and exposures. Whether it's the mass or malignant growth or tumor resulted from the division of abnormal cells or it's a challenge to isolate and treat, the journey of getting enough information to make good decisions and help yourself or the person you're caring for can be challenging. You need a champion, whether it's someone close to you, a support group, an old friend you can talk to any time of day, or medical personnel you can trust. You can be a "cancer lancer." I call us "cancer lancers" because I see us using all the resources (lances) we can access to focus on winning the battle with all the tools available for cutting out (lancing) the cancer, growing healthy cells and an enduring positive mindset to conquer the challenges along the way.

I know so many people surviving and thriving after years of treating and recovering from a variety of cancers—all ages, cultures, backgrounds, and occupations. The American Cancer Society is available 24/7 with detailed information and resources to help us through all aspects of the diagnosis to treatment, recovery and emotional healing. One essential oil helping me cope with anxiety is the Tranquil™ Roll-On, an aromatic blend of lavender, cedarwood, and Roman Chamomile that calms me to enhance my focus on what I want and settles the "what-ifs" of the moment.

For me, wandering through the maze of doctor visits, more questions, eight months of health insurance approvals for tests after the initial bleeding surprise occurring years after menopause ended, I was filled with doubts, fear, and confusion. I'm a perpetual student and researcher, and I discovered more healing tools like meditation, affirmations, yoga, research advancements, Neurolinguistic Programming (NLP), tapping (EFT), energy medicine, Tai Chi Chih, sound therapy, REIKI, reflexology, hand yoga, and more patience. As I learned more about the specific bladder cancer treatment options and "gold standard" options, I found diffusing Peace and Calming® essential oil blend helpful to focus on methods to manage the frequent anxiety.

A lancer is defined as a soldier of a cavalry regiment armed with lances, which are long weapons for thrusting, having a wooden shaft and a pointed steel head. I imagine cancer patients standing tall, armed with the support of encouraging friends and family as their "lance of positive mindset" to live well walking in to the chemo room and sitting straight as the nurses and pharmacist do the prep and start the IV drip of hydration, anti-nausea, and chemotherapy medicines for hours. A warrior in the journey takes focus, rest, hydration, good nutrition, and a positive attitude to fight and thrive through and beyond the cancer journey. My biggest hope is to learn more about the treatments, holistic alternatives, and testing to be able to help more people prevent cancer and maintain optimal health.

When your oncologist tells you you're in partial remission, it may mean you can take a break from treatment as long as the cancer doesn't begin to grow again. Complete remission means tests, physical exams, and scans show all signs that your cancer is gone. Some doctors also refer to complete remission as "no evidence of disease (NED)." The typical time frame ranges from three to five years of follow-up until the doctor or you are satisfied there's no more cancer.

I continue to find good self-care options by doing more healing activities and sharing with other cancer patients and caregivers as they express a need for support. It is rewarding and encouraging to share tools in which I have found strong support in my journey in healing to wellness. Frequent positive feedback from many survivors and their families gives them hope and keeps me motivated to continue to carry the lance to thrive.

It becomes imperative early on to have a clear vision of what you want to achieve beyond the treatment and create a plan for after NED, imagining how you will feel accomplishing the goal or outcome. Whether your goal or desire is travel, creating a nonprofit support organization, planting a vegetable or flower garden, volunteering in your neighborhood, or your top item on your bucket list, you may access AARP, local hospital oncology support groups, and other survivors who will gladly share resources and tips.

Janie Becker is The Encourager (self-appointed), certified massage therapist, raindrop specialist, energy healer, caregiver coach, speaker, author, cancer survivor, and volunteer. Janie works with people one-on-one, in groups at health and aromatherapy education workshops, supports caregivers in creating their self-care action plan, and shares a monthly newsletter focused on hope, healing, and peaceful living. She welcomes your questions and collaboration toward healthy living.

www.lessbrainstressnow.com

"NEVER GIVE UP, GIVE OUT, OR GIVE IN" —LIFE'S LESSONS FROM MY MOTHER

Kelly Bennett

I believe our path in life is determined by decisions we make. If you fall down, get up, dust yourself off, and keep going. Below in italics are life's lessons I've learned from my mother: Loretta L. Petersen 1/20/1922–7/7/2019.

My mom was born poor during the Depression to alcoholic parents. Her dad ran out of money for drinks and made her dance on the table at four years of age, doing the "hoochi coochie" to pay his tab. *Dance, even if you don't want to. Mom made it fun, regardless. Make life fun!*

She walked barefoot to school and had barely enough to eat. She went to the local orphanage often to survive. *If you don't like what you have, change it.*

She went to business college to get out of poverty. After graduation she landed a great job typing. She loved to dance too. She went to the Arthur Murray Dance Studio to take lessons. They hired her to be a teacher instead. *You never know what might happen; taking a risk is the first step.*

In 1944 she was the first woman locally enlisted in the Marine Corps. Her commanding officer tried to break her down, but she never quit. *When you put your mind to something, finish it. Don't let others get in your way; if they say you can't do it—show them you can.*

She was asked after bootcamp where she wanted to go, and she chose El Toro, California. *Find another place if you have the chance to make your mark.*

The women's barracks weren't finished, so they shipped her to the base in Miramar. She partied and danced. *Have fun while you can, make every moment count, even when you're waiting for something else to start.*

At El Toro, she wanted to work on airplanes; instead she was a secretary coordinating housing for incoming Marines. *Play with what you have until you're on to the next chapter—make what you have the best you can.*

At the El Toro Marine Base pool, she met a handsome lifeguard named "Pete." At a party, she got pregnant with my older brother. The Marines told her to marry "that Marine" or get dishonorably discharged. Two years later she had another boy, and I came along eleven years later. *Make lemonade out of lemons. My mom didn't like my dad at first but grew to love him. Folks back then fixed things before they threw them away.*

Married for fifty-six years, my dad died in 2000. When Mom finally went to a senior dance, she met Dale, a man ten years younger than her. He loved her unconditionally. They danced three to four times a week. Living separately, they were still inseparable. *Be aware of change, accept what life offers you, and be thankful for a second chance.*

Mom broke her ankle in October 2015; I moved in to care for her, getting her back on her feet by May 2016 so she and Dale could go to the famous Senior Prom. They had so much fun, and it was nice to know my job was done. *Enjoy the time you have with your parents. I was lucky I did, and I'm thankful for that.*

Life was great as Dale tended to her. I kept the house running. She loved people and talk to folks everywhere. She'd see everyone's head down looking at their devices and say, "I don't compute!" *Go out and meet someone face-to-face. Have a conversation with your neighbor, the checker at the grocery store, or even your own family.*

September 2018, she awoke with her left side of her face fallen, and I immediately called 911. Doctors said it was Bell's Palsy, and we discovered she had Non-Hodgkins lymphoma. If not treated, she'd live only three months at most. We opted out of treatment; her quality of life wouldn't be the same. Celebrating her ninety-seventh birthday was the goal. *Life is fragile, do those things that you want before you're told you can't do them anymore.*

She loved hugs; she had every senior at the dances hugging. Dr. Louis Profeta, MD, in an article for EmergencyCareForYou.com entitled "ER Doctor: It's Time to Bring Back Hugging—Everywhere," wrote: "The need to be hugged and experience human contact is in the root of our DNA. It is the building block of our soul. It is as much a part of each of us as the air we breathe. We curl up and we die inside without it." *Go out and hug someone before it's too late.*

Dale's health started to decline. Dancing stopped, but they still talked for hours. When Dale died in November 2018, it seemed that Mom's spirit died as well. *Make every second count. We are not promised tomorrow.*

After six months, Mom's health was getting worse. We called in hospice to keep her comfortable and out of pain. On July 5, 2019, I called the family, as now it's just a matter of time. July 7, 2019, at 8:08 p.m. she is gone. *Surround yourself with loved ones and say those things that matter, even if it's hard.*

She taught me to *love people for who they are, forgive your past, and make today count.* My mom lived her life with passion—and now so am I.

An award-winning broadcast journalist, **Kelly Bennett** has been a reporter, anchor, TV host, radio host, and senior assignment manager who transitioned into public relations and managed community affairs for two Fortune 500 companies. She founded Bennett Unlimited PR, giving her clients local, national, and international notoriety and connecting them to influencers to further their goals. Seeing the need to help more, she created Purpose Driven PR, which gives online support through videos, webinars, events, and masterminds consisting of experts and guidance on "How to Unleash the Power of Media to Launch of Grow Your Mission-Driven Business."

www.PurposeDrivenPR.com

#GOINGFOR81
ZEN IN MOUNTAIN AND LIFE PROJECTS

Eileen Bistrisky

A passion for adventure has led me to climb mountains on all seven continents. With each expedition, I've learned lessons not only applicable to mountaineering, but also to facing challenges in life and in business. My Zen in my current project is a result of these lessons.

In 2005 I traveled to Argentina to climb Aconcagua. Having learned to take time to acclimatize, I was doing well with my acclimatization until the day we carried gear to 19,500 ft. That day, altitude hit me hard! I spent extra time down at 18,000 ft camp where I found out I could recover while still at altitude. The next lesson was around team dynamics. I had met my trip partner through an amazing site: SummitPost.org. He and some others had tighter travel dates than I did, and bad weather was coming. They wanted to go for the summit a day ahead of schedule, and I wasn't ready. They moved up to 19 camp while I stayed down at 18 by myself, deliberating what to do. It was a very emotionally challenging time, wrought with loneliness and self-doubt. On their summit day, I got up to Independencia Hut at around 21,000 ft on my own, and turned around while still feeling strong enough to do so. I ended up leaving the mountain without summiting as I lacked the confidence to stay and complete the journey without teammates.

On Denali in Alaska in 2007, again with trip partners from SummitPost, I spent two weeks at 14,000 ft waiting for storms to pass at higher elevations. Once cleared to move up, time was running out for some who had earlier flights to catch. During the move up to 17,000 ft, bad weather came in and my two partners and I hunkered down at 16,000 ft. I woke up the next morning to clear weather but feeling like crap due to the altitude. My partners decided to make a summit attempt from there, while once again I was left alone to deliberate what to do. I received encouragement from a passing group to continue up to 17 camp where many of my newfound friends were returning from the summit. Still not feeling fantastic, I congratulated those who had made the summit and watched them leave the next day. It was challenging to be in such a similar situation to Aconcagua: alone on a mountain, not sure whether to go up or down. Again the feeling of loneliness and self-doubt kicked in. I took a couple days at 17 camp to better acclimatize. There was one last group going for the summit who welcomed me to follow their schedule, so I sucked it up, and went for it the next day. The acclimatization made such a difference! It was one of the most comfortable summit days ever. I was so stoked to make the summit and get down the mountain on my own. I learned that it really pays to stick it out!

In 2014 I set out on a leisurely trekking trip through Nepal with some friends. We were going to trek from Jiri to Everest Base Camp, to Gokyo, to Lukla. Knowing the benefit of acclimatization, I had created a schedule that would allow us to see everything over a five-week period. The trip started well, but as we got to higher elevations, my partners wanted to accelerate the schedule. We began traveling separately on some days, meeting at the next village. This was somewhat demoralizing. By the time we reached Gorak Shep and visited Everest Base Camp, we were well ahead of schedule, and they wanted to move on. I was no longer enjoying the trip. I had no idea what I was going to do, but I knew that I couldn't keep chasing them. I was devasted that for the third time, I found myself alone in the high mountains, unsure of which way to go.

I went for a solo hike up Kala Patthar, a peak my long-gone partners had done the day prior. At the summit, I met a fellow who was planning to climb Island Peak, and he invited me to join him. Not sure yet if I had it in me, I agreed to at least meet him in Dingboche the next day. We did an acclimatization hike together that went well, so I accompanied him to Chukung, where we would see if I could join his Island Peak trip. It turns out that I could, and I did. Island Peak, similar in altitude to Denali, offered excellent scrambling, glacier travel, and a fixed-line ascent to a summit ridge. Despite the uncertainty when my original partners went ahead, my trip had evolved to be even more exciting and rewarding than originally planned.

A trip to Antarctica to climb Mount Vinson in 2015 was showing all the typical patterns previously encountered. Weather had delayed our progress, and we were running out of time. A speedy ascent to high camp left me feeling less than stellar and completely unready for the group summit attempt. Something about this trip was different, though. Rather than the loneliness, self-doubt, and devastation from previous trips, as I sat alone at high camp, I felt a sense of optimism and Zen. I had the confidence that I could recover at altitude and that new opportunities would present themselves. Sure enough, they did! I was able to comfortably summit the following day.

It's these cumulative experiences that have brought me Zen when facing life and business challenges. As for my current mountain project, I discovered that there are eighty-one peaks in Vancouver's North Shore Mountains. It is my goal to do them all in 2019. At the time of submitting this chapter, I have done forty-eight of them. With proper recovery management, team dynamics, sticking it out, and being open to new opportunities, I am confident that I will remain Zen while everything is unfolding, and the season will work out exactly as it was meant to. #GoingFor81

Eileen Bistrisky, MBA, CSEP, CMC, ACC, is an award-winning entrepreneur who helps business teams with their systems and strategy. Organizations come to her when they want to improve their operational effectiveness and enhance their leadership skills.

Her firm, Effective Leadership Consulting, gets teams beyond plateaus they have hit to achieve profitability and efficiency through clarity of vision, effective communication, and empowerment. Eileen speaks internationally both about her mountain adventures and her Six Ingredients for Profitability & Growth. When not empowering teams to profitably benefit people and the planet, you can find her on remote mountain expeditions and sharing her stories to inspire others.

www.effectiveconsulting.ca

How I Flunked Kindergarten But Got a Master's Degree in Life

Christine Blosdale

OK, so I didn't really "flunk" anything. But I did manage to repeat kindergarten after the elementary school convinced my parents that "Christine just isn't ready to be around children yet."

Excuse me? Was I throwing tantrums if I didn't get my milk and a nap? Noooo. Perhaps I had massive meltdowns about being away from my family? Nope.

I was required to attend kindergarten *TWICE* because I was . . . (drumroll please) . . ."developmentally too old and sophisticated." I kid you not.

So how does an otherwise normal little girl with an above normal obsession with Jim Morrison and her Baby Alive doll manage to get such a diagnosis?

Well, let's start with the fact that after my parents divorced, at the ripe old age of five, I sat them both down and thanked them profusely for making such a wise decision, as it was blatantly obvious they were not meant to be together. Seriously, that's what I said.

For the first two years I lived with my mother, but in those days it was incredibly difficult for her to care for both me and my older brother as she received zero child support (or alimony).

Looking back now, I realize just how dirt-poor we were, but my mom always made me feel like a princess. Eating out of a can of black olives was my caviar. Trips to Zuma Beach with a bucket of KFC was the French Riviera. I never knew how much she suffered, nor did I know how much she worried about feeding her babies. I didn't have a clue.

Because she was having such a hard time providing for us, she reluctantly gave us back to my father. Enter Montclair College Prep in Los Angeles, where my dad was employed as both a teacher and football coach. The year was 1970, and as the only child on campus with full access to anywhere I wanted to go, I was King. Or Queen. Hell, at that age, gender identity was not an issue. For the entire school day, five days a week, I ruled the school.

Like a stealth secret agent waiting for their intended target, I would lie in wait behind the athletic field for that annoying, yet oh so liberating, school bell to RINNGGGGGGGG!

After what sounded like millions of locker doors slamming shut at the same time, yapping teens crisscrossed the campus with books in tow until every one of the classroom doors finally closed. The campus was finally mine. All mine. *Muahaha!* It was pure fucking heaven to a kid.

Once the teens were held captive in class, I began my adventures. First on the list was an empty school bus (my castle), and then I'd have deep conversations about life with a young hippie couple who were building an ark of some sort for some natural disaster yet to come.

After helping the hippies sand the deck of the ark, I'd saunter into Madame Sublette's French class. "Bonjour!" Then it was on to the creepy-yet-cool science lab that reeked of formaldehyde. I will never forget that smell, nor the sight of various scattered mason jars full of floating parts.

I held lengthy philosophical conversations with anyone, from the hippie couple, Madame Sublette, the creepy science teacher, the janitor, and the principal to the cheerleaders, scruffy school cat, football coaches and linebackers—hell, even a spider or two I found on my favorite empty bus.

I would engage with anyone interested enough to talk to prekindergarten me. So when it came time for me to go to school, one thing became very obvious: I had spent so much time interacting with adults that I wasn't able to relate to children my own age.

"Really, Corey? Are you actually eating paste? Hey Beck, could you let up on the crying? It's seriously cutting into my getting-to-know-my-beautiful teacher crush. *Sheesh*."

I was a five-year-old body walking around with a fifty-year-old mind.

That's why they held me back—so I could learn how to socialize with my peers. And I am eternally grateful that they did. It taught me a huge lesson in life that I rely upon time and time again.

The moral of the story is this: sometimes in life we don't get to move forward. Sometimes we get held back from what we think we need or deserve. Sometimes we take a bit longer to get to our destination. But it's the beautiful details in the journey that make it all worth the wait.

It has taken me over half a century to know for certain that I am exactly where I need to be.

And that solid knowledge (along with the ability to see and feel things deeply) has served my family, friends, community, and clients well. I have a gift, and I'm not ashamed to let people know. I can be talking to anyone and ideas flash in front of me about what they should do.

I will see a "best plan of action" or a product name or service that they need to embark upon, and sometimes it's accompanied by goosebumps. It just happens. I'm not some fortune teller with a crystal ball. I just see shit.

And I see and hear it clearly. It's a lot like a persistent voice that keeps bugging me to speak it out loud. But its 100 percent real, and I have faithfully used it in all aspects of my life; from that five-year-old on campus to my fifty-five-year-old current self.

What a lovely gift to share! The best feeling in the world is to help lift others up to a place and space they couldn't imagine. Invariably they will then lift others up as well. That's the magic of it all.

And doing it all from a child's heart? That is graduating with a master's degree in life!

Christine Blosdale is the award-winning radio personality and host of the podcast *Out of the Box With Christine*. She is an author, personal development speaker and business consultant who guides her clients with an internal GPS (Goosebump Producing System) that's garnered her the nickname "The Idea Coach." She recently launched AccelerateYourDreams.com, a global online platform of workshops and webinars on Health, Wealth, Love, and Life. She's raised well over 17 million dollars for both non-profit organizations and private companies alike and recently became an "Icon of Influence." She continues to expand her coaching and consulting business globally.

www.ChristineBlosdale.com

CLIMBING OVER ROCKS

Naomi Carmona-Morshead

I am committed to climbing over boulders; overcoming obstacles. I've reached the top many times: marriage, children, entrepreneur, business owner, awards, achievements, grandchildren, prayer warrior and more. I've also experienced many valleys: car accidents, death of spouse, financial loss, and miscommunication. I've learned it's when you have mountain-top life experiences, your perspective changes. The higher you climb; the better the view! Thank you, God, for mountain top experiences!

I climb mountains. In 2015, I climbed 8 mountains in 8 months. But it wasn't always that way. I was born in 1954 with a congenital heart defect. Even with surgical intervention, my chances were only 50/50. I survived pioneering open heart surgery 50 years ago at age ten. But I wasn't strong. I didn't know I had the potential for physical activity. I chose to conquer mental, physical, emotional, and spiritual obstacles starting at age fifty-eight. I decided to make a "Brave Heart Shift" and was trained with doctor's advice using resources & focus to become stronger than ever!

I climbed the tallest free-standing mountain in the world—Mt. Kilimanjaro, Tanzania, Africa, 19,341 feet elevation last year. At 13,000 feet, before we reached the summit, I woke up at 2:00 a.m. I fumbled for my jacket, my knit cap, head lamp and unzipped the first door of the tent, and then the outer door. As I made my way out, I had to close each zipper in freezing temperature. I stood up in a pitch black night. Above me were four trillion stars. My eyes adjusted and I discovered right in front of me that I was standing equal to the Big Dipper. Really! I had climbed the mountain to the stars to save "little hearts" for Mending Kids. I had reached my goal! Today, you are exactly where you are supposed to be. There is someone who needs your service, your hug, your smile, your love, your "Big Dipper," your "Brave Heart Shift."

Next we climbed to 16,000 feet elevation. It was seven difficult hours climbing UP, UP, UP to hike 2.3 miles. Why? One step forward; slide back; one step forward; slide back; one step forward; slide back. In the game called LIFE, You are a virtual mountain climber and you need to know HOW to climb the mountain of life, don't you? One step at a time. We stopped after a rock scramble at 18,652 feet, Gilman's Point. To recover and rest, they served us hot tea and biscuits. Daily life needs rest!

We hiked to Stella Point, 18,885 feet. The air is quite thin. In fact, it's harder to breathe; you must walk slowly. "Naomi, you lead; follow the path down into the crater. I couldn't see more than three feet ahead. As I walked down into the fog, there were rocks as big as a VW car. Walking slowly through the fog; the air was freezing; it began to snow. "Don't you want to lead the group?" I said. M'hina, the guide answered, "Keep walking."

I walked slowly for one and a half hours. Suddenly there was a big darkness with a man standing just in front of me. It was our mess tent with hot food, refreshments, and rest! Who supports you as you climb the mountain of life? Do you ask them for help? Do they say "Keep walking!"? You are a virtual mountain climber: you climb UP and you help others reach the summit and then rest.

In 2009, I met a little Ecuadoran girl (9), Maria Jose, visiting the USA for open heart surgery and scoliosis. Her procedures were provided by Mending Kids, Burbank, CA.

In the ICU watching Maria, I re-experienced my ICU days (fifty years prior) when I was ten years old lying in an oxygen tent with tubes everywhere. Seeing little Maria survive two surgeries inspired me to dedicate the rest of my life to raising money to provide heart surgeries for underserved children around the world.

Today I am a healthy sixty-two-year-old. From a non-athlete, my husband trained me to summit real mountains and virtual mountains of life.

Why was it important to get to the summit? I received a vision; I understood that God had a message for me that I could learn at that top of Mt. Kilimanjaro.

M'hina started talking, "Naomi, you prayed for snow and it snowed. Because of the snow, it's too foggy. There won't be any sun today until we hike down in a few hours."

"But there's going to be sun, I just know it!" I said.

The first 200 yards it was foggy, a bit of pink in the sky. As we reached the summit sign, yellow light burst through the fog; it was brilliant sun! It lasted for twenty minutes. There was something to experience at the summit. M'hina was right. I could not see the ground for a cloud covered the entire summit of the mountain. But I got the message. "Leave the darkness behind and walk into the light." Is that message for you? What darkness is holding you back? What obstacle is keeping you in the dark? Darkness will speak, "There's not going to be any sun." You don't have to listen. Leave the darkness behind. You CAN climb up no matter how many steps you take backwards. You will reach the summit of your life.

I call this process "The Brave Heart Shift." YOU make the decision to Shift toward the light. Combine resources and training and focus both toward a goal. You will gain courage and compassion which become heart-centered: SHIFT! Your goal may be big or small incremental steps. I challenge you to turn toward the light and make a Brave Heart Shift in your life today.

Naomi Carmona-Morshead speaks internationally, climbs mountains, and escorts tours. She is a wife/widow, mother/grandmother, entrepreneur, and health architect. She tells tales about hiking trails so difficult, she could only take 100 steps before resting. She has overcome physical, mental, and emotional obstacles to reach the summit of Mt. Kilimanjaro in Africa. Mending 100 Hearts fundraising has already saved 146 children. If you'd like to help, donate here: www.Mendingkids.Org. REF: 100 Hearts. Follow Naomi's adventure blog at www.Mending100Hearts.wordpress.com.

www.TheBraveHeartShift.com

Two Weeks Before My Sixteenth Birthday, My Dad Died—I Thought I Killed Him

Toni Caruso

I was so excited that hot summer day, two weeks before turning sixteen. Soon I would get my driver's license. It was a lazy day, and I was laying on the couch relaxing. There was no internet or cellphones back then. Around 3:00 p.m. that afternoon, my dad came home from the Air Force base job he had two weeks a year. He was in the reserves, a major with over twenty-five years of service. He had served in World War II and the Korean War. Now he gave one weekend a month and two weeks a year to serve his country. He wanted a nap before going to his night job as a movie theater projectionist. Being the spoiled fifteen-year-old, I didn't want to get off the couch, so he laid on the floor. At 6:00 p.m. he left for work; I never saw him again.

My best friend Pam came to sleep over that night, and we laughed until late. I woke up to a ringing phone; a woman's voice was asking my name and age. I answered; she hung up. I found out later it was the hospital. Standing there confused, I saw my mom's friends walking into our backyard. Something wasn't right. They told me my father had been in an accident and died. I was in a daze. They wanted me to find my older brother; no one could reach him. My mom was coming home, and they wanted us all there and strong. I was fifteen; how strong could I be?

My brother's friends had been with him, helping him grieve and getting him ready to be the man of the house. He came home and went to work helping. My twenty-one-year-old sister lived and worked ninety minutes away in Squaw Valley. My mom's friends said they would go tell her personally. I thought the news should come from family, so I volunteered to go with them. It was a long drive, and an even harder conversation. I had to tell my big sister, my dad's first and favorite child, that he was gone. Worst of all, it was all my fault.

The truth was that my dad had fallen asleep behind the wheel less than two miles from home. He had hit a tree. Not wearing a seatbelt, which was not mandatory at the time, he had crushed his chest. He got out of the car and walked across the street to a home owned by a doctor. He worked on my dad immediately. At the hospital he was stabilized, but just a few hours later he died. My mom went from frightened to hopeful to devastation. She was a forty-five year old widow, with no job and no high school diploma.

I couldn't believe he had been so close to home; if only I had let him sleep on the couch, he wouldn't have been so tired, and he would have made it home safe. It was all my fault.

I watched my mother cry late at night for weeks. On my sixteenth birthday, I got my license, but I didn't want to celebrate. I held my thoughts and grief about killing my dad for many months. How do you tell your family you did this to them? One day my sister started asking me what was wrong. I decided I had to confess. She said it wasn't my fault; in fact, Dad was known to fall asleep at the wheel. I had done nothing wrong. He would wake up on the other side of the street or swerve off the road. There was nothing I did that would have caused this accident. She told me we were lucky it hadn't happened earlier, lucky he hadn't hurt someone else. It didn't feel very lucky, but I did experience some relief. I still don't know if things could have been different, but I can't change what happened.

Mom grieved by getting out of town. She traveled internationally for a month, then drove around the U.S. for an additional month. That left me to handle the bills, the house, and as well as attend my junior year of high school. I became the kid who drove her friends to and from parties safely. I was the Designated Driver before that was a thing. I became the adult at a very young age.

I quickly learned how men would take advantage of a widow. Contractors and repairmen would promise the moon, yet not deliver. Car dealers were the worst. At eighteen, I wanted a brand-new Dodge Colt. I had been driving my mom's hand-me-down Dodge Charger (I know now, bad idea). After twelve hours at the dealership, they were not going to let us leave without getting me a car and getting them that Dodge Charger trade-in. It was a horrible experience. I used language my mother had no idea I knew. The entire process was shady and demeaning, but at the time we didn't know what we didn't know. At one point when we started to drive out of the parking lot, they stopped us and gave me a "sweet deal." We got screwed; life lesson learned. I decided in that moment that I would never have to depend on a man for money, decisions, my happiness, or my future.

This is the core of who I am today. I don't trust easily, but when I do, we are friends for life. I don't let people get close. Men especially, which is why I didn't marry until I was forty. I am very deliberate in who I work with and bring onto my team. I have built a life that I love; I have a family I adore and a business I am very proud of. It's those defining moments in life that either make us better or worse. It is a choice. I thank my sister for listening to me that day when I was sixteen. Who knows what that guilt could have festered in me and the direction my life would have taken? I miss you, Dad!

With over thirty years of event production experience, **Toni Caruso** has handled events small and large for the entertainment, corporate, and business-to-business worlds. Toni has taken her knowledge, skills, and experience and brought them to business professionals so they can help educate, inform, and share their genius live on stage. Her mission is to produce live Signature Events that are exciting, engaging, unique, and informative—where business professionals at all levels can connect, collaborate, and learn tools to move their business forward. She creates an experience where they walk in with a dream and walk out knowing how to make that dream a reality. She wants to support small business owners and entrepreneurs as they share their stories live on stage, which is the fastest way to build and grow their community. She is wife to Keith, Army mom to Rocky, and advocate for our military worldwide.

www.CarusoSignatureEvents.com

STARTING OVER

Laura Cipres

The year was 2001. As I opened the door for my husband-to-be, I noticed a forlorn look on his face. "The company let me go," he said. The weight of the world seemed to rest upon his shoulders. John had help jump-start a new business; he had the knowledge and the contacts they needed to succeed. His partner, on the other hand, seemed to have ulterior motives. Once the company was up and running, he no longer thought he needed John. We were a few months away from our wedding day.

"Don't worry," I replied, "we'll have more time to spend together and plan our wedding."

"I'll start looking for a job," he said as his eyes looked intently into mine, reassuring me that I could count on him to provide for us. I knew that we would be alright.

John was offered odd jobs helping friends, but I knew he had envisioned starting a company of our own. It was his dream, and now it was mine as well. I told him he could count on me, that I would support and help him. After the wedding, we put our thinking hats on and our funds together. We applied simple, practical principals. Our approach was this: 1) take what we know; 2) find a need; and 3) fill that need.

John's experience was in the gas industry, having worked for over sixteen years as a field service technician for the local gas company. He was an expert at customer service. I had over twenty-five years of experience in business management and customer service. That was the beginning of our adventure. We started in our spare bedroom with two computers, one inkjet printer, and a cat as our secretary/mascot—a real motley crew. We found a supplier for the product needed, got a cashier's check, and sent it off to Canada. A week later we received our shipment of product. Now, all we needed to do was sell. We had never designed flyers before. Everything we did was from scratch; stock art saved the day. We burned out our printer printing all the *(what seemed like a million)* flyers. John set off day after day to deliver them to real estate offices and homeowners alike.

A few weeks went by in silence while we waited. Then the magic happened! Our first call from the advertising came in. We went from being virtually unknown to an active business. Referrals through word of mouth increased over time. One real estate agent after another started calling. We provided one service at the time that was needed if they wanted to close escrow in the city of Los Angeles area: a mandatory city ordinance requiring an automatic gas shut-off valve installed at the gas meter was our niche.

Then one day, a real estate client asked what else we did. She said it would be nice if she could call and have a one-stop-shop to take care of all the compliance work. Because of her request, we acquired the necessary certifications and licenses to serve our growing clientele. By the end of the year, we had hired a secretary and had a crew of seven installers and service technicians working six days a week. John and I were together almost twenty-four hours a day. Dispatching and handling the back end of the office was my specialty, and John's was acquiring clients and managing the field technicians. I could see the deep joy and enthusiasm with which he worked. However long the hours stretched, John was the hardest worker, and never once did I hear him complain. Everything he did was out of love for our family, and it brought me great pleasure to finally see his dream come true.

Then, on December 30, 2008, the Case–Shiller home price index reported the most significant price drop in its history. The housing bubble burst. It affected approximately three-fourths of the housing market across the United States, and 99 percent of our business was tied to the real estate market. To say it caught us by surprise is a bit of an understatement. We did not expect it when the phones stopped ringing; at the time we billed everything through escrow. When contracts fell out of escrow, we did not get paid. The checks stopped coming. We let all our employees go. Like many around the country, we too lost our home and our business; everything was gone.

Our commitment to one another was more significant than our circumstances; we decided to reinvent ourselves and our business. We pressed the reset button on our life and decided to move down from Newhall to Orange County, California. We rented a small condo and used a spare bedroom for an office. We worked long hours, most nights until one or two in the morning. This time, we worked with Real Estate Owned (REO) agents, and serviced bank owned properties, preparing houses for resale.

Our hearts were heavy as we witnessed the devastation of abandoned dreams in each home we inspected, trashed out, and fixed up. So many families were displaced. We saw it all, from the sheriff's lockouts on the foreclosed home to the vandalism left behind in some of the properties. It was gut-wrenching.

John and I were committed to finding a way to give back and help. We partnered with Mercy Housing and other similar organizations who are committed to affordable housing for families, seniors, vets, and more.

Time heals, and time mends. Our business has been growing exponentially. We have not only survived—we have thrived, gleaning many life lessons that we now share with others. Be flexible, reinvent yourself, never give up, hang on to one another, never lose hope. Your dream is worth fighting for and always remember to give back. "Each one teaches one" (African Proverb).

Laura Cipres is co-founder of Andreas Fault Property Services and Premier Success Trainings. She has over forty years of business administration and customer service experience. Laura has worked with companies such as So Cal Gas Company, John Hopkins University, and General Mills. She is a certified executive, life coach, and mentor. Her hobbies include traveling the world with her husband. John and Laura joined families to create a nuclear family of five adult children, eight grandchildren, and one fur child, Tato the Gato.

www.andreasfaultpro.com

IT'S SAFE TO BE ME

Natalie Clayton

In January 2018, I birthed a coaching and consulting company, TILT Synergy, Inc. Our mission is to assist individuals and empower their way of thinking to become their best selves personally and professionally. But let me take you on a journey where I discovered my Faith in God like no other and my "Purpose Through Stillness." My journey started in 1995 with an amazing twenty-year career span in law enforcement: police officer with San Diego Police Department, special agent with the California Department of Justice, and a parole agent with the California Department of Corrections and Rehabilitations.

Besides my career I was a divorced "supermom" with three kids. I walked around with a large "S" on my chest and was involved in every aspect of their lives: school, church, sports, and extracurricular activities in the community. I was a track and field sprint coach and competed as a sprinter in the Police and Fire Olympics.

In 2007 I remarried who I thought was my dream man and soulmate, and everything was great! Then the unthinkable happened. In March 2011, my twenty-two-year-old son was in a horrible accident. He (a pedestrian) was hit by a large party bus. The party bus dragged my son three hundred feet. He had multiple severe injuries and was in critical condition. He was in the hospital for ten months and had thirty-nine surgeries.

I stopped working for eight months to take care of my son. During that time my husband became a nonsupportive roommate and requested that I choose him over my son. We divorced a year later. I turned to the Word of God for strength. I believe the Word of God is the Breath of Life. In the Bible Palms 46:1 reads: "God is our refuge and strength (mighty and impenetrable), a very present and well-proved help in trouble" (Amplified verson). The Word of God kept me afloat above what felt like hurricane flood waters in my life. I put my complete trust in His Word. The Hand of God was on my life.

In October 2011, I went back to work hoping to get promoted to a Parole Agent III position (equivalent to a Captain). At the same time, my son was released from acute hospital therapy. Within seven months, in May 2012, I was diagnosed with stage 3 colon cancer. I thought to myself, *You've got to be kidding, right?* It felt as though my world crumbled.

Within two weeks of my diagnosis, I underwent colorectal surgery and endured six months of chemotherapy. I had to fight cancer and take care of my son in his post recovery. I decided to stay positive, peaceful, and have a heart of gratitude with STILLNESS . . . and the Living Word of God. When faced with circumstances you think are impossible or unbearable, be still and know that God is God!

I believe God is the Lord over all things and nothing is impossible for Him. He is my

Healer. His Work was already done on the Cross! I believed I was healed by the Blood of Jesus. Prior to the chemotherapy treatments, I researched alternative treatments for cancer, and I decided to seek treatments from a holistic practitioner three months prior to chemotherapy treatments. This decision was totally against my oncologist's wishes.

Faith requires action, and I had to be proactive toward my healing. God is a Way Maker, Miracle Worker, and Promise Keeper. I believed in my spirit—regardless of what I saw in the natural—that I was healed. My hands and the bottom of my feet turned black from the chemotherapy treatments. It was difficult to drink water; it felt like I was swallowing broken glass and nails.

Despite the side effects and discomfort from the chemotherapy, I was determined and diligent. I went to the gym and worked out seven days a week and detoxed in the sauna. I changed my diet and eliminated sugar, white flour, and dairy. I juiced every day with the "magic juice": beet, granny apples, and carrots. I drank between 70 to 100 ounces of ionized hydration 10 pH water a day.

In the Bible Psalm 46:10 reads: "Be still and know, recognize, and understand that I AM God. I will be exalted in the Earth. I will be exalted amongst the nations." I had to Be Still. Everything I planned and knew to be true in life—my career, my husband, finances, and my income was gone. The State of California laid me off.

In stillness I reflected on the seasons in my life. I had to reset forgive some people and move on in Love. In my stillness I prayed, rediscovered who I was, and renewed myself. I discovered an amazing Trust and Faith relationship with God. I reconnected to my passion. I love motivating, empowering, and inspiring people. No matter what you're going through or facing in life, God Is Able to Do All Things.

God is a Healer, Provider, Redeemer, and Restorer. In my walk with Christ, I discovered Faith as a way of life. A couple of days after my surgery, I took a shower after meditating and praying. I heard the voice of the Lord say, "The only 'C' word that is manifesting and dwelling in you is Christ! Every challenge no matter how impossible it may seem can be overcome by Faith."

I realized that I had a lot of toxic people and situations in my life. I cut out every toxic relationship from my life. The layoff from my employer proved to be a blessing. I had worked in a very toxic and dysfunctional environment with a toxic boss. My second marriage had toxic red warning flags that weren't visible at the time of my wedding.

A dear friend of mine shared that God would reveal the reason why I was diagnosed with colon cancer, and like clockwork it was revealed that I held on to things with unforgiveness from the past. I discovered that the colon is a holding tank of waste. I had been holding on to somethings that weren't serving me, and through my stillness I grew to forgive and let go. It's not an easy journey to get to a place where you forgive people, but it is such a powerful place—it sets you free to live the life you want and desire.

"Be, Do, Have": Be what I believe. Do what I believe. Have what I believe. The acronyms for TILT, my coaching and consulting corporation, stand for: Transformational Integrated Leveraging Team—an affectionate playful nickname my amazing late father came up with.

Natalie Clayton is a Thriver and More than a Conqueror. She is the creator of TILT Synergy, Inc., Coaching and Consulting Group. A retired police officer of twenty years, she is originally from San Diego, California. Natalie is the mother of three adult children and grandmother of her precious little angel named Nylah!

She has a MS degree in Human Services–Organizational Management and Leadership, and is a volunteer mentor with the Big Brother, Big Sister organization of Orange County and Inland Empire. She is a believer and follower of Christ and an outdoor sport enthusiastic! She loves to road bike, workout, fish, and is a die-hard Chargers fan!

www.iamnataliej.com

A Backyard Roller Coaster

Hayden Duswalt

I have always loved roller coasters. The thrill of riding them is so exhilarating that I couldn't get enough of it.

One day, my brother Ryan and I had the crazy idea of building a roller coaster in our own backyard. I was around six years old when we first thought of this, so we started out small. We took some wooden boards we found in our garage and used them as tracks. We lined them up down a hill and used a skateboard to ride down. We had a ton of fun, but we were inspired to go bigger.

Later that week, we decided to use PVC pipes as the track instead of the boards and built a small cart out of wood and little rollerblade wheels. We loved it so much, and we even made a series of YouTube videos about the small roller coaster we built.

But many years later, we got the itch again and wanted to go even bigger and build a realistic roller coaster with a drop and everything. It took tons of convincing to our parents over the years, and even when they declined, we would still watch videos of other people building roller coasters in their backyard.

After years of persistence, our parents finally allowed us to build a big roller coaster when I was fourteen years old. We immediately began designing it on paper and buying supplies at our local Home Depot. We bought PVC pipes for the rails of the track and wood for the supports and crossbeams. And we bought tons of screws. We found that drilling screws into the wood and PVC pipes was so much fun.

My brother and I had had a clear design in our head for so many years, so we knew what we were doing. We woke up early in the morning every day and worked day and night, nonstop; the motivation was shooting through us every day.

It only took us one week before the roller coaster was ready to ride. The final product was thirty feet long with a seven-foot drop, a camel hump, and a spike at the end. I was chosen as the first one to ride our roller coaster. It was somewhat scary to ride a roller coaster that was homemade, but it worked perfectly.

It was so rewarding to finally ride the rollercoaster I had pictured in my mind ever since I was six years old!

Hayden Duswalt is a sophomore in high school. He enjoys swimming, guitar, piano, music, performing arts (theatre), and of course, building roller coasters.

I Found My Passion

Ryan Duswalt

A lot of my life I had been set on being a golfer and wanted to pursue becoming a professional. I practiced every day and played many tournaments on the weekends. I even traveled by plane to a few national tournaments. I was a very successful junior golfer, and I even had a social media presence with the tagline ZeroDaysOffGolf, where I would post a picture of me playing golf every single day.

Once eighth grade hit, I started playing the game Rock Band a lot with my brothers; I was the drummer and got really good at it. So good, in fact, that I actually asked for a real drum set for Christmas.

I transferred all the grooves I had learned playing the video game to the actual drum set, and it kicked off my hobby of playing the drums. I played quite often, and I initially found that it was an awesome way to let off some steam.

I also learned my favorite metal songs to jam out to, and it was always really fun.

It soon became clear that I enjoyed drumming and music way more than I enjoyed playing golf. I had played varsity golf at my high school since ninth grade, and now I'm a senior in high school, and while I will probably play varsity golf again this year so I can graduate as a four-year lettermen in golf, I have completely lost my passion for the game.

I've realized over the past few years that the reason for this is that I love to make people happy. Golf is a game with no team—you are playing by yourself, and it's a pretty lonely sport. Yes, I was on my varsity golf team, but you're really playing the game by yourself, whereas music is always about the fans and making people have an enjoyable experience, which I love.

After hours and hours of practice (I practice drums four to six hours every day), I became the core drummer in my high school's jazz ensemble my junior year of high school, as well as the main drummer in my school's worship team and my local church's worship team.

Every year, my high school puts on a huge show that features many well-known tunes performed by the music students. I played most of the songs on the set list, and I had such a blast doing it—experiencing a joy I had never felt before, even after winning a golf tournament.

I recently went to NYU this past summer for a two-week music program, and I auditioned for a band and was blessed to play a set at the famed The Bitter End club in Greenwich Village, a place where all the top names in music have played. This changed everything for me, and now I know exactly what I want to do with my life.

Playing at all these live events has finally inspired me to put together a concert of my own called Ryan Duswalt & Friends. At this concert, all of the proceeds will go to charity through the Band Together Foundation, and the concert will feature many of my favorite rock songs from the 80s and 90s. I put together the band and have asked a few celebrity RockStars to sing their hits as well.

Ryan Duswalt is a senior in high school. He plays drums and aspires to be touring in a successful band one day. He is also a golfer and enjoys building things.

CHILDLIKE COURAGE

Tyler Duswalt

My experiences speaking on seminar stages have been extremely valuable in contributing to the person I am now.

I first spoke onstage at my father's marketing seminar when I was ten years old and had just published my book, *The Short Book on How to Become a Blogging Expert*. At that age, without any real capacity for embarrassment or intrusive thoughts about what is and isn't possible, my fear of speaking was crushed by that sense of childlike wonder.

Through the years, maintaining a piece of that courageous mentality was admittedly a tough task. Public speaking—namely in front of my peers—started to become more daunting as other insecurities surfaced. What enabled me to persevere through those fears was the knowledge that I had done it before: I'd commanded a room at a very young age, and I could do it again—this time with more life experience under my belt.

Getting over this mental hurdle has affected the way I interact with people in only positive ways. It's helped important aspects of my composition, such as my confidence and conviction, and things seemingly incidental, like the volume of my voice.

Speaking has taught me that doing something for the first time makes the next time easier, continuing until it's another skill in my arsenal. I am aspiring to be a film director, so the ability to lead or control a room with a plan and poise is vital. Making myself completely vulnerable to the ears and opinions of others is one of the hardest things I've had to consistently do after I raised the bar for myself at such an early age, and I couldn't be more thankful for my actions a decade ago.

When starting anything, put yourself into the shoes of the child whose bravery is unwavering; you will only have yourself to thank down the line.

Tyler Duswalt is a student at Texas Christian University. He is majoring in Film and Business; he aspires to be a film director.

Don't Stop Believing

Maryann Ehmann

Have you ever had a pivotal moment that transforms your life and sets you on a whole new trajectory, a day that can only be described as a complete set up by God? Yes, that happened the day I met Craig Duswalt. But first, the backstory . . .

For most of my teen and adult years, I struggled with feeling inadequate and undesirable. Picture a little half-Korean girl in an all-white community during the Korean War era in the 1950s, the product of a biracial couple. While there were many blessings growing up, often it's the embedded messages of insufficiency that secretly control us.

I have found that this is a highly common belief that trips up even the most accomplished high achiever. Striving to prove themselves, they often burn out, lose their way, become highly developed perfectionists, or just quit.

I did all of that, relentlessly pursuing degrees and prestigious professions. But no matter how hard I tried or worked, it never seemed like enough. Striving, rather than dealing with the real issue, resulted in alcohol abuse, prolonged migraines, relationship difficulties, financial insufficiency, and bouts of depression. It would be years later that I recognized this as the product of not resolving that old underground belief that I was inherently defective. Praise be to God, through a series of miraculous events, I began to discover my true self, growing in freedom and joy as time went on.

I had left my career to be a stay-at-home mom, but now it was twenty years later and time to "get back out there." I was inspired at a conference to write a book, as I had many messages to share. Investing in a program that would help me do that, as well as launch whatever business I wanted, establish an online presence, and thus be on my way to a life of my dreams, I dove in. But with little clarity as to what I really wanted to do and more limiting beliefs to plague me, I ended up quitting after three years of trying, feeling defeated and determined to never, ever put myself through this torture again.

Six months later I agreed to accompany my husband to a conference for authors, with the caveat that I would not be sucked into buying any more programs. Despite the bevy of inspiring speakers, I held my ground. With no real interest, boredom was setting in. Unable to sit through one speaker after another, I kept fidgeting. In the middle of wondering why I was there, it happened. Fun blaring rock music. Old familiar tunes. The compulsion to dance! And bursting through the doors, this crazy guy, throwing t-shirts like we were teenagers at a rock concert! Rising to our feet like star-struck fans, singing along as we ridiculously plowed into each other for these simple articles of clothing as if they were hundred dollar bills. The stagnant air filled with electricity that woke us up and commanded our attention.

This was my introduction to Mr. Craig Duswalt. Using what he learned from his Guns and Roses days, he captivated us. This was the moment my purpose was waiting for. Yes, I signed up for his very attractive package, and within six weeks my book was done, within a few more months I was on stage presenting it, my online presence was established, and almost like magic, speaking engagements flooded in. Speaking gigs turned into clients, and my business was born. Within a few years, I had a six-figure coaching business, making more than I ever made as an attorney and doing what I was born to do. As I look back, I can see some key elements that contributed to my success.

Borrow someone else's faith, if you have lost your own. Craig had an unwavering faith in me and constantly communicated this. When we lose faith in ourselves, sometimes the only way to keep going is to borrow someone else's.

Clarity is essential. But it doesn't always come easily, especially when the real you is trapped under a pile of limiting beliefs. As much fun as I was having sharing my message around the country, I was spending more than I was making. Through Craig's encouragement, I stayed the course and eventually clarity—and money—came.

Make mistakes and be yourself. If there is anyone who does this well, it is Craig. One of the most transparent and authentic leaders you will ever meet, Craig set the stage and helped me get over that damned perfectionism. He always made it safe to experiment and be adventurous. Genius!

Join a community of like-minded believers. We all need to feel like we belong, that we matter, and are held accountable to the desires of our heart. Being an entrepreneur is not an easy path to forge, and often it incites every fear of being weird and undesirable that lies within. Ten years later, I still belong.

Dig deep and share the love. Everyone talks about mindset, but because of misconceptions, most people avoid it. While this is my forte, Craig always gave proper due to the mindset work. Sometimes, to be honest, people's resistance to digging deep made me question if I was wasting my time. But it is part of why I am here, and Craig never lets me forget it. As my skill and belief grew, so did my ability to share the love, my passionate work.

As of today, I have helped thousands of people clarify their purpose, transform their mindsets, and create the lifestyle business of their dreams. I have led teleseminars, workshops, and intimate breakthrough events in luxurious locations (my favorite). When it comes to marketing myself and sharing my God-given goodies with the world, I have pretty much tried it all. However, it is love-inspired belief that keeps us going. I know I speak for many when I say: "Thank you, Craig, for always believing in us."

Maryann Ehmann, founder of Magnificent Love Mindset and Business Coaching and a member of the Forbes Coaches Council, is obsessed with helping people find their truest selves, walk in the purpose for which they were created, and prosper themselves and others abundantly while doing what they are born to do. Adding spirituality, neuroscience, and quantum physics to business, marketing, and life strategies, Maryann, a former prosecuting attorney and financial adviser, offers a uniquely refreshing approach to living life and doing business.

MaryannEhmann.com

WILDERNESS SURVIVOR

Vivian R. England

Winter, spring, summer, and fall! These are the four seasons in which the earth evolves and regenerates itself. During these seasons, the earth goes through a period of metamorphosis, if you will. What do I mean? Well, in the winter, things appear to be drab and lifeless, as nature takes a well-deserved rest. The sun sets earlier and is replaced by darkness. The majority of the trees are barren with no leaves in sight. The weather is cold and frigid, and periodically snow falls from the sky and covers the ground. Animals are in hibernation. People are seen donning heavy coats. The thermostat is turned up to heat up the home.

After the winter season, spring sets in. During the spring, nature begins to awaken from its slumber. Birds and animals come out of hibernation. A big thaw is on the horizon as snow is replaced with rainfall. Trees begin to bud again. Flowers start to emerge from the ground, while seeds are being planted for vegetation. Heavy coats are exchanged for jackets. The thermostat is turned down, for the chill in the air is subsiding. As the weather gets warmer and warmer, spring turns into summer.

During the summer, people shed their jackets. Closed-in shoes are replaced with sandals and flip-flops. The trees and flowers are now in full bloom. Vegetation has grown and ripened. Animals are grazing the hillsides and back into their natural habitat. Days are longer with the sun blazing in the sky, and nights are much shorter. People flock to the beaches to bask on the sand and get suntanned. Nature has revived itself.

The fourth season is fall. What happens during this season? The trees begin to lose their leaves again. Days begin to get shorter and nights longer. The weather begins to get a chill, and the sun sets earlier. Jackets are being donned to offset the chilly air. People now replace their shorts and sandals with long pants and closed-toed shoes. Harvest time is in full swing. Animals prepare for hibernation. Seeds are sowed to bloom in the spring. This cycle repeats itself year after year. In so doing, the earth revitalizes and replenishes itself.

Nature goes through four seasons. We, too, encounter different seasons in our lives. Although some of the seasons may seem more joyous than others, they are all designed to help us mature in the things of God. The season we may find the most difficult is the winter season. I like to refer to this season as our wilderness experience. During our wilderness experiences, things are more gloomy and disheartening than at other times. We may feel like we are all alone while the world is crashing down upon us. No one really understands what we are experiencing. Trials and tribulations are on every side. It's like the old saying, "When it rains, it pours!" The Bible says, "Many are the afflictions of the righteous: but the Lord delivereth him out of them all" (Psalm 34:19, KJV).

Wilderness experiences vary from one person to the next. For one, a wilderness experience may be the death of a loved one. To another, it can be the loss of a job. To yet another, a wilderness experience might be a divorce, poverty, famine, homelessness, sickness, and the list goes on. It is evident that everyone will encounter a wilderness experience. As we go through our wilderness experiences, we must maintain the right attitude. It is our attitude that determines whether we are overthrown in the midst of our wilderness or come out victoriously. Our attitude also determines how long we stay in our wilderness experience.

For example, in the Book of Numbers, we are told how the children of Israel were journeying to their promised land via the wilderness. This journey should have taken only eleven days. However, they spent forty years in the wilderness due to their murmuring and complaining. Those individuals who were twenty years of age and over died in the midst of the wilderness, with the exception of Caleb and Joshua. These two made it to the promised land because of their belief and trust in the Lord. We are meant to learn from their experience.

Therefore, I encourage you to prevail over and rise above the cares of this life. Do not die during your wilderness experiences. Recently, we have heard in the news of others who were well-established in society that allowed their wilderness experiences rob them of their will to live. They committed suicide. Suicide should never be an option as a way out. I implore you not to allow this to be your fate.

I must admit that there was a time when I wished I were dead because of the pressures of this life. At night, crying myself to sleep had become the norm. Depression was closing in on me, choking out my joy. Nevertheless, it did not rise to the point that I wanted to take my own life. I can only attribute this to my relationship with the Lord. When I crawled into bed, it felt as though He were holding me in His arms. This gave me the comfort I needed to make it through the night. Also I clung to Romans 8:18, "For I reckon that the sufferings of this present time are not worthy to be compared with the glory which shall be revealed in us," this gave me encouragement to face another day.

As I have survived numerous wilderness experiences, you can too. If you believe you can, you will triumph. Remember, your state of mind will give you the victory you seek. The Word of God lets us know we are more than conquerors through Christ Jesus. Keep the faith, and you will become a wilderness survivor!

Vivian England is a native Washingtonian, international speaker, sign language interpreter, spiritual counselor, ordained minister, and co-author of two bestselling books, *Rock Your Life* and *Women Who Rock 2* with Craig and Natasha Duswalt. Having risen from tragedies to triumphs, her mission is to empower women to rise above the pain, hurt and agony of their past, embrace their self-worth, and pursue their destiny. Her motto is: "I can do all things through Christ which strengthens me."

living4purpose@yahoo.com

LIVING HAPPILY EVER CYBER!

Sandra Estok

When I was eleven years old, my family was evicted from the place where we were living. The only house my family was able to afford the rent on was a shack in the middle of an owners' property. This house was a rectangle box of concrete with a metallic door, an uneven ceiling, and one small window in the front. There was no bathroom or water service inside, just a latrine in the middle of the yard. It was certainly different from the other nice houses that looked like family homes.

Every day, in front of the house, I watched kids playing volleyball. I never learned to play any sport, and I dreamed of playing with them. However, they rejected me every time. Then, one day, one of the kids yelled at me: "Get out of here! You live in an ugly shack, loser, you are never going to make it, and you will never be one of us." As I was walking away, another kid said: "Hey, come back—of course you can play with us—a new game called "la ollita." In this game, the first person who drops the ball would kneel in the center, and everyone would hit that person with the ball.

I went home with many bruises and a broken pride. I wanted to cry, but instead I remembered what my teacher Ms. Marleen had said: "Happiness is a choice, because we are the architects of our own life." So, I promised that no matter the situation, I would always choose happiness and take action for my dreams to come true. I declared, "I am going to learn to play volleyball right now!" But first I needed to figure out how to make money to buy a ball.

Based on that goal, I got my first job with a nearby family, helping their thirty-year-old daughter Shelly to read and write. Her mom told me she would pay me based on results. Every day for the next four months we worked together. Shelly wanted to read, write, and spell her name, so we focused on achieving that.

Finally the day came when Shelly could write and spell her name, and we were both so excited! Though I was happy for her, I was also happy for me, because I would get paid and my dream of buying a ball and learn how to play volleyball would become a reality.

Shelly's home was beautiful, we were at the dining table when her mom entered the room. Shelly started spelling her name and wrote it in a piece of paper. I was so proud! But her mom looked at me and said: "Is this all you have done for four months? What a waste! I am not paying you for this," and walked away. Shelly was devastated, and my dream of playing volleyball was gone.

I went home and cried for hours, but remembering Ms. Marleen's quote and my promise to choose happiness, I decided to explore selling something, so I went to my mom. "Mom, how do you make tamarind juice?"

There was a tamarind tree in the yard, so I made the juice with the fruit and poured it into one side of a plastic bag, tied the corner, and froze it. Because of its shape, I made the sign "Boobs for Sale."

A couple of weeks later, I had earned fifteen dollars and bought my first volley ball. Every day after school, I practiced volleyball for hours against the front wall of our house. As I learned the basics, I joined a local team and got some coaching. Fast-forward five years later: I was playing many tournaments and our team even attended a national championship!

A month later, our landlord passed away, and his family came and told us "to get out." We were being evicted again. Our family packed up and went to live with my stepfather's family. I was only sixteen years old and had just graduated from high school. I enrolled in a government program to become a secretary.

I kept playing volleyball, and life started to get better when I got an internship at Heinz Venezuela Company. One day, one of the executives' administrative assistant told me: "Sandra, please go to the Intercontinental Hotel and deliver this envelope."

The hotel's lobby was stunning and luxurious. The floor was tiled in polished marble. There was a gorgeous chandelier in the center of the high ceiling, and a sophisticated flower arrangement adorned the side. I had no idea that places like this existed except in movies. The concierge walked me to the restaurant area, and as I handed the envelope to the man who was waiting, he said, "Sandra, have a seat; get breakfast and charge it to my room," and walked away.

I stood there speechless and finally decided to sit and eat. There was so much food! As I was enjoying it, people started showing up for breakfast, some in business attire and carrying briefcases. At one of the tables, I saw a woman using a small computer. This world was very different to mine!

As I continued to observe everyone, my mind started to visualize myself wearing a suit, carrying a briefcase with a small computer, traveling, and making an impact in the world. From this point on, a new life of possibilities opened in front of me. I thought of my mom and little brother at home and how they were counting on me. Then I declared: "I am going to become a businesswoman. I just need to figure it out how to pay for my night's college degree."

I have achieved almost everything I have dreamed of, and in some cases even more. I feel an immense gratitude for all the blessings I have been given. My life is full of realities that once upon a time were only in my mind because I never believed others would limit how far I could go.

Throughout my journey, there was someone—a kid, familiar or unknown person, a boss, co-worker, or even subordinates—that were pushing me around or bullying me; it was from those moments that I grew the most.

Today, choosing happiness continues to be the focus of my life, my family, my health, my relationships, and my business. Founding Way2Protect allows me to fulfill my promise and act on my dream to change the way our cyber world is perceived by leveraging our day-to-day stories, relating and connecting to protect what matters most to us, and Live Happily Ever Cyber!

Sandra Estok is passionate about helping business owners protect themselves against cyber threats. Through her company services, speaking engagements, and simple but highly effective cybersecurity training and awareness content, businesses can focus on protecting what matters most to them. She brings over twenty years of multicultural and cross-functional experience in Cyber Security, IT, and Data Privacy. She holds an MBA and industry certifications in Cyber Security and Data Privacy.

www.Way2Protect.com

WORTH FIGHTING FOR

Susie Fabrocini

I was five years old. Sitting on the floor of my parent's bedroom, I was crying to my father through the closed bathroom door, telling him that Eric Shuletsky, the bully who lived across the street, had pushed me, and I fell down and hurt myself.

My father, through the closed door, said, "Go back over there and push him back."

"What? I can't do that!"

"Why not?"

"Because he's bigger and stronger than me!"

"It doesn't matter. If somebody pushes you, you have to push them back. If somebody hits you, you have to hit back, and if somebody hurts your brother or sister, you have to fight for them too."

Reluctantly, I did as he commanded. To my great surprise, he did not chase after me when I pushed him and ran back home. That was the end of it. It was an empowering experience that brought out the fighter in me.

Fast-forward to October 1998. I was leaving my husband and buying a house for myself and my two little girls.

My phone rang. It's my realtor. "Did you just leave your job?"

"It's OK. I have another job. I just switched."

"IT'S NOT OK!" she yelled. "YOU CAN'T CHANGE JOBS WHEN YOU'RE IN ESCROW!"

"What? Why not?"

I didn't know. Nobody told me about that rule. How was I supposed to know? Not only that, I made the down payment on the house I was buying with a loan from my 401k at the job I had just left. Imagine my shock upon learning that I would have sixty days from the day I left to pay back that loan. Seriously?

Fortunately, my new job offered me an advance on my salary to pay off the loan. Unfortunately, the new job was on a TV series, so the advance was set up to come out of my paycheck over a very short time frame, which meant that now my paychecks were not enough to cover my living expenses!

It seemed like every step I took was another financial booby trap set up to take me down. I was getting pummeled by my financial situation, and before I could recover, I would get knocked down again. There was no opportunity to push back. What could I do?

As luck would have it, I met a woman who had taught herself about money and was able to retire at twenty-seven years old! She encouraged me to do the same and recommended that I start by reading *Rich Dad, Poor Dad*, and with each book I finished, she would tell me what to read next.

My eyes were opened up to a whole new way of looking at money. There were two sides to this new viewpoint. There was the immediate, consumer economics side that I needed to master because this was the part that tripped me up to begin with, and there was the bigger picture of building something for myself and for my future.

I had a lot to learn, and I was up for the challenge. It wasn't quick, and it wasn't easy.

I read books, I sat down with people, I attended seminars, I took classes. I learned about business entities, asset protection, trusts, real estate, stocks, options trading, insurance, annuities, retirement planning, loans and financing, compound interest, taxes, etc., etc. I learned to read contracts, ask questions, and negotiate.

I'm pretty well set up now, and I'm going to be OK. But I look around and I see the old me in so many other women, and I want to empower them too. First from the consumer economics side, and then from the big picture/building a future side.

It won't be quick, and it won't be easy. But it will be worth it. To that end, I've written a very simple book on the basics of financial planning. I've held workshops on money management and created an online class on winning the wealth game and another on creating a simple budget. I've done webinars, podcasts, and spoken to women's groups and students.

But really, the biggest thing standing between the majority of women and financial empowerment is the social taboo against talking about money. Money is a private and personal thing that we don't speak about (sort of like sex without partners). I remember my own mother warning me against discussing money, politics, or religion.

If we don't talk about money, then how will we learn?

I feel like the most effective and beneficial thing I've been doing is hosting a meet-up group for women to gather together in a casual setting with wine and chocolate where we talk freely about money issues pertinent to whoever is in the room at that moment.

If more women would gather together to support and share in this manner, it could be the fastest, easiest, and most delicious pathway to women's financial enlightenment, strength, and security.

Susie Fabrocini is a speaker, writer, and advocate for financial empowerment through education, as well as an award-winning filmmaker and photographer. She founded the Economic and Financial Education Council, which offers free financial workshops for her community, and she was on the board of directors for the Soroptimists of San Fernando Valley. She is currently doing research for a documentary on women, money and power, and is running a financial services company out of Los Angeles and a real estate investment company out of Boise, Idaho. Susie's proudest accomplishment to date are her two brilliant, delightful, fun-to-be-around, daughters.

SusieFabrocini.com

Harness Your Vision and Rewrite Your Life Story

Elayna Fernández, The Positive MOM

Elayna's daughters are so sweet. Elayna's daughters are so confident. Elayna's daughters are so happy. Elayna is such a positive mom.

When I hear those comments, I am in awe. Three decades ago I never would have thought that I would be connected to those statements. As a child, I was constantly beaten up and told I didn't deserve to be alive, that I was worth nothing, that I could never do anything right.

I was seven years old, and the Caribbean sun was especially hot. Waste was everywhere. My brother and I would regularly visit the dump behind the little dirt-floored, tin-roofed wooden shack we called home to find objects and artifacts we could play with.

Right before going back home to finish up the long list of chores I dreaded, fetch water, and do homework, I noticed something unusual. It was an old, soggy, smelly magazine with a name we couldn't pronounce.

I eagerly flipped through the pages and was completely fascinated by the bright pictures. Those children were wearing jeans and sneakers, owned books and real toys, and had the time to play with them! They had loving moms—they even read together!

In that pivotal moment, I forgot the stench and trash around me and resolved that these happy faces were a vision of what my life could be.

What if I could learn that language? I wondered. I set out on a journey to not let my circumstances define me and to find the secret to living this dream.

I told the only person who believed in me: my dad. He said "Yes, ¡*Tu puedes!* (You can do this). He taught me a few words he'd learned in English and built a wooden box with a slit so I could save all my "coins."

Since our slum didn't have power at night, I started my first entrepreneurial endeavor: a cardboard puppet show! I told stories about my vision, and besides infusing hope in others, it fueled my passion like a forest fire. I also tutored my classmates and used my writing skills to make extra money.

After saving for four long years, at eleven years old, I had enough money to enroll in the English class I had dreamed of.

Having that picture engraved in my mind and heart got me through a few more years after my parents' painful divorce. My home was a battlefield, and I constantly thought about taking my life.

I finished high school at fifteen, graduated from my English class with honors, and became an ESL teacher at that young age. My perfect grades and impressive achievements failed to prove my worth, and I hoped that maybe I could do that in the big city.

But adversity had other plans. In 1996, while on my way to college, I was kidnapped, raped, and almost murdered by a stranger in a car. Later that year, a near-fatal car crash left me in a coma for eight days.

I felt doomed and defeated but knowing English (and then learning Italian) helped me gain the financial security I was proud of and had always craved. To many, I was a success story, but there was a void in my heart, because I had never found the joy I saw in those vivid illustrations. Was it all a fraud?

In my quest for happiness, I would soon get married, leaving everyone I loved and everything I had built behind to move to the United States and start a family of my own.

I poured my heart into motherhood, and that gave me purpose. And though I'd love to tell you that we all lived happily ever after, history soon repeated itself: again I was being knocked down physically and verbally by the person I thought was meant to protect me . . . and my daughters.

Suddenly I was a single mom of two toddlers, left to start over again: alone, ashamed, and without a penny to my name. I was stuck in a 100-square foot room I couldn't afford. I didn't have a bank account, a job, or a car. I didn't even know how to drive!

Curled up in the fetal position, drowning in my own self-pity, self-blame, and self-defeat, I felt my world was over—and I wanted it to be over. When I looked up, seeing Elisha and Elyssa peacefully asleep completely transformed my experience: something was awakened in me.

I finally understood why I found that old magazine while sifting through revolting garbage, why that picture had been my compass, and why I had to uncrumple the page, and tell a new story. This vision had been for my daughters all along, for what was possible in *their* childhood. I couldn't give up—not now! It wasn't *my* dream—it was *our* dream!

In that moment of divine inspiration, I couldn't come up with a to-do list, but I did something that has become a daily power practice: I wrote a to-BE list. I stopped focusing on what to do and focused instead on who I could be.

I could be the mother I didn't have. I could be the joy I wanted to see in the world. I could be a positive mom!

Armed with the power of a new mindset, I was ready to embrace my sacred purpose. I created The Positive MOM platform to empower moms to free themselves from the confinement of their own mind and decide who they can BE in their life story—on their own terms.

I am certain that when God gives you a vision, He gives you permission to pursue it and provision to fulfill it.

As I write this, I have a thriving business, I have conquered cancer, I freed myself from a disempowering marriage, and I added Eliana and Elydia to my joy. My four daughters inspire me each day, and I'm grateful because my vision has been manifested—and I wholeheartedly know that yours can be too!

Known worldwide for her bestselling books, life-transforming training programs, and highly-acclaimed blog, **Elayna Fernández** is a Latina Storyteller, award-winning Story Strategist, and avid Student of Pain. Certified as a coach, teacher, and master trainer, Elayna empowers moms worldwide with the mindset to transform pain into peace, purpose, and positive growth so they can experience JOY, FREEDOM, and MEANING in motherhood and mompreneurship. Born and raised in a slum in the Dominican Republic, many times a survivor, and a single mom of four daughters, Elayna is living her best life in Fort Worth, Texas. Her philosophy is *"BE Positive and You'll BE Powerful!"*

www.thePositiveMOM.com

SOME WHISPERINGS RIGHTFULLY NEED INCREASING AWARENESS

Jay Fisgus

Years ago one of the great names in real estate sales training, Tom Hopkins, presented a definition of success, live, in Los Angeles. Success, he said, is a continuous journey toward the realization of predetermined worthwhile goals. Years later my lovely lady made a commitment fitting that definition. Her goal was: Mitigate the threat of ovarian cancer by raising awareness.

Her journey began a few years back, late in spring, just before I discovered her doing something highly unusual. As she was from Austria, English was not her first language. Dismissing her lack of proficiency in English, she felt more comfortable speaking English among friends. Suddenly, she became assertive, regularly striking up conversations with total strangers. What gives? She told me a story, describing a conversation she overheard among some women. The subject was cancer. A remark was made about ovarian cancer: "It whispers." The initial symptoms are commonly subtle. Women and doctors themselves reasonably dismiss minor random aches and pains associated with common ailments, saying: It's nothing. It will go away. It comes and goes. It's not gone, but it's still minor." The "whisperings" camouflaged by suggesting other common issues allow the cancer to progress undetected. The "whispers" continue. Ultimately, the woman decides that something is just not right; the cancer has likely entered its later stages.

Doctors describe the progress of ovarian cancer and its expected range of possible patient outcomes by stages. Stage One is earliest in cancer development and has the most favorable range of outcomes for the patient. Stage Four is the last stage and is characterized by advanced development and diminished probability of patient's favorable outcomes. Doctors counseling ovarian cancer patients have no crystal ball to predict outcomes; instead they address uncertainty using statistics to advise patients of expectations and possible outcomes. No matter the stage at initial diagnosis, not everyone dies immediately; not everyone survives to category five years plus.

Every stage has its examples, but those who discover the cancer in Stage One are far more likely to have the most favorable outcomes. So the level of patient awareness early on can be critical in making a difference between outcomes. It's early patient sensitivity. It's early patient willingness and ability to communicate with their doctors. It's also persistence. If unusual symptoms become persistent, then it's time for patients to be persistent. It's time to make an appointment. It's time to review once again any unusual, suspected "whisper" symptoms with the doctors. The overwhelming response regularly is that the suspect concern is not serious, but the question is worth asking anyway.

My lovely lady saw opportunity in what she heard. Women have reason to be cautious, yes, but certainly no reason to be alarmist and no reason to be complacent either. If women were more aware and less complacent, it's possible to make a difference in mitigating the threat of ovarian cancer.

She felt something had to be done, and she did it. She started conversations. Perfect stranger or not, someone might hear, "Got a minute?" or "Heard about ovarian cancer? It strikes about one of seventy women. How many women are important to you? Count them. The closer to seventy, the more likely ovarian cancer will strike one of them." She often ended quickly with, "Know what you can do about it? Just talk. Who do you care about? Talk with them!"

She encouraged people to go online and search "ovarian cancer." There's lots of good medical information available. My wife-to-be hoped that, as a result of one of her conversations, one more woman somewhere, sometime, would be more aware, more suspicious, and make an appointment sooner. If ovarian cancer was discovered, her doctor might have what must always, for doctors, the preferable Stage One discussion.

Early in July my lovely lady asked me to join her. Her hope became mine. We were a team with a mission, in more ways than one! People thanked us for sharing the information. Ovarian cancer survivors from all stages shared their stories. My lovely lady was buoyed up with emotion. She felt the awareness! She was fighting back! She was making her mark! We considered results. What to measure? Asking every direct contact to pass the awareness on to five women important in their lives, we could assume one woman would act on the conversation we started. We celebrated often. She celebrated every woman. She celebrated daily and with good reason—it might be her last.

You see, my lovely lady's diagnosis—late Stage 3 ovarian cancer—was October 2 the previous year. Despite prompt action, the cancer discovered was inoperable. Her surgeon broke the news to me gently. Chemotherapy doctors and nurses likewise did their best. Retiring the month before her initial diagnosis, I served her as caregiver. It was our opportunity to share a lifetime in the time remaining. She celebrated opening day of the LA County Fair, of course, front and center, in Wine Class. By October, my lovely lady had lost so much weight that she was too weak for more chemo. She passed away in January, fifteen months after the date of that initial diagnosis.

Spreading word about ovarian cancer has not stopped with her passing. I continue making conversation, almost daily. My hope is that one day some woman, sparked with awareness by our efforts, would be a bit more suspicious of "whispers," make an appointment with her doctor to discover her body was alerting her to ovarian cancer early on, in Stage 1. Prompt action might reward her with additional years of quality time with friends and family. Somewhere, my lovely lady will celebrate. So will I.

Now, I'm asking you to start conversations like my lovely lady to help mitigate the impact of ovarian cancer on the lives of women you care about. Who is your lovely lady? Who are the top ten women in your life? Whose life might you change? Join our journey; celebrate successes. Cheers!

Jay Fisgus is a lawyer and entrepreneur helping people resolve collection, judgment enforcement, and real estate issues. He's not a doctor, but he advocates for women becoming more vigilant to the threat of ovarian cancer. He urges them to make sure their medical information is from reliable sources. Women, he declares, must necessarily serve as their own personal first line of defense to this cancer threat. He advocates for each woman to recognize that the best strategy for taking care of family and friends is to look first to their own health and well-being. He welcomes the opportunity to speak to your group.

thejayfisgusgroup.com

A CLEAN COLON EQUALS A FOCUSED BRAIN

Elle Flores

Which is more important, the brain or the colon? What is the answer to this question? Most people say the brain. What they don't know is that when the colon ceases to work, the brain ceases to think.

I was invited to a family reunion where I had the pleasure of meeting a new sister-in-law with her four-month-old baby girl. The baby was crying nonstop; I could tell something was bothering the baby. After introducing myself and commenting that her baby seemed obviously very upset, the look on the young mother's face was desperation and embarrassment. She immediately apologized for the baby crying and being so disruptive. After some time talking with her and becoming acquainted, I learned that the baby had colic and was on some type of medication for either gallstones or kidney stones; she couldn't remember what her doctor had said.

Knowing how rare this is, I was shocked, especially after she mentioned that she was breast-feeding the baby. I asked her what foods she was consuming. She looked puzzled and asked, "What would that have to do with my baby?" I looked puzzled right back and responded, "Everything!"

As we became better acquainted, I discussed with her the subject of her diet and how that affected the quality of the breast milk she produced for the baby, and I explained how her diet was affecting the health of the baby.

She worked with me for six months, long after her baby got well. She noticed results immediately; after two weeks the baby was much calmer. I coached and educated her about nutrient-dense foods based on her and her baby's blood type, the importance of implementing pre- and probiotics to her diet, and I taught her how to make her own fermented culture at home and how to consume it to add flavor and variety to her meals. I taught her the importance of understanding food labels and why she should purchase food at farmers markets rather than supermarkets.

By the end of the first three months, the baby was happy again and no longer on medication, and the doctor told her that they must have made a mistake and misdiagnosed her because the baby didn't have the stones anymore.

A natural by-product of this young mother's newfound education was the profound health benefits she also experienced. Her face cleared up, she lost weight, and she noticed a difference in her eating habits. She found herself naturally making healthier decisions; she wasn't craving junk foods anymore. She was amazed at how her newly acquired knowledge of foods created profound changes in the baby's health and mood, and what kept her motivated to continue to work with me was noticing that her own health and mood improved as well. Fast-forward a year later: she has kept the weight off and is enjoying a healthier lifestyle. She teaches her family what she has learned, and they too have benefitted and are making healthier choices.

With so much information available about what it really means to be health-conscious, it's a conscious choice to be ignorant about this subject. Every successful client tells me that they can't believe that something as simple as food can make such a profound improvement on their health. People are funny, though. It is rare to see someone make the conscious decision to make that empowering lifestyle change. Sadly, what I see more often is that they prefer to gamble with their health and put their faith in diet pills and invasive surgery to lose weight.

The young mother and her four-month-old baby girl is a great example of how the food the mother was digesting directly impacted the health of her baby. The introduction of the fermented culture was a game changer for this baby. The gut needs to be maintained with a proper balance of the microbiome in the digestive tract, and when the mother consumed the pre- and probiotics from fermented vegetable culture "good bacteria," she and her baby were finally receiving dense nutrition. The nutrients are created through the fermentation process as the bacteria go through their life cycles; microbial cultures create B vitamins, including folic acid, riboflavin, niacin, thiamin, and biotin as well as a nice array of antioxidants.

The baby's mood changed almost instantly! The brain-gut connection is very real; the gut affects our mood. What happens when you skip breakfast or lunch? Yes, you are hungry, but you're also grumpy and in a bad mood. The reason you feel that way is because your organs need food. All our organs are made up of minerals, and without them the organs function poorly and become starved. Introducing fermented culture to the gut is easy on the digestive system, and through the process of digestion, the bloodstream carries the nutrients and oxygen to all the organs, especially the brain.

Everyone wants to look good and be healthy, and the answer is in our gut. Eating foods that agree with our gut is the first step in listening to what your body is telling you. If eating a hamburger and fries makes you gassy, this is your body communicating that it is not digesting. Today many children are suffering the consequences of adult illnesses and diseases, including obesity and diabetes, and those numbers are steadily climbing.

This can be reversed through education. A healthy gut means excellent overall health and longer life spans. It is my pleasure to coach and help you do exactly that!

Elle Flores is a Certified Natural Holistic Practitioner (CNHP) and Life Coach who turned to nutrition when she experienced problems with her own health. She was on several medications, but intuitively she felt it was her diet. This was life changing and empowering, and she now shares her knowledge with her clients, who achieve wonderful results. Elle now controls the foods she eats by growing her own food, and she plans to show her clients to do this for themselves.

LIFE GOES ON—BENT BUT NOT BROKEN

Katrina Garcia

When it comes to success, many look at this as material things. I look at success as a survival story of life because of the many challenges that were thrown my way. First, at the wee age of seven, I was molested by the one person I trusted the most, my father. I know it's not a pretty start to this story, but trust me, it gets better. This is simply the preface of the many challenges I faced through my life and came out my own hero.

At six years old, I was a modern medical miracle. I stumped many doctors with high fevers of 104 and paralysis, only to come out of the situation with a stronger resolve.

During my school years I was taunted and made fun of due to ears I had not grown into, a bubble butt due to a swayed back, and a name no one could pronounce. But through it all I learned to laugh as I made fun of myself, many times before someone else could.

While I was growing up, my dreams were lofty. I always wanted to be the boss, the one who sat in the big office at the very top of the building looking out over a city I dreamt of dominating. I also swore I would never have the little family, the husband and the 2.5 kids, that my sister so badly wanted. Instead I wanted to conquer the world with my brilliance. I also really wanted to be just like Barbara Streisand—a singer, dancer, and all-around entertainer. I did try several times to start my own band, tried out for other bands, and took dance in school. Just when I had my break, I found out I was four months pregnant. Back to the drawing board I went.

I worked hard to instill in my son great values and integrity. I love my son very much, but he was like having ten sons. You see, at a young age he was diagnosed with ADHD, and boy, did he work to test the boundaries each day. In fact, he got kicked out of three preschools. Imagine, if you will, the rest of his time in public schools. But that will be in my memoirs one day for another fun read. Today he is a highly functioning thirty-two-year-old filled with hope for the future and is managing on his own without meds. In fact, we had a saying before he got dropped off at school: "Think before you talk, think before you walk, think before you act." It worked to retrain his brain to think on his own and not rely on meds. I'm so proud of him.

At the tender age of thirty-six, I married the love of my life and began a life I never thought I would have. The house with the kid, two dogs, and a future with the man I loved. Not bad for never wanting a family.

When I turned forty-two, I found myself facing another medical challenge and had one of my kidneys removed. Ever since I was little, I had struggled with bladder and kidney infections, never realizing that one was working great while the other one never really grew to the proper size. My right kidney was the size of a quarter, while they are supposed to be the size of a fist. Well, off with the old and in with the new, I say, so off I went to surgery and no more bladder or kidney infections. All in all, I felt ready to conquer the world again. But the universe had other medical challenges for me.

At age forty-nine I found myself facing the big "C"—cancer. However, luck was on my side, and I survived ovarian cancer. The doctors told me only 25 percent survive this type of cancer. Not only did I survive two surgeries, I didn't even have to go through chemo or radiation. I truly believe it was due to my belief system. I repeated over and over, sometimes screaming in the shower, "They will remove all the cancer in the first surgery, and I will be cancer free forever!" And here I am, cancer-free today, and by God, I won't ever have it again, EVER!

In 2010, we took in the true hero of my life, my mom. We cared for my mom 24/7 as I watched the life slowly diminish from her each day. Dementia robbed me of the mother I knew and loved. This was the biggest challenge I faced, and this journey brought me compassion and patience I never thought I had. But if I had to do it again, I would.

When I was forty-five, I had started my own business. That was a huge challenge in itself. I took risks I thought I never would, but my business is still going strong today. I've proven to many, including myself, that success is not only possible but also rewarding. I get to change people's lives every day as I work to build their websites and help them achieve success. It brings a smile to my face and heart knowing that together we can all achieve our dreams. My true success is taking life's challenges and coming out ahead with laughter and light. As you know, we all have choices—what's important are the choices we make.

Katrina Garcia started her entrepreneurial journey during one of the worst recessions our country has seen. Through it all she has managed to build a successful business. Her ultimate goal is to provide quality service to her clients with integrity along the way—no hard sales, simply results.

She has worked tirelessly to build KG Website Designs to provide website and membership builds with an emphasis on customer service. Each client is treated to the highest standards possible, ensuring true results.

www.KGWebsiteDesigns.com

Passion and Persistence

Jason A. Gardner

At fifteen, after stumbling through childhood in a haze of abuse, fear, and self-doubt, I found myself across the table from my father voicing my desire to end my life. He laid a gun in front of me, a nice silver .357 that he still owns to this day, saying, "Here you go; do it." I eyed it and him and then made a critical choice that would shape my future—a conscious decision to take all the challenges, fear, difficulties, hardships, and sorrows and appreciate them. Yes, genuinely appreciate them. To embrace the lesson and grow in the knowledge that every hurt is crucial for growth and that growth is the very key necessary to unlock the next step in my future.

I'd love to say that from that day forward, life was success after success, but there were more keys required to unlock my potential.

At sixteen, I moved out on my own and dropped out of high school. I had no plan, a minimum wage job in a grocery store deli, and a tiny cabin I rented with a friend that barely kept us from freezing to death in the snowy winters. I know, I was a genius even then. Have you ever looked back on your childhood and realize the reason for your faith as an adult is that without divine intervention the odds of you being here today are about the same as winning the lotto jackpot . . . consecutively, while dodging lightning strikes?

At seventeen, I did what every kid with glorious ambitions and little direction does. I enlisted. Now don't get me wrong, I'm proud to have served; it was one of the best experiences of my life. Then I decided the Naval Special Warfare Command was the way to go and I signed up for BUD/S. In doing this I discovered my passion for learning about nutrition and physiology. I wanted my body to be ready for anything, so I started taking college courses. I accumulated unit after unit in nutrition, physiology, kinesiology, endocrinology, biopsychology, and so on. It became an obsession of mine for years. After retiring minus part of an eye, I finished my formal education only to realize my practical education had just begun.

My first move on the quest to fortune and success was to become a bodyguard for strippers. What I found was plenty of excitement. Guns, bats, pipes, cars, bottles, you name it, I dodged it and somehow managed to keep my charges safe. To this end, I spent quite a lot of time in the gym where I decided to hire a trainer to get some better results. After months of working with all the trainers in the gym, and realizing I knew more than them, I was offered a job. I was hired as a personal trainer to sell packages and train clients. After five months, I had sold exactly ZERO contracts, which made me quite popular with management. My boss pulled me aside and gave me one month to get it together.

Enter my new manager, who took an interest in me and changed my perspective entirely with life lessons on the brick steps outside that 24 Hour Fitness in Yorba Linda, California. What's the magic secret he taught me in all those hours on the steps sitting in the OC sunshine? That I had value. Worth. Innate gifts. God-given talents meant to be shared with the world. He taught me that to serve my true purpose, I'd have to let go of pride, ego, deceptions, and insecurities and embrace being myself. This man became a lifelong friend and mentor, who twenty-plus years later continues to play an integral role in both my personal and business life.

That month, as my perspective shifted, I sold my first package. Three months later, I was one of the top ten trainers in a company that employed over 1,500. I set records. Broke them. But most importantly, I found a passion for educating others in health and wellness which allowed them to both heal their bodies and live their healthiest lives. Shortly thereafter, I began consulting with doctors regarding patient nutritional needs, often even educating them in human nutrition and physiology, how supplements worked, and why most of them didn't. This extended to great success in working with patients suffering from cancer or other diseases who elected to pursue nonmedical paths of treatment.

It became my obsession, and I was good at it. I continued to pursue knowledge, started businesses, helped more people, learned more, and began to find true success-es—and larger failures.

In 2010 I took nothing but my clothes and my pups and headed to Arizona for a fresh start. Shortly thereafter, I switched careers and started a very successful financial services practice helping people grow, manage, protect, and understand their wealth, all while adding my expertise on how to live longer, healthier lives.

To ensure my place in every sad country song, my puppy, Dobbie, got terminally ill. After spending thousands of dollars on prescription foods that made her worse, drugs on top of drugs, and then more drugs to treat the side effects of those, I'd had enough. Following months of vets suggesting that I let her go, I decided to learn canine nutrition and fix her myself. I did, and Dobbie is now a happy, healthy thirteen-year-old papillon, that was, according to her vets, not healthy enough to live past age six. This experience culminated in the creation of a fresh, organic dog food company that has twice been voted healthiest in the U.S. and is its own self-funded rescue organization. To learn more, visit BarksandBerries.com.

Then, just eighteen months ago, to reaffirm once and for all that success and posi-tivity breed success and positivity, I was presented with an opportunity through a few close friends to open the Arizona market for one of the largest, and fastest-growing network marketing companies in the U.S. Once again, I took the risk and found yet another life-altering period of growth that has allowed me to own my life. I travel, I work when, where, and with whom I choose, and I'm building the life I could once only have dreamed of.

My friends, embrace the pain, for it holds the key to your potential. Embrace the hurt and sorrow, your own and that shared with others, because without the risks and peril, the rewards of life available to you will never be what God intended or created you for.

———————————

Jason Gardner is a highly successful financial advisor, owner/operator of Barks and Berries fresh organic dog food and rescue organization, and a top earning network marketer currently building teams in California, Arizona, Texas, Nevada, Wyoming, and Montana. A U.S. Navy veteran, nutrition guru having owned and run companies in the fields of nutrition education, exercise and nutrition endocrinology consulting, and has been a guest speaker, keynote speaker, and authored several articles in the wellness and nutrition field. He currently resides in Gilbert, Arizona.

www.JasonAGardner.com

THE MAKING OF A CHAMPION

Del Gerard

As the high school varsity track and field coach, I had one burning question for my students, most of whom chose events they weren't very good at just because it sounded easier or better than other events. The students also didn't have much training on even the basic skills of running, jumping, breathing—let alone competing and pushing themselves to the max, which was a clear sign for real injuries. This one burning question was the key to any future success and would take away any excuses as well.

"Would you like to be a loser in the thing that you love, or a winner in the thing that you hate?"

Dead silence.

This question gave these kids—who were more interested in transferring out of PE, hanging out with friends, and having fun than real training, working out hard, or being their best—a new perspective on who they could become and what they could accomplish.

One by one, each student was asked the question. Amazingly, not one of them said they wanted to be a loser. They all wanted to be a winner . . . a champion.

But what does it take to be a champion?

It was time to show them.

The *plan* was simple: to win league next year. One problem, though: it had never been done before in the school's fifty-four-year history. Thus the students' mindset and belief system struggled. They also had never been trained properly to meet the daily required physical demands, which meant it would take time to develop them. Champions are made in the off-season. We started immediately to *prepare* for the next year. Over the next several months, students were given information on the differences between, as well as instructions and proper training mechanics on all league track and field events. Weight training, exercise recovery, and healthy diet and nutrition were also included.

As the new season came, so did the time to see who had readied themselves to *compete*. During the first two weeks, every student was tested daily for their personal bests in all track and field sprints, hurdles and long distances, and their strengths and abilities in all jumping and throwing events. This was crucial to figuring out who would be best qualified to compete in what event, based on real results. No one was excluded from anything.

Once they realized what they could do in each event, we showed them league stats and statistics of previous league championships for the past several years. Students could now see where they would have placed in comparison to other athletes over time. They were also able to quantify the exact percentage of improvements each year. This surprised and encouraged many of them, as they saw new possibilities in events they would not have even thought to compete in before.

This set the stage for all future practices, workouts, trainings, drills, values, habits, leadership, confidences and beliefs. Now they knew what they couldn't have even imagined before. The coach no longer had to get them to buy in to anything because now they had living proof. The timing was ripe to fully train and develop them on how to *"plan, prepare, compete, and win."*

Each week a trophy was given to any athlete who got their personal best or broke any record in any event they participated in (paid for by Coach). Our local sporting goods store helped us design personalized sweats for each athlete with their favorite number on it and provided all track and field shoes and equipment with a discount.

But even with all that, many decided to quit. Pressure from friends, injuries, and the structure was too challenging for many. Two-thirds of the program dropped out, leaving only fifteen boys on the varsity squad.

Wanting to be champions, six sophomores stepped up to the varsity team to take fifth and sixth place in events that they would have otherwise taken first place in.

We are not here to win track meets! We are here to win a championship!

This was our #1 principle, goal, mindset, and guiding philosophy. Others were the following:

- If you lose every single-track meet but win the championship, do you care?
- You are not competing against outside competition. You are competing against yourself.
- You must personally improve and get better a little bit more, each day, every day, period.
- You want to peak (be at your best) at the end of the season (at league) and not before.
- Never say *can't* around Coach Gerard unless you are trying to get more running practice.
- League championship is won by placing first, second, third, fourth, fifth, and sixth, not speed or times.
- Know what place you need to finish in each of your specific events at league.
- If you did the absolute best you could, would you, should you, have any regrets?
- "Team partners" must lead, support, help, and encourage each other no matter what.
- Believe in yourself and what you can do. Your coach does. You have been trained well.

In the end the team did everything they were trained to do. Many of them surpassed all expectations. Personal bests were made. Limiting beliefs were shattered. What was possible for them and their future changed radically, all because that year they won the league Track & Field Championships.

From coaches to the athletic director, from parents to friends, even from the opposing coaches to the teams they competed against, everyone congratulated the team. They had done what no one thought possible. They had accomplished a dream. They were champions now, and they did it despite losing over 70 percent of the meet's they competed in. Of course they celebrated. They worked hard over the past several months. They earned it. Well done.

After it was all over, the team got together for their final meeting. The question they asked me was "Coach, if we did the same thing, do you think we can win again next year?" *Hmm . . .*

Well, I am proud to report that yes, they did it again the very next year. Back-to-back champions. Awesome!

Del Gerard is a number-one bestselling author, speaker, spiritual mentor, and real-life coach. He has impacted the lives of thousands, identifying and eliminating the obstacles that stand in the way of their success. Creator of Higher-Level Development Training, Del combines his specialized knowledge, training, and experience to teach the principles and strategies that lead to transformational breakthrough. A gifted teacher and great communicator, Del leads with his unique fun-loving style and enlightening process of guided learning and discovery. His honest, straightforward, no-nonsense approach gives his clients the tools and skills they can use today.

www.delgerard.com

LIVING ON EMPTY

Marsha Gleit

On my road to happiness, I ran into self-care. After thirty years in corporate America, moving from job to job and letting my career take me where it wanted, I found myself extremely stressed, overworked, underpaid, and unhappy. Morning after morning as I entered the office through the double wood doors and headed to my glass-enclosed cubicle, I felt like a combination of a caged animal and the ring-leader in a circus.

I was the controller for a mid-sized insurance company. I managed the accounting department, the IT department, the sales administrative staff, and the front desk. I was indirectly responsible for human resources and everything else that was needed when the owners were "out of the office." And they were rarely in the office. Yet with all of this responsibility, and the stress that accompanied it, I was not the ultimate decision maker. I could not make any of the major decisions without the owners' approval. That wouldn't have been so bad if the owners could only make a decision. This circus act went on for ten long years, and the many sleepless nights and hours of negativity slowly wore me down. I was unhappy!

Shortly after my fiftieth birthday, I took a close look at my life. I came to a very pivotal epiphany: I had one career left in me. What would that be? What would that look like? I created the list of what I wanted in a job and what I did not. The top items on my list were the freedom to work from anywhere, financial independence to travel, and working with women who were facing the same challenges. Lastly and most importantly, I wanted something I could do for a long time, as I did not see myself retiring at sixty-five.

Fast-forward: I got certified as a professional life coach, I resigned from my position, and I started my company, Burgeon Coaching, which coupled my business acumen with my new life coaching skills. I was on the road to HAPPINESS.

Well, not so fast . . .

As with all type A workaholics, my identity was my job. It was who I was, it was what I did, it was where I spent most my time, it was where most of my friends were, it dictated my mood, and it was all encompassing. So leaving my unfulfilling job should have made me happy, RIGHT?

But no, something was still missing. *A lot* was missing. But it was not until I was hospitalized twice and had three toes amputated that I ran into the missing element: SELF-CARE.

To back up a bit, in August 2018, while on vacation in San Francisco, I started running a fever, I developed an incredible headache, and my entire face was on fire as if I were the devil. The blister that wouldn't heal on my toe started to throb terribly. We returned home early, and the next morning I visited a walk-in clinic. The doctor who was about to treat me told me I should go immediately to the emergency room. By this time. I had a high fever, a black toe, and what I came to learn was an infection in my bloodstream. As I rode up the freeway in an ambulance that transferred me to another hospital, the only thought going through my head was *How did I get here?* After a five-day hospital stay and one amputated toe, I decided it was time to get my health in line. I began a healthy eating regimen. I lost 20 pounds. I was back on the road to happiness.

Three months later, while on vacation in New York City, I was taking my socks off in the hotel room and noticed that I had broken my toe and the bone was sticking through the skin. I knew then that another hospital stay was in my future. Another infection in my toe? Another hospital stay, another vacation ruined, and another two toes amputated— but why? I loved my new business, and I was eating healthy.

So, like all analytical A-personality types, I began the research process. What I found is now my life's work and passion: self-care—the balancing of our physical, emotional, and spiritual well-being. Self-care: putting me first and my needs above all others. Self-care is not a selfish act, but a *selfless* act. Self-care is not a luxury but a necessity and a priority.

Today I live by this mantra. On my road to happiness, I ran into self-care. And I found my happiness.

———————————

Marsha Gleit is a professional life coach and the founder of Burgeon Coaching. After thirty years of working in C-level positions, she found her passion for helping others grow. Combining her business acumen and life coaching skills, she helps her clients begin living the life of their dreams. During her personal journey, Marsha found that caring for her needs was missing. Her unhealthy and stressful lifestyle lead to the amputation of three toes. Practicing daily self-care changed her in unbelievable ways. Self-care is the cornerstone of her practice, and she believes that if you put your oxygen mask on first, you'll be your best.

www.burgeoncoaching.com

FROM INVISIBLE AS A GHOST TO PRESIDENTIAL LIFETIME ACHIEVEMENT AWARD RECIPIENT

Raven "The Talk Show Maven" Glover

If someone had told me just fifteen years ago that I'd be the recipient of a Presidential Lifetime Achievement Award for my service of giving others a voice, I'd have said they were crazy.

But here I am, proud that Barack Obama chose me in 2016 for realizing a dream I had set in motion at the "seasoned" age of fifty-five.

The dream started long before then. It was with me for forty-plus years—stifled and unrecognized—reflecting on the outside how I felt on the inside: like Casper the Friendly Ghost, invisible and voiceless.

But it took hearing just *one sentence*, as I sat at the hospital bedside of my mother. That *one sentence* struck a chord and triggered me into inspired action. That *one sentence* had such a profound effect that it set me on a path to empower hundreds of people to find their voice.

It took hearing that *one sentence* at the right time, from the right person, to get me into motion to make real the dream I held for as long as I could remember.

I always had wanted to be on the radio. I marveled at the idea of deejays "spinning" records that could be heard by people all over the world.

I remember, as early as age thirteen, a wide-eyed girl in Cleveland, Ohio, wandering down the street from my mom's restaurant to the local radio station to hang out, until the owner would call my mom to come get me.

By age sixteen I had become such a familiar face at the WJMO radio station that the program director invited me to be a junior disc jockey. I felt right at home.

Soon after, I was offered an internship to spin jazz records to motivate patients at the local Veterans Hospital. Call it foreshadowing, call it irony, but it's too coincidental that my radio career would have a major revival at another hospital almost forty years later.

Growing up, I felt unheard, ignored, misunderstood, and invisible. Even though I had that dream of being on the radio, I couldn't imagine it coming true. I felt so unworthy that I gave up on it early on.

But that dream didn't give up on me. Nearly forty years later, it found me, at a time and place that I would least expect it—in the ICU of Methodist Hospital at the bedside of my mother, where I lived for weeks waiting for her to recover from a heart operation.

Mom went in looking like Lena Horne, and I watched her deteriorate. It got me to thinking, *Are there any dreams left inside of her?*

I spent hours in the hospital chapel praying. I was not ready to lose my mother. One day, I heard a message loud and clear—call it God or my inner voice. It said, "Mother's going to make it. She's going to be different, and she's going to need you. It's time to step up, show up, and grow up, and do something that's going to impact her life. But first you have to impact *your* life."

Here I was, in my fifties, and Mom was helping me pay my bills when I should have been helping her. She needed me to do much more than that now. I found my why.

I was working twenty hours a week, making ten dollars an hour, and I couldn't see any other way. But right before Mother went into the hospital, somehow, I found the money to make payments on a course by Alex Mandossian called *Teleseminar Secrets*, where I'd learn how to interview people.

I would get on the conference calls while at the hospital, hanging on Alex's every word, but it was this *one sentence* that stood out and made me stand up. On one of the calls, I heard Alex say the *one sentence* that would turn my life around:

"The quickest way to become an expert is to interview experts."

WOW! He talked about how I could record a podcast and *thousands* of people could hear me. . . . It set me into motion. I grabbed a sheet of paper and brain-dumped. My mind was racing. What do I need to do? Make a list of people to interview, equipment I would need. . . . Where do I start? I figured it out, and less than twelve weeks later, I launched *Women Power Radio*.

I set my sights high, interviewing celebrities such as Fran Drescher and Montel Williams and business icons such as Lisa Sasevich and Brian Tracy. One of my proudest moments was when Jack Canfield said on the air, "Raven is one of the best interviewers on the planet."

But what touches my heart most is that one of my clients felt I was worthy of recognition by the forty-fourth president of the United States. I had made such a difference in her life; I had raised her self-esteem, and she saw this as a huge service that I was providing to the world. All it took was *one person* who happened to be in the company of one of Barack Obama's business ambassadors and said, "How does one get this award? I know someone I'd like to nominate."

I had no idea. When you think nobody is watching, somebody *is* watching, and you don't know the impact you're making.

I'm now heard all over the world, but my mission is to empower others to come out of the shadows and into the spotlight . . . to share their message using the power of their voice.

Too many people are holding back because they, too, feel invisible, like Casper the Ghost. My message to them is:

Don't wait to be great. It's never too late. Your dream was planted inside of you for a reason.
Don't let it die inside of you. The world needs your message. Speak it loud and clear.
You never know whose life you are going to touch.

Raven Blair Glover is known by many as The Talk Show Maven and the "Queen of Interview Marketing and Conversion" for her work in broadcast media. She is the founder of Amazing Women & Men of Power Radio and Raven International Broadcast Media Empire. She is a five-time award-winning host, a former CNN radio personality, recipient of the RockStar Marketing 2016 Talk Show Host Award and the Presidential Lifetime Achievement Award signed by Barack Obama in 2017. Raven inspires her clients to be the Oprah or Larry King in their niche with their own TV show or podcast.

www.amazingwomenofpower.com

CRAFTING A PATH FORWARD

Ayse Gokdemir

I have an amazing job that allows me to create—but has also provided me with the opportunity to recreate myself. I am inspired by my dream world, reflections of my mood at the moment and my emotions to create deeply personal jewelry that I present to others for their enjoyment . . . and this is a central and sustaining part of my life.

I didn't pursue a formal education, but I have always been fixated with diverse aspects of fine art production. Indeed, I have a natural aptitude for handcrafts. This especially includes working with natural stones, beads, fabric from a wide range of color palettes, and accessories that compliment these core materials such as lace, ribbons, and flowers. These fine art "building blocks" have always excited and inspired me. I can spend hours in shops or foundries that produce and sell these materials. As I watch them, I configure and reconfigure component parts and create designs in my imagination.

For a number of years, I was very busy with this work. I started by making gift pieces as a means of sharing my creations with people I loved. Later, I started accepting orders. As everything was going well, I suddenly stopped. My son, one of the most precious parts of my universe, passed away in a car accident. I lost the joy I needed to infuse into my work.

I experienced very difficult times—a darkness that I never thought I would be able to escape. With the support of my dearest daughter and my beloved sisters, I decided to try to hold on to life and start working again. Why did I do it? In life, so many things can be taken away, and so much is outside of one's control. What I can control is what I do and what I leave behind. Art is the medicine for sadness. The act of creation is an act of defiance against helplessness and uncertainty. As Albert Camus says, if the world were bright, there wouldn't be art.

But how does one begin to create again? Grief is incapacitating and saps the desire and ability to do the most mundane tasks, let alone engage in a creative process. Is it even appropriate to think about art in difficult times? The simple answer is to simply do it. Like an engine that won't start, sometimes you have to start rolling the car downhill and hope that the ignition sparks. I paired coral with a silver heart to make a simple necklace. I had done something, maybe just one thing, but *something*. Once you begin, every day gets better. In art there is no end to growing and improving yourself, and if you can focus on process rather than product, then the product will come. I noticed I could focus on my work more every day, and this made me better and healthier and happier than the previous day. My art gave me direction—a trajectory out of the darkness.

I had a tremendous support system. My sister Sengul provided constant motivation, pushing me to extend beyond previous boundaries, explore new media, and show my work to a broader audience. I began to take my work more seriously. I took metallurgy classes and started learning essential metal crafting techniques. I started to add silversmithed pieces to colorful natural stones and beads. I began to make jewelry-shaped silver plates by cutting silver threads and welding them together. Every new technique brought new challenges, but I was focused not on becoming the artist I was but rather on the artist I could be. I was re-inventing myself. While crafting metal pieces for jewelry, I was forging myself back together.

The jewelry I started to make was simply better than it was before. I gained broader attention and have been taking significant numbers of orders and selling this work. My sister and I are in the process of expanding our scale of production and distribution, and we intend to become an emerging force within the market. Indeed, this interaction with my sister has galvanized our relationship and brought me closer to my family during a period that can be extremely isolating. Additionally, while this work was initially life-sustaining, creating jewelry has become more and more enjoyable. I like to compete with myself to make the work better every time, and I have found the joy that I thought I had lost forever.

I still feel part of myself and my life missing, and this will never heal. I miss the person I was when I was with my son, Arif. However, art is an amazing way of not focusing on the missing. The act of creation fills voids and decorates empty spaces. Does this mean forgetting the past? Absolutely not. Indeed, we show respect to lost loved ones not by dwelling in sadness, but by channeling their love into our everyday lives. Am I a better artist than I was before? Simply put—yes. Every piece I create has meaning. Every piece is infused with my process, my direction, my movement away from sadness. If you can imagine turning your back and moving away from the darkest spot in the universe, every new step brings more light. This hope and energy is reflected in my pieces. What was a hobby is now a passion and a profession.

Perhaps the greatest part of this work is that, once started, it is self-sustaining. I infuse a lot of emotions into material things. I work with an abundance of love and desire. This love is present in my art and grows as I share my creations. Indeed, after experiencing a great deal of sadness, I am more than ever captivated and overwhelmed by the power of love. I love my work, myself, my family, and my friends. Even in the darkest hours—indeed, particularly in the darkest hours—we need to remember that we all have the power to create and put love into the world around us.

Ayse Gokdemir and her sister Sengul are the founders of Ayse's Jewelry. Ayse uses her unique vision to create high-design jewelry art pieces that combine diverse sets of naturally sourced materials with experienced metallurgy and craftsmanship. This work is represented in seasonal collections as well as made to order for individual clients. Her work reflects her culture and life experiences, as well as her aspirational vision for the world. Love and vibrant color permeate throughout her work. Ayse and Sengul's overarching goal is to impact and improve the daily lives of people with her unique jewelry pieces.

www.Aysesjewelry.com

FROM STARVING ARTIST TO AN ABUNDANT LIFE OUTSIDE THE BOX

Lisa Gold

Before there was a top-ranked business in New York/LA connecting thousands of actors with agents and casting directors (Actors Connection), before an acting career consulting company, twenty-six audio/video/online courses, and over one hundred networking parties (Act Outside the Box), before the thousands of loyal subscribers to my blog, email list, Your Talent Agent membership, and social media pages, before I headed up the commercial division of a bi-coastal, mid-sized, full service agency—there was a desperate actress.

While my high expectations were supported by my parents, and I was gifted with a naturally talented singing voice, my navigation into the real world after school (North Carolina School of the Arts and the University of Cincinnati—College Conservatory of Music) was a slap in the face. I thought that with my drive, training, and talent, I was ready for an agent, auditions, and work. However, the shift into the *business of show* was anything but "Welcome, Lisa, we've been waiting for you; let me show you to your dressing room."

When I finally did begin the journey of finding and taking professional-level classes, vocal coaching, pursuing auditions on my own, and seeking representation, I was plagued by a chronic case of second-guessing myself. I had shiny-object syndrome, going from one direction to another and thinking that *that* new choice would surely be the better and faster one. My zigzagging made everything a thousand times harder than it should have been.

The first few years were emotionally and financially rough, and I didn't hit the boards of an Equity theater for quite some time. My television debut was a decade away. In fact, my first few gigs were in theme parks, cruise ships, and wedding bands. Even though I was working at my chosen profession (in addition to my flexible side hustle as a waitress), every small gig singing at bar mitzvas and birthday parties, jingles and print work for mom-and-pop shops, hosting, and MC work was marred by a hint of self-doubt that taunted me with a sense of "not enoughness." Even singing at the twentieth anniversary of the first lunar landing with a twenty-one-piece orchestra felt too small and local.

When will someone recognize my talent? When will my big break come? When will I become a union member? Will fame and fortune ever be mine? I had painful heart-to-heart conversations with friends and family, desperately trying to convince them that real success was just around the corner. A thousand missteps, botched auditions, rejection, and depression filled my days. Half-finished classes and programs, self-doubt, and analysis paralysis created an industry contact list so small I could literally recite every name by memory.

And when I finally did start to get a bit of traction in my career, I finally realized: "I'm in a freakin' business"!

What I discovered was that building my own dream acting career was NOT at odds with treating it like a regular business. It was exactly like owning a restaurant or selling a widget. My lightbulb moment came during the time I had just taken over ownership of Actors Connection in May of 2000. In speaking daily with the agents, managers, and other industry folks that made up our business, they explained to me that acting was the commodity being traded and actors a product in a very saturated marketplace. They had their pick of thousands of actors, and *marketing* is what distinguished those gaining representation and auditions *along with* their talent. They went hand in hand—only most actors hadn't a clue. I sure never thought of it that way before.

Around the same time, someone had given me the book *Rich Dad, Poor Dad*, and upon reading it, it solidified everything I was learning on the job. *Every* business, including show business, is designed to solve a problem, help people, serve people, and inspire people, and successful ones also have the purpose of making money with the value that is created. This was the beginning of my own acting career flourishing.

So I doubled down and learned how to do what "normal" businesses did. I learned how to rapidly grow my knowledge of the people, projects, and companies I wanted to work with and get to know their names, preferences, and ways to access them. I learned how to leverage time by focusing on one medium, the "lowest hanging fruit" where I could create income and visibility easily and quickly. I learned how to create and promote myself with the thought of what I offered and not what I wanted. I learned how to target agencies and casting opportunities by narrowing my niche instead of running around trying to be all things to all people just to get a job, any job, in the industry. I learned how to communicate with assurance what my product offered, uniquely and consistently, in person and in writing, and how to attract the right representation for my unique type and skill set.

And best of all, since learning and discovering these things and becoming successful as both a business owner and an actress, I've had the honor of helping thousands of actors and artists sidestep years of struggle and build amazing careers of their own. Over the decades, I've developed a reputation for teaching concrete and attainable actions that, combined with passion and purpose, make a dream acting career a reality.

I'm able to do this because I teach what I know. I teach what I've learned from my own mentors as well as personally done to build a successful and reputable acting career in TV, theater, commercials/print, musical performances, hosting, and more. I also teach the skill set I've developed over educating myself for twenty years in marketing, which has served both my traditional businesses as well. I've learned and I teach that creating amazing teams, taking inspired action, and building momentum around a passion, are the main keys to creating an inspired life *and* profitable businesses.

Lisa Gold: Started in the biz with my first professional paying acting/singing job when I was sixteen years old; Have made money every single year since then as a performer . . . so a couple of years now (tee hee, I can't help but joke a bit because my dad was a comic); Can't get enough of *General Hospital*; Embarrassingly obsessed with my dogs Lil' Bear and Chica and cat Georgie; Love to travel, travel, travel and drove my RV solo for a year around the US (with the fur babies of course!); Can be overheard singing along to music in elevators, grocery stores, and elsewhere and not even know I'm doing it.

www.ActOutsidetheBox.com

How to Create your RockStar Brand and the Five Things I Learned While Touring with a ROCKSTAR!

Amber Griffiths

I have created a life that is punctuated by music. From the rock song that inspires impromptu dance parties in the kitchen to that ballad you listened to the first time your heart was broken, music moves us. Music is powerful and can impact lives in less than three minutes. I believe that at least part of that power is because, on some level, we want to *be* that RockStar. We want to share our story and impact the world.

A few years ago, I had the opportunity to do exactly that. I toured with several '80s bands (my favorites!) and got to experience what a RockStar looks like backstage, on stage, and the real life in between shows. I want to share what I learned, and how that experience inspired my story, my Vision, and my commitment to help you share yours!

1. Everyone Is Human. It doesn't matter how much money you make or how many people know your name, you are still human. This means you have flaws as well as things you do really well. You owe no apologies for being who you truly are. The more you embrace and claim 100 percent of who you are, the more you will shine. The more you claim your Voice, the more easily your Ideal Client can connect with you. RockStars claim who they are, and they stand on that stage, in the spotlight, feet planted firmly, and they share all of it! Own who you are, claim it, and share it, 100 percent.

I watched a lead singer struggle, unapologetically, to put on his t-shirt for nearly three full minutes. Just hours later, he walked out on stage, and made 4,500 raving fans scream and swoon. Flaws and genius, all in one fabulous human.

2. Always Share Your Genius. You have a talent, a skill set, that no one else can touch. No one does exactly what you do, exactly the way you do it. Your zone of genius is that thing you would do for free if your business didn't depend on it. This is the thing that lights you up and drives you to be more. Always, always share it! There is something in your business that comes as naturally to you as breathing. And the more you share 100 percent of it, the more your Ideal Clients will flock to you. By the way, when someone shares their genius with you, say thank you.

The dancers were professional hair and makeup artists. They shared their genius with me by doing my hair and makeup for each show. They truly were talented and gracious humans.

3. Live in the Moment. Respect your season. Take a moment to revel in the life that you call yours. Not everything has to have a huge impact and push you forward. Some moments are just meant to keep you on track, while others are meant to move you a little to the side so you can get new perspective. If you are always planning and living two weeks ahead, you will miss the best moment of all—the one RIGHT NOW! You will miss a smile, or an opportunity to laugh from your belly and sing at the top of your lungs. Celebrate every moment! Don't get so worried about what comes next that you miss what's happening now. Revel in the encore, soak up the roar of the raving fans, and just breathe.

The drummer and I went sightseeing in Hollywood, and I watched her giggle over the walk of fame, ask for photos with celebrities, and so on. This famous, international musician took time in between shows to be absolutely present in the moment.

4. Let Others Shine. Not everything is about you—and that's OK! Stand in your genius and be amazing and, while you do that, support others doing the same. You can't do it all, so please stop trying. Inspire others to thrive in their genius zone. You will make more money and have more fun doing what you do best and creating opportunity for others to do likewise. You will have opportunities to speak up and promote those around you. Write testimonials even when you haven't been asked. Refer people, often. Share the wealth. Invite people to share your stage. Say thank you.

The band manager rarely slept, making sure that everyone was at rehearsal, had the instruments and supplies they needed, and were in the best possible shape for each show. He was never on stage himself, but not one of us could have done our jobs without him doing his.

5. Say YES and be ready to JUMP! For years as an entrepreneur, I was pretty content. And then one day an opportunity presented itself. It seemed unreal, too good to be true. But it was something I wanted, and I knew it would change me forever. I took a risk, I said yes, and I jumped. Forty-eight hours later I was standing on the stage of the Greek Theatre in Los Angeles playing some of my favorite childhood songs with the man who made them famous.

I challenge you to be so clear about what you want that when something shows up, you are ready to JUMP! You know you will land just fine. You know you're great at the show. What else do you need to know? Say YES! When something amazing presents itself, just jump!

The clearer you are about what you want, who you are, and what you offer, the more successful you will be in life and business. The clearer you are about who you serve, the more likely you are to draw them into your space. And the more committed you are to your Vision, the more likely you are to achieve it and make the impact you want on the world.

Amber Griffiths is Branding Expert and RockStar of Your Brand by Design. She has spent more than two decades dedicated to helping business owners and entrepreneurs create their RockStar Brand so they can exponentially increase their profits, work with people that excite them, and revel in the genuine thrill of getting paid to do what they love to do. Amber is a member of EWomenNetwork, Public Speakers Association, and Unlimited Woman Alliance. She is an international speaker, a two-time Bestselling Author, and was recently awarded the Best of the West in Branding Award.

www.yourbrandbydesign.com

It's All in the Details

Stephanie Hastings

Have you ever felt the discomfort of your underwear riding up to places unknown or walking in new shoes that are wearing the flesh off your heels? Well, this is something like that . . . but worse! It's the knowledge that you are being audited by the IRS . . . for the last seven years . . . for $8 million dollars—and you have no idea how things could've gotten so off track.

As an executive assistant, I have had many roles within the various companies that I've worked. One company specifically required my bookkeeping expertise and data entry skills. The two partners of this company had just received notification of an audit that would encompass the entire seven years they had been in business.

I had initially been hired as the personal executive assistant for just one of the owners who had several other business entities. Fortunately for them, I previously represented clients with tax and IRS situations and was able to jump right in when asked to do so. When they received the audit notice, I was able to ask the right questions and do the research to alleviate some of their fears and request more details as to what the real problem was.

It turns out the real problem was that the previous bookkeeper didn't really know the accounting system and only knew how to enter the income received! That's right—not the expenses and not the liabilities!

I was given a brown paper bag and several office filing boxes filled with receipts. As you may or may not know, with time and from the oils on your hands, receipts and thermal printouts fade and degrade.

At our first meeting, which took place in the IRS agent's office, I had to play the part of the head schoolmistress and muscle one of the owners into silence. I actually made him leave the meeting. He was so nervous and downright obnoxious in his stance of innocence that he was getting the auditor all riled up. (By the way, making an IRS agent angry is NEVER a good thing. Especially if that agent is an official auditor!) I, along with the other (saner) owner, was able to get her to understand our position and outright shock—and ask her for lenience and what would be needed for us to reduce and/or remove the bulk of the fine and fees.

Being the diligent and detailed person that I am, I scheduled the follow up meeting (the evidence meeting) with the IRS auditor for six months later WITHOUT either owner being present. Who needed the hassle?

During this time, I went through all the company receipts and invoices, called all their current and past vendors, and worked night and day to input all the data. I stayed in contact with the auditor to let her know of my progress and whenever I had any questions. Truly, I'm such a nut that I even scanned in as much as I could and worked the first two days while on my HONEYMOON in beautiful Aruba.

Long story short, when the auditor arrived at the conference table for our evidence meeting, she was quite impressed with all that data that I collected, scanned, and had detailed both in the accounting system and in the printed reports I was able to hand to her.

She was so confident in the work that I did that upon further review of the documentation, the statements, and letters I acquired from the vendors as to the business ethics of the owners, the auditor reduced the $8 million-dollar audit charge down to $1 million dollars!

I hope my story has inspired and encouraged you to seek knowledgeable help to make sure the numbers in your life are accurate and detailed. When you have the right person on your team, it alleviates a great deal of worry and oversight.

This is what I know to be true: when you let your passion and talents take you to new levels of excellence, you will succeed in all that you do. Remember, it's all in the details!

Stephanie Hastings is a certified bookkeeper, enrolled agent, licensed life producer, speaker, author, wife, and mother. After more than eighteen years in various executive assistant roles within corporate America, she struck out on her own to realize her passion to make a positive ripple effect by helping individuals and small business owners to accomplish their entrepreneurial dreams. Stephanie's business and financial expertise along with her background in hotel/restaurant management has allowed her to "humanize" the numbers and relate to her audience and clients.

Through her various personal trials and triumphs, Stephanie has been able to hone her skills and expertise to grow a community of resources and affiliates. She knows how valuable it is to have a solid network you can refer to and rely on. She is always learning and striving to do better.

www.taxdaybaby.com

WHEN DO YOU CHOOSE YOU?

Annette Jacobson

When I was thirty-five years old, I had it all—a successful career in IT, a one-year-old baby boy, and a husband with a good career.

But that spring, memories from my past began to surface.

I would walk down a tree-lined path in the park, smell the damp dirt, and be transported back to my childhood, where I was eight years old again, playing in the fields at my grandmother's farm; and I was smelling the Easter ham, and watching my mother take the meat out of the oven.

Other memories surfaced as well—scenes with my dad. Those were the most disconcerting. I decided to see a therapist to help me figure out what these memories were about. She told me, "When you get a revelation about what this means, you need to call me right away." Not quite sure what she meant, all I could say was "OK, I can do that."

Two days later, I came home from work and walked upstairs to take a shower. My hands were filled with suds, and as I washed my hair, suddenly *boom, boom, boom*—the mismatched scenes clicked into place. "Oh my God, oh Daddy, what did you do? You really did do those things to me!"

Bursting into tears, that was the moment my life changed forever. Except that's not quite true. My life had changed forever years earlier, when I was a child and those things actually happened.

I ran down the stairs to tell my husband. As I sobbed, he looked from our son to me and said, "Shh, you're scaring the baby."

I called my therapist that night. That was the first decision. I loved my husband, but he could not help me.

I had to keep going with the day-to-day. I found myself running to the bathroom at work, trying to hold back tears, sobbing quietly behind a locked stall door. It seemed most of my days were spent crying, hiding in the bathroom. Eventually, I stopped caring about my face being all blotchy when I came out.

I was falling apart. Even working with my therapist, I still asked, "How can I keep doing all this, working, being a wife, mother, homemaker, while trying to make sense of my past?" She began to explore options that would help me.

A few weeks later, the forecast was for a beautiful day. My husband and I decided to take the afternoon off to go golfing. We walked up to the eighth hole, both pulling our carts, and I felt the pressure of needing to say what I wanted to do, the sentences I'd been rehearsing in my head for several days.

"You know how I've been having a really hard time at work?" I hesitated, anticipating his reaction, gathering the courage that was buried within me. I knew this wasn't going to be pretty. "Well, my therapist found a place for me to go in Grand Rapids for three or four weeks where I can get the help I need."

"In Grand Rapids? That's three hours away!" He was incredulous, responding as if this was totally unnecessary to even consider. "And for *how* long?"

"Uh, for three or four weeks." Didn't he see how I was completely falling apart? Where had he been?

He turned to me, anger and frustration evident in his entire body. "How much will *that* cost?"

This was the hardest part of the conversation. His fury filled me with fear as I gripped the cart handle more tightly. "Well, if insurance doesn't cover it, it will be about $11,000."

"$11,000? That's as much as your brand-new Toyota Corolla!" he shouted.

Some strong, unknown part of me was birthed as I responded to him. "I don't care —I need this—I need this for me to function, to live. It doesn't matter. I'm worth as much as a car."

I was amazed at myself as I actually realized that I did believe this, in every cell of my body. The air was filled with his anger and frustration along with my determination as we finished golfing.

Two weeks later, with tears in my eyes, I kissed my baby boy goodbye and left for a five-week stay at a psychiatric facility.

I chose me. For the first time, I put me first.

If I hadn't done that, I would not have known my own value. I would not have understood how great this gift of life was that I was here to fully experience, a life I both desired and deserved. And the world would never be receiving what I am able to offer today.

This would not be the way I would have thought that I would choose *me*. I would never have dreamed of spending that kind of money on my well-being or comparing my value to a brand-new car or standing up for myself with my husband.

Sometimes you can't choose when your life pivots or why it needs to, but when you heed the call of your deep desire, you are taking care of not only yourself, but your family.

I'm curious. Have you chosen yourself? I hope you know your own value. I hope the world knows what you have to offer, and I hope you are experiencing all that you are here to be and do—because that's what happens when you choose you.

Annette Jacobson is passionate about helping women say "Yes!" to the amazing life they are each uniquely born to live. She is the founder of Women Rocking The World, leading and catalyzing women to have the impact on the world that is their own to make through living the lives they desire and deserve. She inspires and transforms women into their greatness through her speaking, teaching, coaching and writing as she shares her vision and insight.

www.WomenRockingTheWorld.com

Money Isn't the Root of All Evil: Dishonesty Is

Dee Jones

A dollar bill is a sticky, dirty green piece of paper—an inanimate object. It has no voice, no sight, no sound or the ability to discern right from wrong. Only humans can do that. Only a human can hold a bill and determine its usage. Only a human can become possessed with greed, act lustfully, grow red with anger, be filled with pride, or attack with envy. Only a human can use cash to corrupt corporate deals. Currency is a tool to buy goods and services. The personification given to money as a powerful ally or weapon is a warped concept.

Therefore, it is the human being who needs adjustment, not the monetary system. Like things; love people! We seem to have the premise reversed.

For instance, if a building is raised on a weak foundation, it will crumble, and everyone inside and in close proximity will be injured or killed. Now, I'm almost sure the contractor didn't mean to build on an unstable foundation and the inspector didn't mean to approve it, but it happened. The checks and balances in place didn't prevent the tragedy. Neither did the proper licenses those professionals possessed assure perfection. Maybe it was Mother Nature because of a hurricane, fire, tornado, or earthquake. Maybe it was the owner and all those parties, with hundreds of people jumping up and down to rock classics. Maybe it was termites; California is infested with those gobbling insects. Those scenarios are all plausible yet rare.

The larger culprits are the ones who knew their work was subpar and the ones who knew they approved a flawed project. We all know when our best isn't given, when we do our job halfway, or when we forget to put the pieces together properly.

Our minds make excuses why we shouldn't or couldn't be honest. We deny the truth for so many superficial, illogical, and fictitious reasons. We make false promises just to get someone to "shut up." We play games in relationships to psychologically dominate others to get what we want. We sneak around, hiding in dark corners to cover up transgressions. We lie and claim, "It's just a little white lie; it doesn't matter." We steal someone else's treasures due to laziness or jealousy. We tempt people with bribes that demean both parties. We cheat on our partner for lack of dedication and commitment, which breaks hearts.

Are your intentions in business matters forthcoming or sly, slick, and wicked? Do you know who you are as a human being, or do you spend hours on end living vicariously through sports, reality TV, and video games? Are you satisfied with yourself or secretly wish you were the next Top Model or Batman? Serenity can only be attained through a pure heart and mind.

Honesty is the foundation of all virtues and the pillar of integrity! It is a noble attribute of the human spirit. It is the foundation that supports a resilient, honorable individual. It is the cornerstone of a trustworthy society. Children are supposed to learn how to tell the truth from their parents. Then it should be reinforced by relatives, within a school setting, and in the normal course of interacting with adults. How come the adults are dropping the ball?

You can't teach what you don't know, but you can learn. Grown folks are able do new tricks. Yes, you can! Then you can guide the children. But first you must be willing to change. Yes, I said it. Change is inevitable. Complacency is not a pretty color. As one grows, one changes in looks and character. It's a given, but you do have some control. Your fate is not totally predestined. You can rise up and become a truthful individual who walks with righteousness wherever you step.

In actuality, parents should be their child's first role model or hero. Don't you want your teenager to come to you for advice about sex, drugs, and music instead of listening to foul lyrics, watching lustful movie scenes, or smoking weed with friends at school? Don't you want your teen to brag about your good qualities? Don't you want your adolescent to trust your judgment and not sneak behind your back or lie to your face?

This ideal situation is possible when you and your partner engage in candid conversations with one another. This doesn't mean confessing your sins. It means open, forthright discussions about the two of you joining as one; now is the right time. Then you can discuss the concept of creating an ideal family. People seem to just jump in a relationship with closed eyes, hoping all will end happily. You cannot lie to your partner, ever! I repeat, don't fib to one another. The other person will conduct their actions based on your words. If one makes a mistake, as will happen from time to time, try to correct it or at least mitigate the damage. Perfection is not the aim; wisdom is. This is a good opportunity to self-evaluate and continue on the chosen path or go to plan B. Single parents, you may not have someone to toss around ideas with, but you are surely influencing your children. Bear in mind, some sacrifices have to be made temporarily and sometimes permanently, but the rewards are inexpressible.

It is urgent that we improve this character flaw. The children (unconsciously) are depending on us to teach them morals. It begins at home with the honest adult. When each person embodies this virtue, we can develop into an upright society.

Dee Jones (Lady Dee) grew up in California, catching the tail end of the Baby Boomers. She's been an educator of teenagers for many moons now. She's traveled to six continents on a quest to absorb the wonderful cultures on this planet. She's dropped to the bottom of sea and swam with all of sorts of magnificent fish. She's taken snapshots of wild animals in the bush. Dee says, "The wisdom gained is such an enchanted blessing. Oh, what a delightful world God created. My grandma is 102! We are six generations strong. I hope to pass on the goodness and generosity granted me everywhere I jet. I'm gliding into my next echelon."

MUSIC—A SOOTHING REMEDY FOR THESE ANXIOUS TIMES

Eleanor Jones

Music is said to be the universal language. I believe it is so very much more. Music has a transmutable spirit—it actually has many spirits, depending on the music itself and influenced by its presentation and form, as well as the listener and/or performer.

In a short scene aired on television in which a handsome couple were dining, Vincent Price portrayed a waiter. Accompanying the scene was soft, pleasant mood music. This translated into a very tender, romantic scene.

The exact scene was repeated, with a different sound track. The soft, romantic music was replaced with eerie music typically associated with suspenseful horror scenes. The effect was chilling!

The effects of music can be both positive and negative; I will focus on the positives. A vast background of formal training, research and scientific study is not a prerequisite to be able to comprehend the significant role music can and does play in the lives of individuals. Each of us can determine this from our own experiences.

Not claiming any particular expertise, I share my own experiences and observations. Music to me is many things. As beauty is said to be in the eye of the beholder, I believe music's worth is in the interpretation of the listener or performer. I see music as communication, expression of feeling, sharing, and giving. It can be soothing, motivating, invigorating, calming, stimulating, comforting, inspiring, and spiritual.

How the music is experienced is not significant. You don't sing? Listen. Want to participate? Play an instrument, clap your hands, snap your fingers, dance. Are you creative? Have something to say? Compose . . . whistle . . . hum . . . or all of the above.

Music can take you back to a place and time when you experienced pleasure and joy that just recalling it can recapture. Do you have a favorite song or melody? What makes it special to you? Could it be the person or memories it brings to your mind? I think no matter how popular, well-loved, or profitable a song may be, if negative experiences are associated with that song for you, it won't be one you will want to hear often, if at all!

Long before the events of September 11, I had reason to long for peace and comfort, the easing of stresses, tensions, and fear. When at times the pressures of life as a responsible adult became overwhelming, I longed to be able to go back to that place where everything was safe and warm, where I had no cares or fears. That place was as a child in my mother's arms being held and rocked, and loved, and, yes, sang to.

I can still recapture that feeling through music by allowing my mind to go back to that place in time. I wrote and recorded an unpublished bedtime song for my children entitled "Rock-a-Bye Lullaby," which I sang to them every night before tucking them into bed. In my mind, I became one of them. Over the years I have refined this technique—from picturing myself as one of the children being held to myself being held in the arms of Jesus. The image never fails to bring me comfort and serenity.

Another musical experience I believe worth sharing is something almost anyone can do without needing a great imagination or musical talent. I found that my workweek always started off on a good note (no pun intended) when I followed a certain ritual on Sunday night. When everyone was in bed for the night, I turned on relaxing, soothing, *soft* music, filled the bathtub with very warm water full of bubbles and a favorite scent, and just soaked my tension and stress away. *Wonderful!*

Many possible scenarios can work just as well, even with your chosen other. (The bath can work well here, too.) Just imagine sitting together comfortably, a fireplace softly glowing, perhaps a cup of hot chocolate or other beverage of choice, and soft music! No need for words—just the two of you, and music. *Ahh!*

A favorite event I experienced growing up, and even now at family gatherings, is the sing-along. Whether it's Christmastime with carols or any time the family is together, we have a good time singing. (With nine singing children and two singing parents, we had our own choir!) Just thinking about it brings back warm memories.

Let's not forget the benefits of working out and exercising to music! What can be more motivating to keep up a brisk pace than good, brisk music that you like? Exercise, a great stress easer in itself, can be made much more pleasurable for any couch potato and provide other health benefits as well. You can even use the same inspiration to help you whiz through other often unpleasant tasks associated with housework.

Got a child that's acting out? Try calming yourself first, then take that child in your arms and listen to music with him or her. The music—the *right* music—and your touch can work miracles. The sound of your voice in even a hum can add great dividends. I recall how the Bible tells of King Saul, who had a troubled spirit. How was he soothed? Shepherd Boy David was called in to play music for him!

One of the most important aspects of music for me is in my communication with God. I often find that I am at a loss for words to convey my thanks, praise, reverence, supplication. Although I know that He already knows, He is gracious and loving and puts the words in my heart that come out in song. I may be in the shower, in my car, at my computer—it doesn't matter. The words in song flow from my lips to God's ear. What a blessing!

Eleanor Jones is a speaker, singer-songwriter, and author of a three-volume novel. Her stage name and brand is Eleanor "C-PASS" Jones. She has had a varied background as a senior secretary, administrative assistant, teacher of children and adults, senior financial manager, freelance calligrapher, and performing and visual artist. Her writings include poetry, short stories, handbooks, instruction manuals, proposed legislation, legal briefs, appeals, and written arguments. She has also served on the board of a charter school. She is married with children.
www.eleanorjones.com

INNER TRANSFORMATION

Deborah Kahler

As I walked down the long, cold, dim corridor, following some unknown energy, I came around a corner and saw a three-year-old version of myself in chains and locks. She said to me, "Oh! I knew you would come back and find me!"

In the past, I had hidden my true self. Deep emotional hell is worse than any physical pain. I believe we create physical pain, sickness, and disease in our body so we don't have to think about the emotional pain we hid away long ago.

I am thankful and grateful to my Creator, my Jesus Christ, my Holy Spirit all within me, and to myself for not giving up, even on days when I wanted to or tried to.

In the past I put too much energy into surviving instead of thriving. Being angry instead of laughing. Being sad instead of being blissful. Being in pain instead of choosing ease. Blaming others instead of looking in the mirror. Settling to settle instead of stepping over fear into heaven on earth. Feeling abandoned instead of learning from all of life's lessons and embracing them all. When we put our energy into negative emotions, it drains us so fast there is nothing left for good.

I have gone through many emotional upgrades in the past four years, searching out faster and easier ways to let go, and let go now!

Feeling left out as a child, with jealousy issues most of my life, feeling ugly, always comparing myself to my three beautiful sisters, experiencing sexual abuse, verbal abuse, and weight issues, not feeling I had a purpose, going through divorce, having trouble with relationships, procrastination, and hate are traumas and emotions I have transformed for myself in the past few years, with some amazing techniques I have learned from amazing mentors. I am thankful for all of them, being real and sharing themselves so others can learn self-healing.

I am thankful I am taking part in this book and thankful you are reading this chapter. I am choosing to help you upgrade your life and believing that you will choose more upgrades from me or someone who can help you be your God Blueprint! Thank you, Craig Duswalt, for doing this for many!

When we take on the emotional trauma, it happens in the blink of an eye. We don't contemplate whether or not we should let it in. We just do. Just like that. Owned. And then we realize it doesn't feel good, but we don't know how to let it go.

These are things kids should know! These are things everyone should know! This is life stuff! Every day of our lives is filled with emotions, good and not as good. We all require knowing how to deal with OURSELVES! And then share this knowledge with others!

How many people do you know who are trying to survive? How many people have physical ailments? Feel deep sadness, are nervous, can't sit still? Problems from being in the service? From birth trauma? Can't keep a job? Can't sleep? Wet the bed? Have pain in their body? Sugar imbalances? Problems with no answers? Food issues, alcohol issues, drug issues, gambling issues, shopping issues, hoarding issues? Puking on purpose? Constipation? Thyroid issues? Skin issues? Hearing issues? Eye issues? Spinal issues? Had to be an adult when they were a child? Under all of these are emotional traumas. Please help yourself!

Do you feel great in your body every day? If not, be willing to look down underthe "thing" that you are experiencing and discover the root of the problem. Are you willing to feel tears on your cheeks to cure your body, to put your mind at ease, to put your spirit in ease?

Are you willing to do whatever it takes? Are you worth it? If not, why? What are you hiding that is so painful, you are willing to go through hell to hold on to it?

You are not alone!

I have been a massage practitioner for twelve years, bringing emotional letting go techniques into my sessions as I have learned them. I'm grateful for teachers such as Dr. Carolyn Mein, Bob Proctor, Robert Tennyson Stevens, Peter Levine, and many others who have impacted my journey. I am thankful for Young Living oils, thank you God and Gary Young, which brought me into this healing realm. I encourage everyone use oils! 823770 is my number if you have interest!

Others I have learned from are Dr. Carolyn Mein (Releasing Emotional Patterns with Essential Oils), Robert Tennyson Stevens (Mastery Systems, AMAZING!!), Bob Proctor (Thinking Into Results), Freddy McGaver (my beloved!), Jos Boom (in Amsterdam), Bo Eason, and Peter Levine (Waking the Tiger). All of these amazing people I am thankful for. Please look them up.

And now, my favorite and most amazing piece of the puzzle, is with a woman named Marisa Peer. Her technique, and now mine, as I am certified with her, is called RTT. Rapid Transformational Therapy.

Hypnosis takes you into your subconscious memory, the movie of your life. This movie is in your memory from the moment you are in the womb until this very moment in your session. We ask your mind for specific scenes, three or four, which will give us the exact reason why certain things are happening in your body or in your life. You will be amazed at what comes forth!

I have many stories of clients, with amazing transformational scenes using hypnosis. There have been lots of tears—sometimes a dam lets loose. Sometimes I cry with them. I am humbled as I create a safe space for them as letting go happens and they experience pure peace, pure love.

I am truly amazed and thankful for Marisa's information. RTT is my key which helps you let go now, if you are willing. RTT finds your missing piece of your puzzle. Your answer is inside of you!

You are your own pure cure! You are your own trauma terminator! You are good enough! You are smart enough! You are beautiful! Shine your light and stand in all your power! Speak with your God voice!

Be you! You are worthy! I look forward to hearing from you!

Deb Kahler has a business background and is now enjoying her life as an RTT specialist, author, speaker, YouTuber, massage practitioner, Young Living distributor, wife, mother, and grandmother. She is passionate about guiding others into their own personal transformations and coming back into their vibrant, God-blueprint self. Contact Deb to learn more about transforming yourself now.

www.myinnerblueprint.com

FORGIVENESS TO FREEDOM

Michelle Kavanaugh

The basic truth about each of us is that we are loveable. It is our spiritual DNA. If we were mirrored "I am loveable" by our parents during childhood, we experience our loveliness, trust who we are, and grow up to be confident and well-balanced adults. Many of us were not modeled this behavior by our parents. As a result, we grow up to doubt ourselves, judge ourselves, and engage in negative self-talk. We believe that we are "not good enough," "don't deserve it," and are "not loveable." We go through life missing out on opportunities because we are afraid, unhappy, and angry and can't figure out why; we self-medicate; and we engage in self-destructive relationships with partners, family, and friends. We are not living—we are merely existing.

When we live in fear due to self-doubt, we are unable to foster positive and fulfilled relationships. We tend to attract people like ourselves to our world since we don't have the self-confidence to believe that we deserve better. The result is that we tend to get hurt, or we hurt others, because we are living with the same limiting beliefs that we are not good enough. Rejection and hurt begets rejection and hurt. We become very guarded as we try to protect ourselves from getting hurt again. We hold on to anger and resentment to keep us safe from a similar experience. We will not be tricked or fooled again. The unfortunate cycle continues.

In fact, "I'm not loveable" is not true; it just feels comfortable. It is a learned unworthiness, and it can be unlearned. The solution to most of this emotional pain is forgiveness. Forgiveness is a necessary life skill we should be learning in school. It's the way we heal the pain of disappointing life experiences. Here's the truth: we are going to have disappointing life experiences. But if we can process those things with a healthy mindset that becomes second nature, we find it easier to let go of expectations and negative thoughts. We find ourselves having a more positive outlook, and self-love becomes a more natural way of living.

What Is Forgiveness?

Forgiveness is a willingness to drop the narrative on a situation, to stop telling ourselves repeatedly the story of what happened, what the other person did, and how we were hurt. It's a conscious decision to let the past be what it was, to leave it as is, imperfect and not what we wish it had been. Forgiveness means that we relinquish the idea that we can create a different (better) past. As Bernard Meltzer said, "When we forgive, we in no way change the past, but we sure do change the future."

What Forgiveness Is Not

"Forgive and forget" is old-school thinking. We want to "forgive and remember," as that story was important in our life. We encourage ourselves to "just let it go!" Forgiveness is no small affair, and we can't bully ourselves into feeling it. By forgiving, we are not saying:

- We were not hurt by what the other person did.
- Our pain is gone.
- We no longer believe the other person was responsible for causing harm.
- We excuse the other person's behavior.

Forgiveness is a life skill, an attitude, a mindset. Forgiveness is different for every person. For some, it comes on suddenly without having to think about it much. For others, it's a more deliberate process that requires effort and practice. There's no right way to find or live forgiveness. The hardest part of forgiveness is the recognition that we need it to heal us. How do we do it? We commit to working the steps until it becomes muscle memory. It is just a mindset reset, and then it requires a little practice.

Forgiveness is ultimately about freedom. When we need someone else to change for us to be OK, we are a prisoner. In the absence of forgiveness, we're shackled to anger and resentment, so comfortable in our misbeliefs that it never occurs to us to question them. When our attention is focused outward, on getting the other to give us something so we can feel peace, we're effectively keeping ourselves weak and powerless and diminishing our capacity for self-love. What we want from the one we can't forgive is most often love. Forgiveness is ultimately about choosing to love ourselves. It is not about the other person. It is about us.

When we practice self-love and compassion for others, the universe receives it and sends it right back in the form of new career opportunities, loving and caring people that want to be in our lives, and new adventures that we would never have attempted before. We are more comfortable stepping outside of our comfort zone as we have a renewed sense of self and confidence in our abilities. We begin to make more money than we ever have before. We set boundaries with family and friends instead of building walls to guard ourselves. We begin to see the world as a safe and caring place where there are infinite possibilities to help us grow and thrive. We are able and willing to serve others with love and light. We begin to live our best life and look forward to the future. That is true freedom!

Michelle Kavanaugh, an author, podcaster, and speaker, is passionate about helping others recognize the need for forgiveness and the power it brings to our lives. Michelle tortured herself for years with self-destructive behavior, suicidal thoughts, and bad relationships. Once she made the decision to truly forgive her father, her life changed for the better. Her professional career advanced. Her relationship with her friends and family changed. Michelle delivers engaging speeches, and audiences connect with her powerful and emotional story and her poignant sense of humor. Michelle hopes to be a healing force for those that struggle with anger and forgiveness.

www.forgiveness2freedom.com

LIVING THE MULTI-PLATINUM LIFE

Linda Kaye

Growing up, most kids have a dream, even if it's just to grow up! Mine was to be rich, whatever that meant. A pivoting moment can lock that dream into place, as it did mine.

Raised in a family of nine kids brought its own challenges. Although health insurance was a luxury we couldn't afford, my parents gave us what we needed: a home, both parents, food, grounding, and values. Sibling rivalry was free. With seven brothers and eight years before my sister arrived, family leadership was my survival tactic.

Realizing we were poor didn't happen till seventh grade. Awareness of my classmates' new wardrobes made me want to fit in. Allowances existed but were meager. There was barely enough money for basics, so it was up to me to find money. We're not talking extravagance, just a third pair of shoes, new outfit, movie money. I mowed lawns, babysat, and cleaned houses to earn money. I was tired, but undeterred.

Another skill was already underway when I realized I could earn more money in less time than all the other jobs combined. To earn more I had to be in demand and hone my craft so I was better than my competition. Sibling competition paid dividends. No one practices for you, and I learned the loneliness of discipline. There's only one pianist in an orchestra, band, or choir, and I was the "it girl." The more I practiced, the better I got, and the more money and confidence I earned; a bonus was prestige, awards, acknowledgement. The better I got, the better I got. Money paid for lessons, a college education, my own apartment, and a car.

The choice to play piano was a given. Mother had the largest piano studio in town. Anyone that was anyone took lessons from her. She'd combined talent and entrepreneurial skills to supplement necessities to stay home (where else would a mother of nine children be, right?). While she was teaching, I was watching and learning.

Leadership skills led to me being a musical director and conductor on playbills. When studios called to record jingles, why not write them? This led to studio work in Los Angeles. Those same undergraduate skills led to taking a girl band on an Asian tour. Back in the USA, we got auditions. Everywhere we competed with the Runaways, they ran away with the gig. I couldn't see my faults or shortcomings as the leader (can we say ego) as the blind leading the blind. We needed experienced leadership, not a tadpole from a small town. Lesson learned: management equals shortcuts. We were as good and more diverse than any girl band, but inexperienced leadership and branding—The Cherries?—led to us going our own epic separate ways. Playing side gigs, doing Las Vegas, the Tahoe/Reno circuit, stage A-bookings, and no balance led to burnout. Rock on.

You can reinvent yourself and find something useful to do. During this period quiet riots played in my head while crash and burn relationships masqueraded as failed marriage solutions. Now I'm no Madonna, but it was time for a rewrite! Good news about bad news? It doesn't last forever. It's mindset, true grit, and attitude.

The memory of previous successes got me back on track, but it's hard finding "employee" work with no employee skills! My keyboard skills transferred. In a tiny closet of a film security office, I acquired computer skills while the secretaries clicked away on their typewriters.

Success led to more success. Forgetting the past, like the grim reaper in the rearview mirror, I co-wrote a film-authority encyclopedia with a retired FBI agent; published songs; taught at the LA High School for the Arts, and met a guy. As he moved up the studio ladder, we did too. Perks included front-row seats to sports events, first-class world travel, and the supersonic Concorde, until the relationship ran its course. When one door closes, another one opens.

Returning my focus back to music, another business with a record label executive partner formed. Limo rides to everything from the airport to the doctor's office; front-row seats and backstage passes to every top musical event; having clients like Barry White, Janet Jackson, and other top names were in my funnel of business. Turns out I was good at selling ideas—new artists and my independent promo and personal management company took off like a rocket as artists appeared on talk shows like *Arsenio Hall*, in studios with Quincy Jones. My promo work led R & B artists to number-one hits; Barry White's "The Man Is Back" U.S. Tour led to presales work on Janet's "1814 Rhythm Nation" project, netting a triple platinum record with my name on it! Making others shine was instinctive.

As my star rose, my partner strangled growth, ending the partnership, but didn't know I'd lose my business. Snap! All top artists and gold and platinum records on the wall disappeared overnight. The lawsuit was unexpected. The more I fought, the more I lost, eventually losing the house, business, car, contracts. All sources of revenue dried up. Times were tough. If you can't take the heat . . .

It was early fall, and my first year in San Francisco was challenging. Thumbing through want ads led to dogs for sale, which I knew a lot about. An idea stirred: What if I bought and sold purebreds? Clients would leave a 50 percent deposit; I'd buy the dog and deliver it. Fifty percent profit? "Dial A Dog—get the dog you want and have Santa deliver it!" ran for four weeks. Santa looked like a Hell's Angel with sunglasses and tattoos, but I never had a dog returned!

Financial recovery was steady, but it took a toll on me. I enrolled in law school so this wouldn't happen again. Eventually we stop blaming circumstances, and "if only that hadn't happened "stops. I also learned value. I'm more than a multi-platinum record at my core, and I can reinvent myself with grit, attitude, and spirit.

Linda Kaye is a serial entrepreneur, sales coach and real estate broker. Since early 2000 she's sold and leased over $500 million dollars of Southern California commercial real estate. She is COE of a residential lifestyle-change company, Open Roads. Her knowledge and sales skills are offered in a robust online course and available on her personal website. She's involved in many community projects in Malibu, where she resides and nurtures an abundant hummingbird garden.

www.lindakayetoday.com

FAT CATS DON'T MAKE GOOD HUNTERS

Scott A. Kent

After emptying our cash register, the armed robber moved past me, kneeling on the floor as he ordered, put his gun to my head, smirked, and pulled the trigger! In a split second, I saw his smirk turn to a look of fear and I knew then that he thought the gun would have fired. I sprung up and attacked him with a fury I had no idea I possessed. When the police arrived and pulled me off him, he was already unconscious, but I was still inflicting blow after blow, I wanted him dead! How dare he come into my place of employment, rob me, and then attempt to END MY LIFE? Later as I was reflecting on the events of that day, I decided right then and there, I would *never* put my life (or anything of importance) in the hands of another person who may not value it as much as I do.

Fast-forward about ten years. I'm at a bicycle industry convention, and the keynote speaker starts his talk with "Fat cats don't make good hunters." I don't know why at the time his statement stuck with me so strongly; I just remember laughing at the thought of a bike dealer who has lost his edge and might be living in fear of somebody like me coming and taking the business in the town. At that time, that is exactly what was happening in San Diego where I lived in the mid-80s. With a small investment from a partner, I had quickly built a six-store bike shop chain that owned the retail bicycle space in town, and I did it in a way everyone thought was impossible. I was the alpha predator in the retail bike industry in San Diego.

It wasn't until many years later, that phrase about *fat cats* would make its presence known again. At that time in my life, things were great. I had a busy store in a small town that was doing numbers more aligned with a huge market area, had no real competition for quite some time, and was making a nice mid-six-figure income. I had just started a printing business and was happy to have some new challenges. Then it happened. The world as I knew it came crashing down. We lost our income, we lost our confidence, and we lost our way. Now, any sane individual would have sought help to get back on track, but I had a problem that surfaced from all those years ago: I would never put my life in the hands of someone who didn't value it as much as me, and so I had to figure it out for myself. I tried different ways to reverse our circumstances with poor results. We were living hand to mouth, month to month, and it sucked—but this time I just couldn't work my way out of it alone.

One of my clients who also became a friend called one day to invite me to her office to hear a speaker she had paid to come do a talk. I asked what it was about, and she said he was kind of a motivational speaker but not really. I responded that I had already read enough motivational books to fill a library and politely declined her offer. She was insistent, though, and because I didn't want to upset a good client, I went. That evening would change the trajectory of my life forever. I had expected a rah-rah session, but it was anything but. Michael spoke directly to me, at least in my mind, and I could tell he understood what I was going through. I did something I swore I would never do and signed up for a program I couldn't afford with money I didn't have. I left the meeting scared of what I had just done, but after so much time trying to figure it out for myself, I gave in and put my life in the hands of another. And I had just met him! My gamble paid off, and after the first program, I signed up for a more expensive live event with him again. It was money I couldn't afford to spend, but something told me I had to. Magically, a past-due check I had all but written off appeared in the mailbox a couple of days later and was enough to cover the cost of the event and travel expenses.

It was at this event that lifelong changes started to happen. In fact, upon the conclusion of the event, I couldn't make myself leave the room. If I did, the magic would be over. I have never had such a powerful moment in my life, but now I was equipped with tools I didn't even know existed a mere three days earlier— tools I could use to make my life work again. Armed with a new confidence, I started to build the business at a pace far exceeding our past efforts. With my newfound trust in others, I hired a coach, then another, and with their help, I was able to craft an idea for a once-in-a-lifetime business that would disrupt the market, scale past anything I had ever hoped for, and allow us to retire however we like. What a massive shift compared to the "play not to lose" mentality I once had!

Today I pay it forward, helping other Baby Boomers and late Gen-X entrepreneurs who like me, have become fat cats in their industries or those who are having trouble finding success as entrepreneurs. I help them generate an extra ten to thirty thousand dollars per month working ten hours per week or less leveraging their knowledge, skills, and experience. I've been through what they're facing and made it out the long, painful way. My goal is to make their journey a short and prosperous one.

Scott Kent has founded, consulted for, and rescued over 300 businesses in his career and today is the CEO of a printing and marketing firm as well as a business coach. Developing his 10K in 10 Hours program to help entrepreneurs ages forty to sixty-five maximize their golden years, he enjoys helping his clients go from overworked and underpaid to debt-free and time-rich. In his free time, you'll find Scott boating, sailing, SCUBA diving, and spending time with his family and friends.

www.ScottGetsResults.com

IF YOU HAVE TO HAVE A DISEASE, HAVE ONE YOU CAN REVERSE

Shannon Kent

Y*our A1C is 11.0.* With those words, my health just took a front seat. I have relatives with type 2 diabetes that take medication and insulin to control the disease, but until this point I had never had any symptoms or test scores that indicated any problems. I did have a doctor tell me he thought I was type 2 diabetic based on how I carried my weight around my stomach area. To prove it, he told me to eat a plate of pancakes with syrup and after two hours read my sugar and it would show I was diabetic. I did not eat the pancakes, but I did eat bad foods and my sugar always tested fine, so I just thought he was wrong.

In early 2018 my husband, Scott, kept hearing a commercial on a local radio station about doctors having success reversing type 2 diabetes. He decided to take the leap and attend the seminar. He asked me if I wanted to go along, but since I thought I was fine based on my own medical diagnosis, I said probably not. Several days before the seminar, Scott was taking a sugar reading, and I decided to also test to show him I was fine. The joke was on me. My sugar reading was 225. Since normal is between 80 and 120, I guess I was not OK. I called and registered for the seminar.

There the doctor asked if I was diabetic, I told her I didn't know and then told her about the recent sugar test. She gave me a blood test request to check for all kinds of things, not just diabetes. I don't think I have ever given so much blood for testing before. After the seminar we made appointments to speak with the doctor further, not knowing what he or she would tell us. The fun was just getting started, and so was one of the biggest changes I have ever made.

As we sat in the doctor's office reflecting on my results, Scott said, "You know we have to do this, right? There is no way we can't move forward no matter what it costs." Decision made, we were going to hit this thing straight on and be there to support each other whatever the future brought us. We signed up for the program wanting better health and a longer life.

During our initial appointment, the doctor had more bad news for me. "Your test results indicate the possibly of Hashimoto's Thyroid auto-immune disease, and you have a fatty liver. On top of that, with your numbers, you are a ticking time bomb for a fatal heart attack." As I looked down at the test results, tears welled up as I listened to this devastating news. *How did I get to this point? How could I have let my health get this bad?* I was the one who always had normal numbers when I checked my sugar. Scott was diagnosed years earlier with Type 2 diabetes but chose not to take the medication.

As we started the program, it quickly became clear we were going to have some drastic changes to make in our lifestyle, and it would take some patience and teamwork. We were put on a strict diet and detox program for the first thirty days, which was a little overwhelming for me as all my favorite foods were gone: dairy, grains, some fruits, and my favorite, chocolate. One of the fellow patients said something that made it easier. "Is the pain of losing a leg or your sight worse than not eating pizza?" I won't lie, there were days I almost chewed off my leg wanting chocolate. But within days we started to feel better in many ways. About ten days in, Scott started shedding about a pound a day as his systems began working efficiently. And he felt FANTASTIC! I noticed that foods were not affecting me the same way. I started trimming down but not quite as fast as Scott. Guys have all the luck! We both saw marked reductions in our daily sugar readings, with mine falling faster than Scott's. By the end of the thirty days, I was very proud as I kept to the program without cheating. Thirty days over—bring on the tacos, pasta, and cheese, right? Not this time.

To start the program required another blood test and completing other tests. Based on those results the doctor was ready to start directing us on the journey to reverse diabetes. At the thirty-day visit, I was given the good news that I would be giving up dairy, grain, and soy for LIFE. No more cheese, whipped cream, bread—all my favorites, gone. I was crushed. Over the next six months, we would work on one area of our test results, reaching certain levels before concentrating on another area, until we were again firing on all cylinders the way we should be. My A1C went from 11 to 5.4 in three months, so I was clinically no longer diabetic. It felt great to receive those lab results, but just as important was the thyroid issues I had were now gone. My fatty liver issues were also gone, and I was catching up to Scott in the weight loss area. People started commenting on how good we looked, and of course that felt great.

Our battle to regain our health has carried over to all aspects of our lives, and we no longer are content to be content. Now we approach any challenge that comes along as one we can win as opposed to one we have to live with. The freedom that comes with that mindset is liberating.

Shannon Kent worked as a telecom engineer for twenty years before opening a marketing company with her husband Scott in 2008. They consult with clients to help them with their marketing strategies by utilizing visual media, and they also have an online printing company. Through these consultations it was clear that some clients could benefit from more coaching, leading Shannon to begin her Success and Life coaching business, helping people to achieve their dreams. For fun she enjoys her four dogs and scuba diving.

www.ShannonEKent.com

WHAT ELVIS PRESLEY, ELIZABETH TAYLOR, AND JOHNNY CARSON TAUGHT ME ABOUT PUBLIC SPEAKING

Melody Keymer Harper

When I was three years old, my mom put my twin sister and me in a local community market talent contest. We looked like two little Shirley Temple's with brown curly locks singing, "I Love You a Bushel and a Peck" that our mom always sang to us before going to bed each night.

The audience "oohed" and "awed" while we performed, showing big smiles of joy ending with enthusiastic applause. That was the first time I recognized that what I did on stage had a positive effect on others.

We won! And continued on to a theatrical career of film, TV, and stage.

In my late teens, I had the privilege to be interviewed on The Tonight Show with Johnny Carson. I remember being so nervous behind the curtains and then I heard the words, "Here's Johnny."

That did it!

As I walked out onto the stage with my twin sister, all I could see were hundreds of people in the studio audience and that red light staring at me from the big black camera.

I froze! Yes, in front of millions watching, I froze!

My hands were sweating, my stomach was in knots, and my mind went totally blank. I could not say a word. All I could do was nod my head up and down and smile.

Johnny was such a gracious person. Afterward he came over to me and was so warm and charming and disarming. I said, "Johnny I don't know why I suddenly got so nervous."

He said, "Oh, well, I get nervous every time. Sometimes I even want to throw up. That's why I tell jokes, because I think everybody's nervous and it relaxes them. I know when I use humor, people laugh. They feel good. They feel good, and I feel good."

And that's why whenever I can, I try to insert humor in my presentations, and I advise all my clients to do the same.

Now as Jerry Seinfeld famously said, 75 percent of people would rather be in the coffin than giving the eulogy at a funeral.

That's how prevalent this fear of public speaking is. The technical term is *glossophobia*, but none of that really matters if you've got it. What really matters is if you've got it, you've got to get over it. Because it's going to hold you back in every single way, and once you break through it, the world is your oyster.

Later I had the honor of staring in a movie with Elvis Presley called *Double Trouble*. My twin sister and I were selected to be the twins in *Double Trouble*.

The first day on the set, I said to Elvis, "Elvis, do you ever get nervous on stage or on camera?" He said, "Honey, every time I go on stage I get them butterflies, and them butterflies is what keeps me at the top of my performance. That just means you're alive."

Every time we saw him, he would say, "Here comes double trouble." Thanks to Elvis, my sister and I became the "Double Trouble Keymer Twins" in our performances and in our *Double Trouble Talk Radio Show*, where we interviewed celebrities, speakers, authors, business professionals, and entrepreneurs on the power of success and influence.

Elvis was a very gracious person, and starring in that movie with him was one of the highlights of my life . . . but not the only one. It definitely had a huge impact on me because this nervousness while performing, this fear of public speaking, this performance anxiety that put me in a state of paralysis was something I never wanted to experience again.

And it's also something that factors into a big part of my business today, because I help people to create unstoppable confidence, make an impact with their message, and build their celebrity status as the expert authority in their industry through the use of public speaking.

When I met Elizabeth Taylor, I had won a contest and became the Queen of the Hollywood Artists and Models Ball and was in a fashion show with her for a charity event. I looked into those amazing violet eyes of hers—and yes, they really were the color of violets, some kind of a crazy beautiful purple like you've never seen before—and I said, "Liz, I am so self-conscious in front of all these people; with everyone looking at me and having to talk, it is hard for me to concentrate."

She said, "Sweetie, forget about all those people. As long as you look the part and act the part, then all those people will see you the way a speaker should be seen, and you'll have that power. So just put your doubts aside and have fun."

Johnny, Elvis, and Liz helped me get over my fear of public speaking and performance anxiety, which has made all the difference in my life, my sister's life, and in the lives of my many clients; I'm privileged to help them overcome their fear of public speaking and position themselves as celebrities in the eyes of the people they want to do business with.

It has been proven that those exuding confidence and strong communication skills are more successful in their careers and personal relationships. Thus, I have made it my life's mission to help others create a powerful presence on stage, in the media, and in person as successful influencers in their business and lives.

If you want to stand out as the celebrity expert in your industry, make a big impact, and grow your business, I invite you to visit my website to connect with me, get a free gift, and to sign up for a forty-five-minute complimentary business breakthrough call.

In the words of Elvis, "Don't be cruel, don't be a hound dog . . . just wear your blue suede shoes, and keep on rockin."

Melody Keymer Harper is an international speaker, bestselling author, entertainer, and TV/radio/podcast host of *Ignite Your Influence Now!* She has over forty years' experience in showbiz, business teaching, speaking, and communication strategies. She can show you how to Stand Out as the Celebrity in Your Field, Make an Impact with Your Message, and Magnetically Attract New Clients.

Aside from acting in the movie *Double Trouble* with Elvis Presley, Melody has shared the stage and screen with some of the most highly sought-after speaking giants, including Brian Tracy, Les Brown, Jack Canfield, Elizabeth Taylor, Johnny Carson, and Jane Fonda.

www.MelodyKeymerHarper.com

COMPASSION AND BALLS

Leigh Koechner

In second grade I was seven years old and attending John Diemer Elementary School in Overland Park, Kansas. There were a couple of boys that were being mean to my friend Kim Ifft, so I told them, "You guys better watch yourselves and leave Kim alone or you're going to regret it." Later that day I was walking home on my usual route when *Bam!* I got cold-cocked in the side of my head. It hurt like hell, especially since I had just gotten my ears pierced and the hit landed right on the freshly pierced lobe. I was trying to figure out what the heck just happened when *Boom!* I got shoved from behind and fell to the ground. As I looked up from the dirt, I saw David Bishop and Greg Hyde running away as fast as they could. My ear was ringing, and blood was dripping down my chin. It was so tender, and it stung so bad. I stood up, picked up my backpack, and started running home as fast as I could.

I took the back route by the creek. I ran through all of my neighbor's backyards, up my backyard, and busted through the back-porch screen door. I ran up the basement stairs and down the hall to my mom's bedroom door where I turned the doorknob which was locked. I was sobbing as I pounded on her door and yelled, "Mommy, I need you; please open the door. I got in a fight, and my ear hurts." I knew she was in there, so again I yelled, "Mommy, please help me; I need you." I was crying so hard I could barely catch my breath and there were tears, snot, and blood running down my face. I kept banging on the door, then I slowed down, took a few deep breaths, and tried one more time. "Mommy, please open the door. I need you, please open the door. I got in a fight, Mommy."

I waited for a minute, and then I heard the familiar words: "Go away, I'm sleeping."

I turned away from the door and walked down the hallway into the guest bathroom. I grabbed the hand towel, held it under warm water, and looked at myself in the mirror. I started to wipe away the tears, snot, and blood from my face. I noticed my swollen eyes. I just stood there looking at myself, then I looked even deeper into myself. I wiped away the tears and thought, *I am not even good enough for my own mother to get out of bed for.* I kept looking at myself as tears ran down my face, trying to make sense of it all. I couldn't. I held my gaze, straightened my spine, then stopped the tears and said, "I don't need you, Mom. I don't need anyone. I can take care of myself. I am all alone and I will be just fine."

The next day after school, I crouched behind a bush and waited for David Bishop and Greg Hyde near the same spot they jumped me. When I saw them, I ran with all of my might, jumped them and fought like hell. When I got home, my dad was there. My shirt had been ripped and I had a fat lip. He said, "What in the hell happened to you?" I said, "I got into a fight with David Bishop and Greg Hyde." My dad called for my brothers. "Michael, Patrick, come here! Look at what these boys did your sister. Don't come home from school until you make them pay for what they have done."

The next night when my dad got home from work, he said, "Michael, Patrick, did you make the boys pay for what they did to Leigh?" Both of my brothers shook their heads no. My father said, "Why not?"

Michael said, "Dad, when we walked up to them, David Bishop had a black eye and Greg Hyde was missing a tooth. I think it was one of his permanent teeth."

My dad turned to me with proud, shining eyes, which I had never experienced so deeply before. He was gazing lovingly into my eyes, grinning from ear to ear, and still beaming, he put his big paw hand on my head, messed up my hair, and said, "God dammit, Leigh, you have more balls than anyone I've ever met. I'll never have to worry about you." I had never seen his eyes light up like that before. He was in such delight over me having BALLS! I have balls! It felt like he said, "You are my princess" or "You are my favorite child." Those two days shaped the next twenty-three years of my life. I was unworthy, but I had balls.

I lived the "I am unworthy" story like a champ. I ran fast, played hard, and partied even harder. I got drunk and made out in bars. I didn't date people because I didn't want to actually slow down long enough to talk to anyone. I just wanted to run fast, party hard, and make out. I lived this way until I was almost thirty years old, and boy, was I worn out. I knew this behavior was not conducive to the desire I had to be married and have children.

I tried dating without making out to practice my communication skills. I hated it. I got on my knees and asked God for some help. Boy, did he ever answer! Three weeks later I met David Koechner at the Kansas City airport. We were instantly attracted to each other and started dating. After a bit, I started getting drunk and picking fights. He asked, "What are you doing?" and I replied, "I don't know." He suggested we go to therapy together. After our first appointment, I ended up going by myself for two years, where I began understanding why I acted the way I acted, having compassion for myself, and continued melting the childhood armor I had created around my heart.

David's unconditional love started the melting of the childhood armor. I got to drop-kick my pebble and replace it with the truth: I am made in the likeness of God. I came from the stars and will return one day soon. I have everything inside of me that I need for my entire life. I am whole, worthy, and powerful beyond measure. My younger self created a story trying to make sense of what was happening. My older self got to kick that story to the curb and own her power.

Leigh Koechner is a podcaster, speaker, and spiritual teacher (who likes doing the splits and sipping martinis). She inspires others by being unapologetically who she is and lives life with Compassion and Balls. Leigh is authentic, vulnerable, and funny as hell. The refreshingly unfiltered mother of five is the Parenting Expert for Deepak Chopra's Global Well-being app JIYO, co-executive producer on *The Mindfulness Movement* documentary, and has an intimate Messy Mastermind group guiding her clients to take their hearts desire out of their mind and into their reality. Leigh launched her *messy imperfect life with leigh podcast* where she converses with guests about a messy moment from their life, what they learned from it, and how they are using it as a source of good now. SUBSCRIBE!

www.leigh.la

THE DETOUR

Linda Kruse

> *Two roads diverged in a wood, and I—I took the one less traveled by,*
> *And that has made all the difference.*
> *—Robert Frost*

I've always been a planner. I made very deliberate decisions to set my life on a very specific course. University. Career. Filmmaking. Home. Family. But then one day I started on an unplanned journey down that poetically diverged road which led me to an age-old question: If I knew now what I didn't know then . . . would I have taken that road?

Several years ago, I overheard my brother talking about a trip he was planning with his wife and two kids across a country he didn't know: America. My big brother, Victor—a decorated and soon-to-be retired U.S. Army officer—spent his life defending a country he had never really lived in. He and I both grew up overseas in a military family, and then he went into the Army. He spent over twenty years serving in every major foreign conflict the U.S. was engaged in during that time. For years, he had been planning this huge road trip to find a home for his family, and I only heard about it one month before they were to depart! With little-to-no planning, I decided to tag along and film it, thinking it would make an interesting documentary: *An American Hero's Search for an American Hometown.*

It's widely known that the Number ONE rule in filmmaking is: Pre-Production, Pre-Production, Pre-Production. And being a planner, I would have normally kept that in mind. But given the timing I only had two choices: either join them on this journey, filming as we go, or miss it altogether, bogging myself down with planning it.

I had saved up a lot of money toward my plan to buy a home in Los Angeles—and well, the funds that were supposed to go toward that cute little house instead paid for me to follow them on a two-year figure-eight trip across America, filming in thirty-seven states and conducting over six hundred interviews. It seemed that my *own* journey to find a home was going to be put "on hold" while I took a detour on my brother's journey toward that very same goal.

The idea was that we would seek out one small town in each state that would represent an ideal place to live in America. However, what started as a documentary about a family quickly turned into something more:

> *It's the oldest story known to man, coming home, but with a twist: after spending most of his life living outside the United States defending his country, now back from the war, where does a decorated twenty-year Army soldier go home to—if he's never really had a hometown?*

But this amazing idea was fraught with so many issues: I hired the wrong people, I spent too much money, I lost jobs, I missed opportunities, I made missteps and misjudgments. So many times things got derailed or deterred, and I got discouraged, dissuaded, and just plain disappointed—in myself and my lack of planning. There were speed bumps with sign after sign saying this was never going to be anything. That I should stop, that I should quit. But *quit* is a word I know not of.

> *Quit: to depart, drop out, give up, relinquish, renounce, retire,*
> *surrender, withdraw, desert, evacuate, exit, forsake, hang it up, resign.*

I lost friends, I lost money, and I lost years of my life working on this ONE project. But this is supposed to be a motivational story. So here goes . . .

> *In life, the things that go wrong are often the very things*
> *that lead to other things going right.*
> —*Arianna Huffington*

I don't quit. Ever. I don't depart, don't drop out, don't give up, don't relinquish, or renounce. I don't retire, surrender, withdraw, desert, evacuate, exit, forsake. And I certainly don't hang it up or resign. I just reorganize.

Looking closer, I realized that *this* story was way bigger than just one family. *THIS* was a universal story, celebrating *community*. I regrouped and reworked the material. I saved and spent more money, eventually crafting it all into Season One of *KRUSING AMERICA*, a six-part family travel docu-series that follows Lt. Colonel Victor Krus and his family as they crisscross the country on a quest to find their home, sweet home.

How did I find my way? I went back to the *one* thing that resonated more than the story, the family, or even the trip. The *one* thing that made all the difference: *the kindness of strangers*. In each town, I was reminded over and over of the unexpected human connections that so often transform the experience of travel: those personal connections, those six hundred interviews that celebrated the gifts of kindness and warmth. They restored my trust in mankind. Each unexpected gift left a lasting impression, beautifully realized in the people I met along the way. It was *the kindness of strangers* that made all the difference. It was especially noticeable through the many people who touched my life and continue their generosity and compassion to this day. I needed to honor them.

That revision, focused on kindness, created a ripple effect that allowed *KRUSING AMERICA* to go on to win over sixty awards at film festivals all over the world: from Berlin and Bali to finishing as the Overall Winner at the International Tourism Awards, the Festival Winner at the Directors Awards, and concluding with the ultimate privilege of winning both Filmmaker of the Year and Director of the Year.

Despite every challenge, I don't have any regrets for choosing this road. I'm amazed at how it has grown into something I could never have imagined. After starting off as a documentary film, it's now a completed, TV docu-series available on Amazon Prime and worldwide on other venues with the potential of a Season Two featuring a whole different family in different circumstances who discover *their* home through the kindness of strangers.

I'm not sure what the next step will be for me or in the journey of *KRUSING AMERICA*. But at this point, I'm planning on one thing only—I'm planning to be surprised.

Oh, and I did finally buy that house I was saving up for . . . but that's a whole other story.

We must let go of the life we have planned,
so as to accept the one that is waiting for us.
—*Joseph Campbell*

Linda Kruse is a news correspondent, international spokesperson, executive trainer and documentarian. As a multi-award-winning director, Linda's last documentary *KRUSING AMERICA* won sixty awards, earning her both Filmmaker of the Year and Director of the Year. A three-time bestselling author and accomplished writer, she is currently featured in both *Women Who Rock* and *Rock Your Life*. The owner of Atticus Productions, Inc., Linda has written, produced, and directed projects worldwide that explore challenging and intriguing topics while definitively capturing real people and the worlds they live in. All of Linda's work is presented with a creative elegance that is her signature style.

www.lindakruse.com

FIGURE IT OUT

Janet Kunst

I have a handicap. Even writing those words seems strange to me. Until recently, it never dawned on me that what I've considered an inconvenience all my life was actually seen as a handicap by others. It has given me a new perspective into how I view life and have handled life's challenges, all of which can be summed up in three words: Figure It Out.

Let me explain. Without getting too technical, I was born with a birthmark that affects the muscles in my left leg. As a result, I walk with a noticeable limp. Along the way, I've had other complications—some due to how the doctors treated it when I was a baby, others of my own doing. Yet through it all, the word *handicapped* was never uttered, and I am so grateful to my parents for that. In fact, I was always encouraged to stretch myself and figure out how to do things in spite of this challenge.

Obviously, one of the pitfalls of this handicap is mobility. I can't, for the life of me, run very well. I was always the slowest in any race, and, as you can imagine, gym and sports could be a challenge. Even so, it never occurred to me that I couldn't play—I just had to figure out a way to get on base before the ball got there. What I realized was that if I could hit or kick the ball far enough, I'd be OK. And that's what I did. I actually wound up being pretty good at kickball, and I loved playing second base in the local girls' intramural softball league.

Small challenges like this have turned into bigger challenges in other areas of my life. Things that probably would have stopped others in their tracks were just bumps in the road for me. And looking back, I'm beginning to understand some of the comments (and amazement) people have had at different times.

One that stands out among the rest is when I broke my leg. Yep, same leg. I was in Bogota, Colombia, for a six-month internship during my master's program. There were six of us in Colombia at the time, and our parents were all worried. While we were there, the drug wars were in full swing and there was some concern for our safety. School finally decided to pull us out, and an hour before leaving, I fell and broke my leg—both the tibia and fibula—completely in two. Needless to say, I stayed behind in the hospital for surgery while everyone else left. A week later, I got on the plane to go home.

By then, the others had been relocated for their internships—some to Mexico, others to Costa Rica. My school advisor called me at home in New Jersey to see how I was doing and talked about rescheduling my internship for the following year. My initial reaction was "Why? It's just a broken leg." She was absolutely floored that I would even consider completing the program on crutches in a third-world country. Thankfully, my parents sided with me, and I spent the next five months in Costa Rica. It was challenging, especially since there were no handicap conveniences—but I figured it out.

Probably one of my most daring physical feats that stymied many who viewed me as handicapped was my announcement that I was training to walk a half-marathon for the Leukemia and Lymphoma Society. The only stipulation to be able to walk the marathon was that you had to be able to walk a mile in sixteen to eighteen minutes. That's actually a fairly brisk pace for 13.1 miles. I trained every Saturday for about four months before the event in New Orleans. There was never a question in my mind that I couldn't do it—I figured out what worked for me and just did it. Yes, I closed down each check-in station, but I completed the course—all without being sore the next day! (And no, I haven't walked a marathon since . . . I proved to myself I could do it, and that was enough.) To this day, I only have one speed when walking: fast.

While this "figure it out" mentality has served me well with regards to any physical activity, it has spilled over into other areas of my life as well. I tend to not see problems as obstacles stopping me from achieving what I want; rather, they are puzzles that just need to be figured out.

About ten years ago I was working for a local retail property management company, helping the merchants with their marketing efforts in the community. It was during the last recession, so it wasn't too much of a surprise when they told me they had to let me go. What did surprise me was their request to keep working for them as a consultant. Not in a million years had I ever thought about owning my own business. Yet at that moment I thought, *Sure, why not?*, knowing I would figure it out as I went along.

That one decision launched my small business. I had no idea what I was doing or how to go about building a business from scratch. It was also a time where marketing no longer meant just brochures, flyers, and other offline activities. Social media marketing was just starting to be a "thing," and I knew my business would need to grow with the times or I might as well go back to corporate America. So I figured it out, and now I successfully help my clients get online and get excited about using social media and other online marketing tools to grow their businesses.

I don't know what my next challenge will be. But there is one thing for certain: I'll figure it out.

Janet Kunst is the owner and founder of Recipes for Marketing Success. With over twenty five years of marketing experience, Janet's passion is for the small business owner who has the expertise in their field but struggles when it comes to marketing—particularly online marketing. From social media and blogging to podcasting and everything in between, Janet helps you discover your unique Recipe for Marketing Success—and does it for you or teaches you to do it yourself.

www.RecipesForMarketingSuccess.com

RADIATING HOPE

Janie Lidey

*The key to being blessed begins with believing that you are. The key to seeing miracles begins
with believing that you will. And the key to radiating hope begins with
believing in the brightness of your light.*

November 4, 2017, was a magical day. I was performing at Craig Duswalt's *Rock
Your Life Night*: a faith-based event at the City National Grove in Southern California. I had co-written the theme song for the event, and this was the night I would
perform *Rock Your Life* with Craig's stage band and then share some inspirational stories
and music with the help of my favorite Martin guitar. Several years earlier, I had taken
a leap of faith from my career of teaching music in Alaska and set out to create hope
and healing with my music and message. My dream of raising the vibration of love on
our planet was coming true. I was reaching people in many corners of the world doing
exactly what I had set out to do. Blessings and miracles were flowing.

The next day I woke up with pain surging from my right hip to my ankle and radiating with such intensity that I could barely walk. My leg felt like a tooth in the dentist's
chair being drilled on nonstop with no Novocain. I'm a pretty badass chick with a high
pain threshold, but I couldn't pretend my way through this pain. I cancelled the rest of
my performances and headed home for an MRI.

It's not what happens to you but how you react that matters.
—Epictetus

On December 1, 2017, I came home from an MRI with a new blessing in my life.
On that day, I was given a gift that brought an epic amount of love into my life. On that
day, the miracle I am about to share with you became a possibility. The gift: Stage IV
metastatic breast cancer. The miracle: In just five months, I was cancer free. When my
doctors told me that what I had been diagnosed with was incurable, I told them that just
didn't work for me. I immediately began the process of radiating hope into my mind,
body, and spirit to restore myself to wellness.

When I shared the results of my MRI with my husband Sean, he immediately began
to radiate hope into me. He reminded me of the power of the eight daily habits I created
for my *Leap of Faith* book written just a few years earlier, and we talked about how this
challenge would connect me to more people who would benefit from my music and
message. He said that this would help me become a more powerful speaker and give me
the opportunity to show the world and myself the blessings that appear when we choose
love over fear and faith over worry. I had spent the last several years traveling around

the country doing inspirational talks and concerts on the topic of my latest book and CD, encouraging people to expect blessings and miracles in their lives, and now I was being faced with one of the greatest opportunities to prove the worth of my daily habits.

Imagination is the preview of life's coming attractions.
—Albert Einstein

Two days after the diagnosis, a Super Moon lit up the sky. It is said that there are special healing powers in the Super Moon, and Sean intuitively tapped into them on that magical night. We had gone up to bed in the loft of our log home, and the Super Moon was shining brightly through our window and lighting the room as though the sun were shining in.

Sean got this look in his eyes and said, "Sweetie, take off your clothes and lay on the bed."

I'm thinking, *Shit, I just got diagnosed with stage IV metastatic breast cancer, my right hip is about to fracture, and you wanna have sex!*

He said, "Trust me. Take off your clothes and lay in the light of the moon." So I took off my clothes and lay on the bed. Sean ran down to his shop and returned with a large magnifying glass. He began to place the smooth, round glass over my right hip where the doctors said the largest tumor was growing. You know how you can burn a hole through a leaf when you hold a magnifier over it and allow the sun to beam through it? Well, Sean's thought was that we could harness the power of the Super Moon by allowing its light to reflect through the glass and melt away the tumors. He focused the light through the glass, let the magnifier glide over my body, and we imagined those unhealthy cells just disappearing.

A few weeks later, a very large growth on the outside of my body simply dried up and fell off. I was supposed to have it removed and biopsied that week but had to cancel due to my scheduled surgeries. God seemed to give us that visual to help us understand the ease with which the growths on the inside of my body would also melt away.

The miracle that became a possibility on that December day became a reality on April 27, 2018. Just five months after the diagnosis, I was cancer-free. During those five months, I had a titanium rod implanted into my right femur to stabilize the bone that had been eaten by a tumor, radiation to help escort some unhealthy cells out of my body, and some ongoing heavy-duty drugs to keep those cells from coming back.

Our body's ability to heal is far greater than we are led to believe. During my healing process, my new book *Radiating Hope—Cancer Unplugged* was born. It is my vehicle for sharing this story with you. Whatever you are going through in your life, be it cancer or any other life challenge, it can be harnessed as a blessing and lead you to *your* miracles.

———————————

Janie Lidey is a dynamic speaker, bestselling author, Emmy-winning songwriter, and Grammy-winning music educator. Janie was recently diagnosed with stage IV metastatic breast cancer, and when her doctors told her it was incurable, Janie simply said that didn't work for her. Just five months later, not one cancer cell lit up on Janie's PET scan.

She is using her miracle story to radiate hope into her audiences with her new book and accompanying music CD, *Radiating Hope—Cancer Unplugged.*

www.JanieLidey.com

THE POWER OF A SET MIND

Laura Louise

Have you ever looked back at your life and thought, *How did I do that?* If you are anything like me, we press forward with our task and never think about where we began. We never stop and look at what we have accomplished. Why? I believe we are always looking ahead to the next obstacle or challenge. We press through instead of experiencing the glory of the moment.

Most people do not know that I am a high school dropout. I left home my junior year and moved to Georgia where I married the day after I turned eighteen. I left home at age seventeen because I was full of anger and rage due to the lack of emotional support from my parents.

To be transparent, this was a very angry and rebellious time in my life, which lasted for decades. I was not easy to love at that point in my life. I had an abortion, spent a little time in juvenile hall, ran away from home for two weeks, cut class often, and did the opposite of what my parents told me to do. My life was going in the direction of hopeless tragedy.

I gave birth to my son at nineteen and knew my life needed to change. I achieved my GED when I was twenty years old. I knew it was not enough, and for the first time in my life I had a desire to attend college. At the time, my husband did not want me to attend college, and we argued often about my attending. Today I know the why behind our arguments. He confessed that if I went to college, he thought I would leave him because we were so different. Basically, he had a fear of losing me—which did happen, but not because of college. We separated, and at age twenty-four, I began my college career. I had a drive that was unlike anything I had ever experienced. I never missed class and felt like this was my ticket to a new life. Looking back, it was not easy, and if I knew what I would go through, I probably would not have gone. Luckily, we all get to live one day at a time. I think it's a blessing we don't see the big picture as most of us would not move forward.

My greatest challenge included dropping out of accounting a total of six times throughout my education. I could not get the material and thought this class would be the reason I did not graduate. I would cry and tell my mother how hard it was and that I had to drop out yet again. She would tell me, "Well, each time you take it you learn more of the material; you will pass it eventually." She was right; I eventually did pass it! No matter how hard something is, never give up! If I gave up, I would not be the person I am today. Everything we go through makes us stronger. When we go through a thing, we develop a stronger level of self. Our strength is developed by what we overcome.

My six-year journey from community college to graduating from Pepperdine University with my bachelor's in science management was well worth my tears, fears, and trials. There I was, a single mother at age thirty, graduating with my degree, the first person in my family to receive a university-level degree. The same parents who thought I was never going to make them proud and somehow end up a lifelong burden were gleaming with joy and probably a little astonishment. I am certain they thought, *She actually stuck this thing out and became the first person in our family to achieve what no one else had.*

My story did not stop there, I honestly never thought I would get my master's degree. It was so challenging for me the first time that I did not want to repeat the hardship, headache, or financial burden. It took me twenty years before I thought about getting a master's degree. I fought with the financial piece the most; I did not have the money and did not want to have a bill over my head. The amazing thing is that once I set my mind to move by faith, my life changed!

There I was at forty-seven going back to school to achieve another level of education and feeling pretty old in comparison to everyone else. I admit I had a complex for a while about my age in the mix of all the twenty- and thirty-something students. This time my age was my biggest challenge. I did not drop out of any classes, nor did I have stress, tears, or frustration around the academics. Overall, I was very happy and blessed to be achieving another milestone in my life. Remember when I said once I set my mind and moved by faith, my life changed? Well, my tuition bill was paid in full before I walked at graduation. The money came to me in a way I never would have imagined and, if consulted, would not have wanted. However, at the end of the day everything worked out to be better than I could have imagined.

Today the biggest question I get from my family and friends is "When are you going to get your doctoral degree?" I will get my degree in a few years. Until writing this book, I have not thought about my educational journey. We often keep moving and don't look back. I am a high school dropout with a master's degree. Wow, that is actually pretty amazing!

What I want each of you to realize is I am not special. What set me apart was my ability to set my mind and keep it set. I did not let anything stop me, and no matter what obstacles came my way I kept pushing through. You have that same power in you! Do not let anything or anyone in the way of your dreams, goals, or desires. You can do anything you set your mind to if you believe you can do it. In times of despair, remember, I dropped out of accounting class six times before I finally passed it. My recommendation to you is to keep a success journal by writing out your achievements big and small, and when you need a boost—read it. Your strength comes from your glory of achievements! When you read your successes, you realize the strength you have within which will carry you through.

Laura Louise is an author, mentor, and speaker who is changing lives in the areas of alcohol, depression, loneliness, and anger to bring healing and more love. During her own journey, she made the commitment to gain the insight and education to become a powerful healing force. Laura Louise made a promise to herself during her journey to healing that she would step up and serve as a powerful servant and authentic leader to those who want to be free from the bondage of unforgiveness.

www.IntotheLightwithLauraLouise.com

Overcoming Cancer with God

Pamela Malinchak

For richer, for poorer, in sickness and in health. . . . The past twenty-seven years had been healthy ones for both William and me, but on my drive home from the oncologist's office, it was clear that was about to change. I had just heard the three words that no one ever wants to hear: "You have cancer."

The vows William and I took nearly three decades ago had never been tested in sickness. Little did we know how those vows would be tested now.

"To love and to cherish, 'til death do us part . . . please God, don't let death part us so soon.

Flooded with emotion, I couldn't process all that I was feeling. I felt fear and anxiety creeping over my shoulder and making me helpless and weak, but there were also hints of strength, courage, and resolve that would grow over time.

Mostly I felt confused. I was overwhelmed with questions: *What type of treatment will I receive? Where should I get treated? Who do I trust with this?*

While my brain filled with questions, my heart felt empty and drained. It was as if it had short-circuited from the overload of emotions. All I felt was numb. It was usually my gut-instinct that helped me to make decisions when the choices were difficult. But now it seemed as if that gut wisdom was missing in action. I wasn't sure who I could trust for advice.

I don't remember much about the drive home, but I do remember that as I pulled my car into the driveway, William was already there.

How do I tell him?

As I slowly walked out of the car, I quietly shared my new diagnosis. William said confidently, "We've got this! God is on our side." How I loved to hear that! It wasn't just me going through this; we were in this together!

Thinking through our wedding vows one last time, I whispered a prayer. *What you, God, have joined, let cancer not divide.*

If you're reading this book, there is a good chance that you or someone you love has heard those three terrifying words, "You have cancer." If you're like me, the diagnosis raises a lot of tough questions that need to be answered:

What am I supposed to do now? How will this affect my family? How do I tell my kids, my friends, or my parents? What is the best way to treat this? Who is the best doctor? Is there hope? And if so, where do I find it?

The truth is, life did change. At that moment I chose to trust God completely! I knew that God would give me the wisdom to know what to do, where to be treated, and how to choose the best doctors for this type of cancer. My faith grew stronger every day.

Having experienced rectal cancer, I can honestly say that it was painful, excruciating at times. I chose not to read *anything* concerning my situation. I knew that if I kept a positive attitude and thanked God for being with me every day of treatment, I could get though it. There were moments when I cried out to God to stop the pain, but He has used this to teach me many lessons. When I was at my weakest, God gave me His strength.

I needed hope.

Where else does someone find hope? I've heard the saying that hope stands for Hold On Pain Ends. But how do we hold on? Who and what do we hold on to? I put my hope in the Lord, and I felt peace.

God never left my side! He was with me every step of the way, including our decision to travel to New York City to be treated at Sloan Kettering. He was with me every day in the hospital while I was receiving twenty-seven rounds of chemo and radiation treatments. He was holding me close on the last day of treatment while I walked out of the room with tears streaming down my face because that part was over! He gave me His strength in my recovery (during the most painful time).

God continues to be with me daily.

Remember, God promises to be with us in everything we face. Throughout my journey I have been so thankful to learn how to have joy through all the pain. It's easy to be blinded by the difficult days, but when you look through the lens of gratitude, you see the gift in everything.

The only way I made it through the darkest days were saying this verse over and over again: "I can do all things through Christ who strengthens me" (Philippians 4:13). The Lord gave me the strength every day, and I am so grateful for His love and faithfulness.

Ironically, it was my diagnosis of cancer that showed me that the essential things in life are not *things* but our relationships with one another. Most importantly, our relationship with God who will one day bring us to our eternal home.

Pamela Malinchak is a well-respected assistant teacher at a Christian school. Currently she is a student at Liberty University continuing her education. As a former model, Pamela enjoyed working in the print and commercial industry. In addition, she was a professional cheerleader for the New Jersey Generals. She is the co-founder of William and Pamela Malinchak Foundation which supports charitable organizations.

In September 2018, Pamela was diagnosed with colorectal cancer. Her continued faith and trust in God brings her true healing. Pamela gives God all the glory. Pamela lives in Florida with her husband, William, who is a former NFL player for the Detroit Lions and Washington Redskins. They have four wonderful children: Courtney, Taylor, Ashley, and Michael.

From Shame to Sobriety—My Journey

Sue Mandell

At twenty-nine years old, you couldn't handle me. It was PARTY, PARTY, PARTY! I was a bartender in a Navy town, and I had sailors hitting on me every day, having the time of my life—until I wasn't.

My friend's husband walked downstairs one morning, looked at us still partying at her kitchen counter, and just shook his head. For the first time ever, I felt overwhelming shame and remorse. Here was somebody who lived in the normal world, not in my chemically induced haze.

I don't know where they came from, but the words came tumbling out: "I have a problem, and I don't know what to do about it." I was horrified. My best friend's husband saw me for exactly what I was: a drug addict and alcoholic.

She said, "Go home and tell your boyfriend."

"I can't tell him—he'll leave me," I cried. "I'll quit on my own and IF I can't; THEN I'll tell him.

I just couldn't quit on my own, and I couldn't work up the courage to say something to him, so I left some drugs out for him to find. He gave me a three-part ultimatum:

- You're going to quit your job.
- You're going to get help.
- You're going to tell your parents—or you move out.

If I were to tell you that thirty-one years of sobriety was easy, it would be a lie, one of the biggest I've ever told, and I've told some whoppers. They say to live life one day at a time. Sometimes for me it was one hour at a time, or one minute at a time, one second at a time, or even one breath at a time.

For over three decades I've used these three tools almost daily as I've helped hundreds of people to get sober.

The 24-HOUR RESET. Have you ever heard the phrase "Start your day over"? My DAY isn't from when I wake up until I go to bed. It isn't from midnight one day to midnight the next. My day, my twenty-four hours, can start over *anytime I choose.*

If things aren't going well and my brain is running amuck, I can close my eyes and see myself drawing a line in the sand. All the feelings I want to stop are on one side, and what I CHOOSE to feel is on the other. I get to decide what is on either side of that line, *anytime I want to.*

THE NEW PATH—I close my eyes and breathe slowly. Big, deep, slow breaths. I see myself going down a path surrounded by beauty, and then that familiar cloud of anxiety starts to swarm down around my ears. I see a fork in the path up ahead and *I* get to *choose* which path to take. Instead of continuing down the path of anxiety and overwhelm, I visualize myself going down the *other* path, the one that leads to happiness, ease, and serenity.

THE PINK ELEPHANT—It's ten times harder to stop thinking about whatever it is that I'm obsessing about rather than just changing my thought. If all I can think about is drinking, it's ten times harder to stop thinking about a drink than to simply change my thought to what I want to do with friends after work.

Think of a pink elephant; picture his big, floppy pink ears and his long pink trunk, and his *huge* pink body with his massive pink feet. Do you have a clear picture of a pink elephant in your mind? Now don't think about the elephant. No matter what you do, DO NOT think of that pink elephant. Be sure not to see his pink ears or his pink trunk or pink hairy body.

How's that working for you? It's easier to think about what you want, rather than to try not to think about what you don't want. No more pink elephants.

I won't tell you it's easy; nobody in recovery will tell you it's easy, but it's been more than worth it. The best part is that I get to help so many others by passing along the tips and tricks that worked for me.

If you want the Fed Ex Experience—quick, fast, with results NOW—if you want to get sober, or you know someone who does, if you're really serious—text your name to 951-212-0225 and say "I'm ready."

Sue Mandell is an award-winning speaker, a number-one bestselling author, and an addictive behavior specialist. She has been featured on TV on ABC, CBS, NBC, as well as many cable networks.

Sue has spoken to audiences of up to five thousand at numerous National and State Associations, as well as the Federal Law Enforcement Training Center, and the Department of Justice in Washington, D.C.

For over thirty years, Sue has helped countless people battle their addictive behaviors and come out victorious. She is also a master practitioner of NLP (Nuero-Linguistic Programming), a master life and executive coach, and a master hypnotherapist.

SueMandell@BetterMeSolutions.com

REMEMBERING WHAT IS REALLY IMPORTANT

Fred McGaver

A s of a day of reflection comes to a close, I am remembering some times that really left me feeling complete.

Having spent my younger years in the city of Cudahy, Wisconsin, I have often realized that I wondered "when" I would get to grow up someday. You see, growing up was the thing you do when you graduate high school and pursue college or some other form of higher education. Then, when that is completed, you find a partner and create a family and get your career going and "make a living," whatever that meaning you give that for yourself. I remember going to twenty-six weddings of friends of mine during that summer when I was twenty-four. I learned eventually that standing up in a wedding was similar to going to a funeral of a loved one in that in either event it is likely you will not see them again as they all go on to live their lives too.

Emotional maturity is more of decision that an event. People tend to learn what they live. I did too. I also learned at a young age that education is a business and not the culmination of an enlightened experience that brings you to a point of your ultimate "arrival." That fact did not discourage me to opt out, but merely gave me a heads-up of seeing what the real life lessons are.

As a freshman at Marquette University, I had several prerequisite courses that included Chemistry, Biology, Anatomy, Physiology, Anthropology, and English.

During the summer of my freshman year, I was going through many of the notes from the classes I took and noticed that many of the things I just learned were already slipping away. The most practical of all of them seemed to be Anatomy and Physiology because of my exposure to high school and then college wrestling where you are grabbing your opponent to take them off their feet.

One day I was wrestling one of my teammates, and my college coach observed me talking to him as I was grabbing his wrist. I said, "This is his radius and ulna" (the radial bone is one of the two large bones of the forearm, the other being the ulna.), and then moving my hand up to his bicep, I said, "Now this is his the humorous," as we were pushing each other sparring. My coach chimed in, "What are you doing, Fred?"

I stopped and explained to him that I was recalling the notes I wrote over the year from my anatomy course. He then asked, "How did you do in the class?" and I responded that I passed. He then said, "Well that is great; now you can forget all of that stuff as you start learning what is really important." Asking him why, he responded, "It is unlikely anyone will ask you to take that test again. You can remember it all, but you likely don't need to know that again."

As my classes clicked by, I remembered that conversation and decided that going forward, I would always remember one important sentence, lesson, or conversation from that class that would serve me in my life going forward. As I lived with my new expectation of finding and learning "that sentence," I would often find several lessons that were helpful.

As I closed my five years of college, finishing in the School of Business and having 167 college credits to complete my college requirements of 128 credits, I was speaking with some classmates about what they learned over their college years, and we were sharing our mutual perceptions. After a long discussion, we determined that none of us could write down all of the classes we took with the course name, the full name of the teacher, the room and building we went to, and the grade we got in the class. We agreed that the "game of school" was just a modality where you can learn how to learn.

During that time, I decided that "now that I am done learning their (the assigned books of required classes) stuff," I could focus on my real interests. Those interests from before my college days, many still the same after forty years, include handwriting, understanding my intuition, and several other modalities of person growth that challenge me to be "true to myself."

In that sequence of thoughts, I noticed that my experiences in my late twenties and all of my thirties as I was still coaching high school wrestling and often training with several athletes who were also on World and Olympic Wrestling Teams, after all that time and work, I still had no Olympic or World hardware. (Hardware is term for the medals you get from placing in the top three of international tournaments which included World and Olympic stages.)

I then realized that I do not have any regret regarding the effort I put forth because I do not need to guess what the outcome would have been. I know I gave it my all even though I came up short.

My last competition was at age forty in the U S Olympic Trials. I eventually lost after I had qualified for the finals, being the oldest individual to get that far.

I have grieved what would have been if I could have won thousands of times. But I never regret that I did not "get after it." The failure is not going out and getting your intended result, but not going out at all.

Do not let your schooling or routine daily life interfere with your education. Routine and schools are systems, but education is life experiences.

Fred McGaver is a graduate of Marquette University School of Business. Having been in the life Insurance industry since 1980, he has also started, built, and sold several businesses. As the author of *The Magic of Mentorship*, he has been a guest speaker for businesses and athletic teams sharing about giving your all "every time."
He is the member of the Marquette University Athletic Hall of Fame 1999 and the Wisconsin Wrestling Coaches Association Hall of Fame 2014.

Although he himself does not have any World or Olympic Medals, eight World and

Olympic Medalists signed their names to have him nominated into The Wisconsin Wrestling Coaches Association Hall of Fame. Winning the respect of these colleagues and friends is definitely one of Fred's greatest treasures. Call Fred at 262-565-7900 or email him at fmcgaver@gmail.com.

Rocking Opportunities

Crystal Meisner

We've all heard Richard Branson's "say yes and figure it out later" ideology. I align more with "say yes if you can make it work." I feel you should not say yes if you don't mean it, or if you only plan on finding a way out of it. Opportunities may arise, and they can be beneficial to all parties if you can viably see an outcome.

Many years ago, I was working for a local PEG Access television station that dared to be more. More local programming, more variety, and more WORK! At one point, we were producing over 2,200 hours of local programming a year. That's six full hours of local content produced EVERY DAY. That's the equivalent of Los Angeles' major networks regional news day.

We had shows covering pretty much every aspect of our community: government, news events, activities, recreation, parades, services, seniors, babies, contemporary music, police activity, and sports. Because we were a small crew, we worked most every show in some manner, whether in preproduction coordination, set construction and lighting, and/or production. My favorite position, when not directing, was as floor director, or secondly as CG, aka computer graphics. Most shows were recorded live-to-tape. Some may have had remote field productions for the show in its entirety or for B-roll support.

In 1992 we had one such remote production. I suggested to the director/coordinator of our *Sports Talk* show that we should cover the Los Angeles Kings training camp that was being held in nearby Blue Jay, California. It was the second year the Kings had gone to Blue Jay, and I felt it imperative that if we were going to be a regional sports show, we should cover something as big as an NHL team coming to our local area. As a result, we scheduled a day with our host and our director to go up into the mountains and shoot the show. We had been told by the Kings organization that we would get an opportunity to interview the players at a specific time, so we planned accordingly. As it turned out, the players they were giving us the opportunity to interview at that time were the new young players, not the more established players. As a fan and show director myself, I knew if we were to have a really great show, we needed get some interviews with the well-known players most people in our community knew and loved. We were in a quandary. Our host had to leave due to another schedule commitment, so the director, Ron Harvey, and I stayed with our camera and audio equipment and hoped to get interviews with those mainstay players after the later scrimmage.

Well, it just so happened that Wayne Gretzky's wife, Janet, went into labor with their son, Trevor, and Wayne was suddenly going to be leaving training camp to be with his wife for his son's birth! Prime Ticket, who was the primary television coverage for the NHL in Southern California at that time, had been doing preproduction at the training camp but were without a film crew. Upon discovering that Wayne was leaving, they panicked. "We can't have a show without interviewing Gretzky!" So they came to us, the little local crew who was there, and asked if we would record a segment with Wayne for them. Now, this was back in the days of ¾" U-Matic video tape—no cell phones/smartphones/iPhones, no digital anything—but because I always made sure we had plenty of tapes and batteries, I knew we could help.

Here's where I saw the opportunity. I told Prime Ticket, "Yes, we would be happy to shoot an interview for you, and I would appreciate it if you could ensure we get one as well." Sure enough, they said, "We'll make it work."

Now it was MY turn to panic! We had no show host to do the interview. Our director knew many sports, but not hockey. Since going to the Kings training camp was my brilliant idea, it became my next opportunity. While I wasn't fond of being on-camera, nor of doing interviews—introvert that I am—I couldn't let this slip through our grasp, so *I* did the interview. No makeup, I was in production work clothes, not host apparel, but it didn't matter. We were going to get that interview with Gretzky!

We shot the segment Prime Ticket used for their show, and then I started my interview with Wayne. I could sense his impatience to be on his way, but ever polite Lady Bing Trophy winner that he is, Gretzky curbed his impatience to grant us his time. I started a little rocky, but Wayne quickly realized I not only knew about his achievements, but I was a fan of the game of hockey as well. And the tiny hitch in my breath mid-question when Marty McSorley sauntered past clad only in a towel made Wayne smile, and he enjoyed the interview more after that moment.

What a coup! To this day, when I mention that I interviewed Wayne Gretzky, people are flabbergasted—particularly hockey fans—and their unilateral response is, "No, you didn't!" And I reply, "Yes, I did!" It was one of the greatest, most memorable events of my life, and it was all because an opportunity arose out of unseen circumstances, and I figured out a way to make it work for my team as well as for another company. It was a win-win. To top it off, it gave me the credibility to continue the opportunity as a media person, attending Kings games, doing post-game locker room interviews, and following the team during the course of their run to their first Stanley Cup Finals. THAT was an extraordinary opportunity, and another story!

Recently, I had the opportunity to tell Trevor Gretzky himself the story of how I got to interview his dad the night before he was born (thank you, Craig Duswalt!). How amazing is that?

Crystal Meisner's thirty years' worth of work in local television and cable has been seen on PEG, PBS, MTV, ESPN, HGTV, and more. For four decades, she has been on stage, screen, and behind the scenes for a wide variety of productions and shows and has been privileged to work with many notables in entertainment, government, and history. She was a dancer in the Super Bowl XIX Halftime Show, and she has appeared on Oprah. She recently launched a speaker/presenter professionalism training series, based on her decades of experience helping to make show hosts and guests relax and present their best self on-camera and stage.

www.proselfmedia.com

I'll Fight for Your Brand

Andrei Mincov

She was one of Trademark Factory®'s first clients.

Back then, I was working hard to get people to know my firm existed and would routinely offer our services as a prize at events for entrepreneurs.

I hoped this would give us the exposure and generate a steady flow of customers from those who didn't win.

Spoiler alert: it wasn't working very well.

Anyhow, Silvia Martinelli won the prize.

She made an appointment to see me (we used to meet clients in our physical office back then).

Originally from Brazil, a marketing and communications major, Silvia had worked with brands and franchises for over a decade. She came to Canada to improve her English—and ended up staying. Then she started her own business.

The business of . . . Brazilian cheese puffs—a common treat in Brazil, but virtually unknown in Canada.

She created the recipe, started her business, and everyone *loved* the puffs, but nobody could remember the generic name: *Pão de Queijo.*

So, after many false starts, Silvia came up with the name *Otimo*, which means "awesome" in Portuguese, and created a recognizable logo for her brand.

That's when she entered the competition and won a package that included trademarking services from my firm.

With her marketing background, Silvia knew how important it was to own her brand. However—somewhat predictably—she didn't have a lot of money.

No wonder she was so excited about winning the trademarking prize!

She had a dilemma on her hands, though.

The prize covered only *one* trademark, and she wasn't sure whether to trademark the Otimo name or the logo.

I explained the benefits of each option, and after a brief discussion with her business mentor, Silvia decided to move forward with both the name *and* the logo. After all, she wasn't trademarking her brand because she won some contest. She wanted to trademark her brand because she valued her future.

Back then, Trademark Factory's team was pretty small. It consisted of one person: me.

I hustled to win new clients, designed our marketing materials, wrote code for our website, took all the phone calls, checked and answered all emails, did the trademark searches, drafted and filed all trademark applications, responded to all office actions . . . in short, I *was* Trademark Factory.

So when Silvia became a client, I did the search as best I could, saw no danger signs, filed her two trademark applications, and went back to hustling for new clients.

About six months later, we received two office actions citing the same objection. Apparently there had been a previously registered trademark I'd overlooked. A multibillion-dollar company in the food industry owned the Ottimo trademark—with two t's.

To this day, I have no idea how I missed that one.

Now, if there's one thing you should know about me, it's that I *hate* losing, and seeing that office action was a vivid reminder of how I started my career as an intellectual property lawyer.

Back in 1996, I was a law student in Russia, and a radio station had stolen my dad's song for a Samsung commercial.

At the request of my father, famous Russian composer Mark Minkov, I sued the radio station for copyright infringement. I thought I did great—until we received a judgment saying we'd lost.

I had no idea what to do about it, but my dad came into my room and said if I wasn't going to appeal the decision, I should quit law school and find a different profession. So I appealed the case, which went all the way up to the second highest court in Russia, just one level below the Russian Supreme court—and won!

Hence, when I looked at the two office actions, I knew I couldn't go back to Silvia to tell her that her dream of owning the Otimo brand was over.

I didn't want to even think about a refund, but it wasn't because I was afraid of honoring our 100 percent money back guarantee (by that time I had a team). Rather, it was about making sure we'd left no stone unturned, that we'd done whatever it took to give Silvia the result we'd promised. After all, her success would be our success.

We revised Silvia's application to remove products covered by the multibillion-dollar company's trademark, and we wrote a fifty-one-page sweat-and-tears-fueled response listing arguments explaining why we thought Silvia's Otimo brand was *not* confusingly similar to Ottimo.

Four months later, we received a second office action. The trademark examiner was not convinced by our arguments. It was time for us to put our thinking hats back on. We realized the only way for us to secure Silvia's trademarks was to go to war with the multibillion-dollar company and attack their brand . . . yikes.

To put things into perspective, with our all-inclusive flat fee, Silvia paid once to get the process started (and got one of the trademarks for free as a prize), and was not expected to pay ever again. By the time we'd written the fifty-one-page response, this file had already cost me a lot more than I'd made on it, and now we were about to engage in a huge fight!

And boy, did we!

Incredibly, about a year later, we canceled the multibillion-dollar company's trademark, opening the door to getting Silvia's brand registered. The whole process took slightly over three years.

It's usually the first case that comes to mind when someone asks me why brand owners around the globe should invest $3K with us to own their brand.

Well, *that's* why!

Because it gets you the results you pay for—whatever it takes.

If you are a growth-minded entrepreneur with a brand that helps you stand out from the crowd, secure it *before* you spend time and money trying to build it. Because hoping you can own it in the future if no one claims it before you is *not* a strategy.

As with Silvia, if we can help you, we will.

Schedule your call now at https://trademarkfactory.com/call.

———————————

Andrei Mincov is the founder of Trademark Factory®, a company that offers the easiest way to trademark your brand, risk-free, guaranteed, anywhere.

www.TrademarkFactory.com

Man in the Mirror

Jade Molina

At twenty-five, I'm only a year out of the Navy, I'm drinking every night, I'm a jerk to everyone around me, and my wife, Stephanie, is about ready to leave me.

One day, I come home from work and Stephanie left one of the kitchen cabinets open, AGAIN! In a moment of complete impulse, I go over and open all the cabinets, every drawer, the refrigerator, and the dishwasher. I even open up cereal boxes and lay them on the counter for her to find.

She walks in. "Jade, what the heck happened in here?"

With my hands on my hips, chest puffed up, and an "I'll show you" attitude, I sarcastically respond, "You don't like it, do you?"

Now she's crying, and I come to realize the reality of my pride.

After some time, I attempt to make things right, and I take her on a date night. We see a movie and then have a great dinner. On our way home, we stop by a friend's house who is having a party. It doesn't take long before my buddy, Doug, offers me a beer.

I look at Stephanie, who is standing in the distance. "Jade, you can have ONE!"

I gesture back, "OK, only one. I promise."

It's an hour later, and now I am out in the backyard pouring margarita mix and vodka down my throat. Stephanie comes out, sees what is going on, and with an overwhelming sense of anger and brokenness says, "That's it, I'm done. You promised."

At midnight, I start walking home—ALONE—down this dark, two-lane road. I am stumbling all over the place when a car drives by and honks at me. I don't want to get hit, so I decide to get on the other side of the guard rail that is off to my right. I walk over, have a seat, swing my legs over, and . . . I wake up about four hours later. Half my body is on an embankment, the other half is in water. My sandals are gone, and the bottom of my feet are cut up. I have scrapes all over my legs and I can barely walk because of the pain in my lower back. The guard rail is now fifteen feet above me. I didn't realize I was walking on a bridge over the Kern River. Another three feet and there would be no waking up at all.

I manage to crawl my way back to the top. As I get to my feet and head back down the dark road, a cop pulls up and agrees to drive me home. As soon as I walk in the back door, I get hit right in the chest with a set of keys. Books, pillows, profanities, and everything else my wife can throw at me follow.

As I attempt to dodge the barrage of ammunition pummeling me, Stephanie is yelling, "GET OUT! GET OUT! I'M DONE WITH YOU!"

Unable to defend myself, I yell back, "STOP! I'M HURT! I'M HURT!"

"What do you mean you're hurt?" as she turns on the light and just stares at me, crying.

She takes me into our bedroom and starts putting peroxide all over my wounds. I am screaming into a pillow because of the pain.

The next morning, I can barely move. I'm bruised all the way up the middle of my back. Come to find out, I have cracked my tailbone. And it looks like somebody took a jigsaw to my front teeth. I take an emery board and try to file them down to make them look better. As I stand there, looking into the mirror, I don't even recognize the person looking back at me. I know if I am ever going to become the man I want to be, I am going to have to change.

Only one day and seventeen hours after looking into that mirror, I find myself standing before a U.S. Navy Master Chief in Puson, South Korea. I am still in the naval reserves, and it just so happens that my annual active duty commitment falls on the week following this incident.

I am declared unfit for duty and assigned to a recovery barrack for the next two weeks.

As I lie in a dark room on a cold bed, I feel lost, alone, and completely depressed. I have no sense of direction and feel like giving up.

However, upon my return, my wife agrees to a second chance. Her grace ignites a spark in me, so I start fighting. I decide to get fit. Fitness has always given me a sense of identity, and now I need something that can be a springboard to finding my self-worth.

Over time I come to realize that my greatest limitations are often due to what I set up in my own mind, and that my life is ultimately going to equal the standards I set for myself: spiritually, physically, relationally, and financially.

I finally surrender to this truth, and real transformation begins.

It's been over twenty years since that fateful night falling off the bridge. Stephanie and I have now been married for twenty-three years, bearing the fruit of three amazing kids and a meaningful career filled with crusading, coaching, and influencing thousands of people to find the truth for their own life.

If this journey has taught me anything, it has taught me this: if you desire to become a master in the art of living, you must first master the man, or woman, in the mirror.

God Speed!

Jade Molina is a sought-after keynote speaker, educator, performance coach, host of the Men of Growth podcast, and author of the *4 Pillar Playbook*. Drawing from his twenty years of experience as a military veteran, entrepreneur, professional strength and fitness coach, youth leader, and pastor, Jade helps individuals and organizations move from where they are to where they want to be.

www.jademolina.com

Take a Trip That Will Change Your Life

Shantha Mony

It was a hot summer day in July as we rode down the narrow streets of Kampala, Uganda, to God Cares School. Smiling faces peered out of the classroom windows, waving at us as our bus pulled in through the school gates. We could feel their excitement, and I couldn't wait to get down and meet them. The minute we got off the bus, we were surrounded with hugs and smiles—what a great welcome!

The teachers and the children were overjoyed to meet us. They sang and performed for us. It was so moving to see their beautiful faces radiant with joy as they welcomed us into their hearts.

We watched them run across the field playing soccer with a patchwork of cardboard pieces formed in the shape of a ball. As they spotted the bag of soccer balls we had brought along with us, we could see their faces light up in excitement.

What impressed me most about these kids was the happiness and joy that they reflected. They had so little materially, but their faces were so radiant, and they were so happy. They had the love of Jesus and one another.

Some of them came from broken homes and others were abandoned by their parents. HIV and witchcraft are prevalent, and many of the children had come from homes impacted by one or the other. Some of the kids had no choice but to take care of their siblings while their single mother went to work. There were young girls who carried their young siblings on their backs and took care of them.

Our family has over the years sponsored children from different parts of the world, but I had never had the opportunity to visit them. I was so grateful for this opportunity to take this trip along with our church friends, where we could serve the children and the families of the people of Uganda. Preparing for the trip and getting the financial means to do so was no easy task. I thank all my friends and family who invested in helping these children. I thought that I was going to help these kids and make a difference in their lives; little did I know that I would be the one who returned changed and blessed.

One Sunday morning before church, I got to meet our Denise, a bubbly four-year-old. She ran into my arms when she saw me and was all smiles. I met her grandmother and her little brother; it was heartbreaking to hear her story. Her dad was not in the scene, and her mom had abandoned her along with her brother. Denise's grandmother lived in one of the slums, raising the kids and doing the best that she could for them. She was a regular member of the church and would make the long trek to church events and bring the kids along with her. Buyamba Orphanage stepped in to help and provide for these kids' basic needs.

I spent the morning with this grandmother and the kids, listening to their life stories. Denise is just one of the many kids that need our support.

Walking through the small village in Kampala, with an open drain running through the middle of the street, we made our way to the tiny one-room home of one of the students. The smell of the drain and the animals that were scurrying around was the living environment of the people there. Barefooted little children followed us as we made our way there, and when we arrived, we were met by the loving family that lived in the tin-roofed shack. In that tiny, single-room space lived four generations. We met the matriarch of the family and her granddaughter. She was thankful that her great-granddaughter was given the opportunity to attend school and receive love and support there.

Many of the young people who graduate from God Cares School have the opportunity to go on to university. That is only possible due to the generous sponsorships they receive from people like us. I met one of the young ladies who graduated and returned to work at the school; she wanted to make a difference in the lives of others.

God Cares School was founded by the late Pastor Bethuel and Dr. Florence Dongo, who are affectionately referred to as the "Father and Mother of Uganda." The school was started out of their passion for the orphaned and needy children in Uganda. Dr. Florence Dongo's mission is to provide for the physical care and needs of the children of Uganda, empowering them through education and discipleship to become contributing citizens who will impact Uganda for Christ. They also started Buyamba Orphan Outreach to provide love, care, and assistance to orphans and needy children whose parents were too sick or destitute to care for them. For information about how you can help, visit https://www.ugandabuyamba.com/.

I encourage all of you to take a trip once a year to a place that will make a difference in someone's life. There are many ways you can incorporate a portion of voluntourism into your family vacation, whether it's taking some school supplies to an orphanage or a school or visiting some of the local senior homes and showing them that someone cares. Sponsor a child and form a lasting relationship that will make a difference in both your lives. You never know what a great impact your small contribution will make.

Shantha Mony is the co-owner of Luxury Destinations Concierge. She works with individuals and organizations to create meaningful, memorable trips and includes a give back component to the trips. The company specializes in group travel such as family reunions, social groups, incentive groups, destination weddings, and seminars at sea. She is active in her church and the local community. Her company recently started a program to provide carry-on suitcases to local foster care organizations. This makes a huge difference in a child's life as most of the time, all they have is a pillowcase to hold their personal items.

www.luxurydestinationsconcierge.com

I'm an Artist? That's News to Me

Kari Murata

One of my best retreat weekends ever happened July 12–15, 2019. Yes, that's correct, because up until then, I never thought I was an artist. Going back several years to second grade, I remember my friend Joyce, who back then was my idea of an artist. The teacher would give us a squiggly line, and Joyce could make beautiful masterpieces. It is one of the earliest, limiting beliefs I remember adopting. I was not an artist, because I couldn't do what my friend could do. *Hmmph!*

As I grew, there were all sorts of art to dabble in. I did not even dare to try because, as I believed, I was not an artist. With this thought, I was unwilling and unable to create anything beautiful. Instead, I focused on systems that I did not perceive needed creativity (i.e., accounting, even waitressing).

Fast-forward to this past weekend with Terri Hardin! There are so many words to describe her, yet none do her justice. Terri is many, many wondrous descriptions. If you ever have a chance to talk to her (I much prefer listening, but . . .), by all means, grab it! This woman is one of God's best creations! One of those "give the shirt off her back" types who makes the world a better place to be. Even today, in total panic I texted her about writing a success story that came as a total surprise! This is an Exceptional Opportunity that was not to be passed up.

So here it is. I was given a slab of clay, and within a very short period of time, I sculpted a piece. It is a rendition of my dog, Boo! Those that know Boo say he looks scary and is cuter in person! That's OK! I learned this weekend that I am an Artist! I can create my art, whether a scary-looking pooch or a story for my readers here. It may not be perfect, because neither am I. My aim is becoming the best me I can be and keep moving forward! That's all I need to do. It's enough.

This story is for those people who may have made decisions that may have limited their beliefs in their abilities, so they may realize as I did this weekend, we just make another choice. Even if it's a small choice, it's a success!

Kari Murata has a successful track record starting and growing businesses. As she mentors those around her, she brings her unique style that inspires others both personally and professionally. Her systematic approach helps prepare others to launch their own businesses. She enjoys learning and is committed to helping others. Kari is focused on teaching and sharing Financial Literacy and providing solutions for families in California. Kari invests her spare time in personal development and learning. She is a Certified Approval Addiction Coach, Certified NLP Life Coach, and a Certified and Licensed BANKCODE Level 3 Trainer.

KariMurata@gmail.com

Pushing the Limits Ten Dollars at a Time

Lynn Murphy

The homeless veterans begin to line up outside the dining hall two hours before we open the monthly farmers market. Their ages span five decades. Their countries of service span the globe. Their physical disabilities are sometimes noticeable but often not. Their psychological disabilities are hidden, and hopefully healing. They're patient. They socialize with each other while they wait for us to set up. This is a remarkable group of men and women.

In addition to being here today, they have one thing in common—they all live in a complex that houses almost one hundred veterans who have no home of their own. They each have a clean, safe apartment with their own kitchen. They receive assessment, employment services, and long-term support to help them get back on their feet.

I don't know what these veterans have been through physically or emotionally before, during, or after their time in the service. I don't know what they're going through now, especially on the inside. And none of this makes a difference to me. These often forgotten individuals have served our country and deserve to be treated with dignity and respect.

Once a month, a group of volunteers through Diana Gregory Outreach Services bring each of these veterans ten dollars' worth of high-quality produce at no cost to the veterans. Individuals and organizations make this possible by donating the cost of a bag of healthy food for each veteran.

The closest grocery store is almost three miles away. Without transportation, the veterans find it more convenient, though less healthy and more expensive, to buy their meals at fast-food restaurants and convenience stores that are within walking distance. So when we arrive each month, they are pleased to have something fresh to add to their meals.

In the converted dining hall, volunteers fill the tables with bright yellow bins overflowing with colorful and delicious produce. Along with the produce, we offer them genuine smiles, handshakes, conversation, and sincere appreciation for their service to our country.

As I greet each one month after month, they respond in a variety of ways. Some politely acknowledge me. When I thank them for their service, some thank me for what we are doing. Some extend their hand for a warm handshake. Some chat and joke. Some ask for tips on picking out the best melon or ear of corn, or ask what in the world they could do with eggplant or kale. Others share their own cooking tips with us and each other. They all express appreciation for the produce. Ten dollars may not seem like a lot to many of us, but a bag full of fresh fruits and vegetables is a welcomed gift to them. It's something.

A secondary, mutual gift is the personal interaction. One older man in a wheelchair usually appears gloomy and annoyed. He hasn't engaged in conversation other than to comment on the worthiness of the produce. He pulls each bin to the edge of the table and examines the individual items to determine which is desirable and which is not. He pokes and prods and pulls apart leaves until something passes his rigorous inspection and he adds it to his bag.

Unexpectedly, last month he was cheerful and talkative. He shared stories about his early life, his nickname, and his service. He was smiling and seemed happy and engaged. I don't know what made the difference, but I do know the conversation brought me joy. I hope that continues for many more months.

We encourage the veterans to pick a variety of fruits and vegetables. While Idaho potatoes are a popular choice—tasty and easy to bake and eat—I promote apples or carrots or something green. I was surprised when I first heard one of the veterans say he couldn't eat apples because he has bad teeth. I started noticing many of the vets choose only the softer foods such as bananas, strawberries, and grapes, and I realized it is because they can't bite or chew easily. I was dismayed to learn they have limited dental care. Do *you* think about the health of your teeth when making food choices? Or do you take for granted your ability to bite and chew comfortably? Let's pass the word and encourage dentists and dental students to start a program to serve homeless veterans. That's another program that could change people's lives.

When everyone has chosen their food and we've packed those empty yellow bins back in the van, I feel contented and exhilarated, having connected with and served almost a hundred interesting people. It's only then I start to notice my sore feet, my filthy and broken fingernails, my aching muscles.

In their novel *The President Is Missing,* authors James Patterson and Bill Clinton penned these insightful lines for their character President Duncan:

> The familiar feeling passes through me, the sense that my ability to help people is both vast and limited at the same time. You learn to live with the paradox. If you don't, obsessing over the limits will keep you from making the most of what you can do. Meanwhile, you keep looking for chances to push the limits back, to do as much as you can for as many as you can, every day. Even on the bad days, there's always something good you can do.

Serving these veterans gives me a chance to do something vast and limited at the same time. I cherish this opportunity, especially on the bad days, because it lights me up. Whatever I do to help others, the person who receives the most benefit is me. This feeds my soul and inspires me to push the limits even farther.

For the veterans we serve, ten dollars worth of produce once a month may be a small thing. Or it may make a vast difference in their lives. Whichever it is to them, it's something.

There's always *something* you can do. What inspires you to give back and help others?

How can you use your talents and resources? What limits will you push against to help others? Whatever it is, don't wait. Do it now. Keep pushing as many limits as you can. You, too, will reap the benefits of what you give to others.

Lynn Murphy, MEd, a well-respected speaker, workshop leader, and leadership consultant, is passionate about helping organizations build high-performing leaders and teams. She designs and delivers engaging interactive workshops, seminars, and speeches on leadership, team building, customer service, conflict resolution, and communication. Audiences immediately connect with her vibrant energy and lively sense of humor. Her clients learn powerful techniques they can immediately use to crystalize their vision and goals, communicate more effectively, and achieve stronger and more satisfactory results. Implementing these techniques helps them accelerate their performance and productivity while increasing profits.

www.keyinnovative.com

BORN FOR SUCCESS

Christina Nepstad

I used to think success equaled fame and fortune, only obtainable for the RockStars of the world—the beautiful, talented, "special" people. It was what I craved, and I tried so hard to make it real in my mind. I wanted to be powerful, free to jet-set around the world, and stay in four-star hotels. I wanted to be confident, able to speak my mind without caring about what others thought. Seeing my name in lights would've made me feel important and being rich would've made me happy.

When I wasn't imagining such a life, I was feeling sorry for the one I had. I now know it made me who I am today, but back then it was a curse. As a young girl, I fell victim to the crippling effects of insecurity and anxiety. It wasn't unusual for me to ponder the ways in which I could end it all. My dad was angry and had an addiction to the drink (and I don't mean water). Consequently, we all suffered for it. As for me, I found my comfort in food. With a lack of focus, I quickly became a challenged student, labeled as below-average. My ultra-thick glasses and extra-large frame made me an easy target for bullies.

As I got older, I expressed myself by dropping out of college and changing the way I looked. Losing a significant amount of weight, exchanging my glasses for contacts, and turning my back on what was expected gave me a surge of unexpected confidence. Suddenly I had the potential to become someone the world would see as special. With stars in my eyes, I decided to roll the dice in the land of make-believe. After a few years of trying to "make it" as an actress, I realized I was awful.

On a whim, with nothing to lose, I entered a beauty pageant. I did well and decided to keep trying. Three years later, I was crowned Miss California USA. For the first time I felt important. I was starting to live the life I had always imagined. Soon after, I represented the state of California in the Miss USA pageant. To my own surprise, I had risen to the top ten. This meant I would stand with Dick Clark for a nationally televised interview—my biggest opportunity yet to prove myself as a RockStar.

With my name in lights, I had the opportunity to share inspiring insights through my interview response. My story could have helped young women realize that success isn't a privilege; it's a choice. It's not about what you look like, how rich you are, or how many fans you have. Every one of us is born for success. We all have opportunities to rock our lives and the lives of others if we choose. You can't chase success and expect to find it if you haven't defined it first. It might mean something different for each of us, but the secret to having it is understanding it.

Unfortunately, I hadn't yet discovered such life-changing truths. I was asked unique questions about how I lost weight and how I regained my self-confidence, but my actual interview lacked inspiration. Leading up to my interview, I was tied for first place with

Miss Texas, but I ended up finishing in ninth place. Any chance I had of winning Miss USA was gone.

Life has a funny way of teaching us. . . . At twenty-four years old, I finally started to question my definition of success.

I asked God for clarity, unsure if I would hear anything at all. But I did hear Him—in the still of night—assuring me that I was special and truly loved. He told me that the things of the world were fleeting, but His love for me was forever. These insights from God changed the way I felt about myself.

Soon after, I asked my friend, actress Esther Williams, how she became successful. Her profound response was that she traveled through life as a student. She told me to treat everyone as though they were a gift, because wisdom was within every person. I would need to gather the knowledge of others and put it to use! These insights from Esther changed the way I viewed others.

After meeting with Esther, I remembered one particular life lesson about success that I had overlooked. I had met with Bill Marriott before I went to Miss USA. His life-changing advice: Always remember that if you can inspire others to dream more, learn more, do more, and achieve more, you will become more. The recipe for real, lasting success had to include building others up and investing in their dreams. These insights from Bill, a true RockStar, changed the way I understood my role in success.

I spent so many years chasing the world's idea of success, but when I finally knew what it meant to me, I changed—and so did my life. I will forever be grateful for the insights I gained from God, Esther, and Bill about myself, others, and my role in success.

In life, our mess can become our message if we choose to learn from it. My message became the foundation for an interview and communication program I later developed called the Power Seat. Techniques and philosophies from the Power Seat have been recognized and utilized across the country in our nation's military, colleges, businesses, nonprofits, and the beauty industry to help people know how to influence personal and professional success.

The most rewarding part about my own success story has been watching RockStars emerge from the most unsuspecting people, once they redefine success for themselves.

Here's to your success!

———————————

As an author, motivational speaker, and interview coach, **Christina Nepstad's** purpose and mission to empower others for success has earned her nominations for Educator and Woman of the Year. In 2017, Christina and her revolutionary Power Seat program were featured in *Forbes*. She is the go-to coach to some of the world's most successful individuals and organizations, and is the Communications Expert and contributing writer for *Pageantry* magazine. Christina lives in Southern California with her husband and two children.

www.christinanepstad.com

From Zero to 50K

Rachelle Niemann

My running had always been intermittent at best. I would sign up for a race here and there to force myself to run. Sometimes I would train; most times I wouldn't. I would often end races in pain, barely able to walk. I knew this was no way to treat my body, but I couldn't seem to find the motivation to change. One year I established a new goal: to be in the best shape of my life physically, emotionally, and mentally. This was the beginning of my slow ascent to self-love. I *finally* realized that my health is my responsibility, and I must be the one to implement action into my daily life for transformation to occur.

After working toward healing old injuries, some physical but most mental and emotional, it was time to do something really challenging, so I signed up for my first 50k. I knew this was a big leap, but I had time, a plan, resources, and confidence. I was still afraid that I might fail, but I was not letting fear lead the way anymore. I chose confidence; I chose to believe in me. The following are lessons I learned from training for and running my first 50k race.

PERSPECTIVE CHANGES EVERYTHING. I have never felt like a runner, and I've never claimed to be a runner, but while training it finally occurred to me: I am a runner. This is no longer a hobby but a chosen lifestyle. There is no 'if' when I choose it to be. When a lifestyle is chosen, it becomes a priority and a new standard, and resistance to it fades away.

TRAIN FOR FUTURE CHALLENGES TODAY. I knew conditions on race day would be out of my control, so I embraced the difficulties while training, including training in inclement weather. I could only imagine how many unexpected challenges would come up during a thirty-one-mile run, so practicing responding to the challenges and remaining flexible in training created more resilience for further training and race day.

SOMETIMES THINGS ARE MEANT TO BE HARD. On one particularly hot and long training run, I tried to tell myself it was hard because I wasn't training well enough, but in my gut, I knew this wasn't true. During this training run, it occurred to me that this was actually hard. It takes guts, depth, discomfort, and heart to accomplish stretch goals. I was tired of blaming myself for being a problem. There was no problem—this was actually hard. This big goal was meant to be challenging. I must do hard things to experience the growth I want.

PERSEVERING THROUGH DISCOMFORT IS EMPOWERING. On many training runs, my mind would tell me to walk, to quit, to stop. It was so easy to forget about long-term goals as soon as it felt hard. My mind didn't want to push through the discomfort; it just wanted to stop. By pushing through these mind-driven pleas, I've learned that these are just old habits, the old me, my old limitations trying to keep me where it knows I'm safe and comfortable, but I am not my thoughts. When my mind would start this, I would shorten my goals. I would negotiate with my mind and create new goals: "Just make it to the corner" or even "Just take one more step." Then, when I hit that goal, I acknowledged it and immediately made a new goal, feeling empowered with each step and proving to my mind that I could push through the discomfort by accomplishing each smaller goal and continuing to the next. As this process played out and I kept going, my inspiration grew, and I remembered why I was out there pounding the pavement in these uncomfortable conditions day after day: to empower myself to go beyond my current self-limiting beliefs. To push through this adversity so I can be better prepared for what life throws at me in the future. To become stronger and extend my limits.

ALLOWING FOR FUN. I've always thought of running as a miserable task and something I only forced myself to do, but during this 50k training, I intentionally allowed space for fun. I had great fun on training runs and in races high-fiving trees, dancing down the sidewalk and trails, and leaping over curbs and tree roots. This made training much more enjoyable and desirable.

Going into the race weekend, I felt a lot of emotions: giddy, nervous, excited, prepared, and ready—but still unsure and afraid. I was mentally prepared for the race, and whatever happened I was willing to accept. I was excited about the journey it took to get there and the journey to come. Two years before running this 50k, I never imagined I could run farther than a half marathon. When I chose to do the work motivated by a larger goal, progressing to the next level was possible.

It took tens of thousands of steps to finish a 50k, and it took thousands of steps to build my confidence to know it was possible. It took me a lifetime to prepare for and a little over seven hours to complete. It was hot, sweaty, smelly, challenging, uncomfortable, and hard, but it was also empowering, liberating, and even a little bit fun. Running has been the most powerful tool I have used to move me beyond my perceived limits and empower myself. When I started running ten years ago, I was scared to run a mile. I really didn't think I could do it, but I got out there and took that first step to see if I could. It all starts with that one single step!

Rachelle Niemann, a wife, dog mom, ultra-marathoner, author, facilitator, adventure seeker, and a boundless student of life, is an Xchange facilitator who works with individuals, groups, communities, and organizations to choreograph meaningful conversations, create experiential learning environments, and transform cultures to enhance well-being of all associated parties. She is on a mission to inspire transformations from fear to love and compassion, and she wonders what might be possible if we shifted our focus to wellness over illness.

www.RachelleNiemann.com

LEADERSHIP ON FIRE

TK O'Geary

"What good is it to have a belly if there's no fire in it? Wake up, drink your passion, light a match, and get to work."
—*Simon Sinek*

When I least expected it, life dropped a fiery thought-bomb on my head. At dusk one November evening, I was in the office at work, talking to a woman in another state on the phone. I was interviewing her for a position on my team. As the director of the newly created Process Excellence Department, hiring staff was a priority. As we approached the end of the interview, I said, "Tell me about your favorite boss." Little did I know my life was about to take a turn.

After she shared stories about, and listed traits of, her favorite boss, she emphatically stated, "I would walk through fire for him! I would!" (He had recently retired). Staring at the phone, I felt her flame of passion burst through the handset. After we said goodbye, I stared at the phone and thought, *Wonder what it takes to be that kind of a leader? Wait! I want to BE that kind of leader.*

I set out on a quest to learn how to be the leader that creates a fire of passion and fierce loyalty that team members would be willing to walk through fire for. Yes: Walk. Through. Fire. That meant reading leadership books, listening to experts, finding other walk-through-fire-for-their-leader people and asking what their leader did to inspire that feeling, and talking to leaders whose team WOULD walk through fire for them. I learned three powerful Cs to being THAT kind of leader: Connect, Conduct, Congratulate.

Connect

A leader must connect with the team, let the team know they are important, and connect the team to the vision and to each other.

1. Start at the end.
Answer, "What do we want to accomplish?"

2. Strike out "I need . . ."
Replace with "You need . . ." Tell them "Why."

3. Understand each other.
Synergy comes through understanding each other. Teamwork takes work; it's worth it.

Conduct

A leader must conduct the team (think orchestra) to enable peak operations, whether it is completing a project, processing work, or creating something new.

4. FOCUS: Follow One Commitment Until Success*
Show how to know you are on track.

5. Try-Storm
Take action. Don't wait for perfection. Learn from your actions.

6. R2A2
Clear roles, responsibilities, accountabilities, and authority promote productivity.

Celebrate

A leader must celebrate team achievements, mentor and challenge the team, and promote an engaged and fun environment.

7. Appreciate the team.
Appreciation has an expiration date. According to Gallup press, a leader must show appreciation and praise (authentically) at least every seven days.

8. Share your knowledge.
Mentor. Teach. Challenge others.

9. Make it fun.
Goofy prizes. Celebrations. Team lunches.

All nine are important. A few have a staggering effect. *Understand each other*, #3, can help a broken team unite and help a good team become great. How? By understanding that we are all different and that we are not out to get under the skin of our teammates. Thanks to an incredible boss who used the Myers-Briggs personality index to lead us, I found this tool helpful as a leader and when providing consulting services to a customer.

Myers-Briggs is just one of many good tools that can help (e.g., DISC, The Birds, etc.). How did this help me? While leading a multi-state contract with site offices, there was some friction going on in one of the offices. An extremely productive team member and the solid performing site manager were not connecting—not even a hello in the morning or a goodbye in the evening. There were other team pair friction points too. I went out for a site visit. We had a potluck and talked about people's Myers-Briggs types.

There were some cautious comments as we spoke. When we got to "Are you a planner, or an 'in-the-moment' person," the ice REALLY started melting. By discussing the

---

*Christina Gillick's variation of "Follow One Course Until Success" (author unknown)

natural tendencies—e.g., strong planners often focus on creating plans and tightly monitor deadlines, while strong in-the-moment thinkers may not even engage in planning thoughts until later—people saw where friction occurred.

This discussion brought out comments, such as "I thought they were trying to get under my skin!" When I brought up the humorous items (Star Wars characters by their Myers-Briggs type and Myers-Briggs "prayers"), the ice melted. Soon the site was a more enjoyable place to work, complete with hellos and goodbyes.

Couple #4, FOCUS, with #6, R2A2, and you have a powerhouse effect. As a leader, you are responsible to make sure everyone knows their role on the team and their responsibilities in that role. People also need to know what they are accountable for accomplishing and what authority goes with the role. This is what leadership expert Jim Collins identifies as knowing if you are in the "right seat on the bus."

Did all this work? YES!

While I've enjoyed many large successes, there have been some heart-tugging successes too. One day, after learning and incorporating the three powerful Cs, a woman on the team stopped by my office. Her skill at designing information technology systems? Superb! Her comfort level at interacting with people in general? Not so much. Speaking to an audience? Never going to happen.

I led a work project that required oral presentations. Ideally, we needed key people on the presentation team. She was key, but her fear of speaking was so overwhelmingly high that she got sick just thinking about it.

One day, she stood hesitantly at the door frame. Her face white, she shakily said, "If YOU are willing to work with me, I'll be part of the presentation team." Wow! That was her version walking through the fire—an intense, flaming, heat-producing, raging fire of fear.

Connect. Conduct. Celebrate.

That's how leaders fire up their teams, so they can walk through fire.

TK O'Geary is a sought-after and award-winning consultant, analyst specializing in understanding customers, and creator of the Make Your Vision Stick© system. TK's passions include youth education, especially in STEM and leadership. This passion spurred her to serve on STEM-related boards. TK also mentors young leaders and coaches TEDx speakers. TK advises and consults with organizations and leaders around the world on strategic planning, leadership, communications, improving the human side of process, and understanding customers. Known as The Geek Who Can Speak, she is dedicated to helping people bring a voice to their talents and vision.

www.TKOGeary.com

GRATITUDE: OUR SUCCESS IS NOT ENTIRELY OUR OWN

Ivano Ongaro

As I reflect on the successes in my life, I recognize that although I put in a great effort, there were others who helped me get there, and those persons should be recognized. It is important to realize that success for most people is a team effort.

Our family emigrated to Canada when I was six years old. It was a great sacrifice for my parents to leave behind family and friends to provide a better opportunity for the family and me. Things were tough in post-war northern Italy, and my parents were not well educated. My father had the equivalent of a grade-nine education and had to learn a trade to help support his family. My mother also is one of these exceptional people. She did not attend school because she was needed at home to help with the farm chores and look after her siblings while her parents worked the farm. As her younger siblings went to school, she taught herself to read and write by learning from her younger siblings and copying their lessons in her spare time. My parents placed a high value on education and learning and always encouraged me to try my best in school. I started grade one in Italy, but we moved before the end of the year, and since I could not speak a word of English, I started grade one in Canada. I tried my best and managed to plod along with mediocre grades.

Things changed in grade eight. I was transferred to another school due to overcrowding at my school. My new teacher was a feisty redhead of Irish origin and accent. She had a totally different attitude and expectation for work and study. Perhaps she recognized that I was performing below my capabilities. The first thing she addressed was my penmanship. (I was naturally left-handed and had been forced to write right-handed, with nearly illegible writing as a consequence.) Her solution, after unsuccessful attempts to improve writing, was to stick with printing. This made my written work legible, and we moved forward. This small success lead to others, and by year's end all my grades improved from mediocre to excellent.

When I returned to the old school, the new habits and attitude came with me, and I had another successful year. The new plan was to enter the matriculation program in high school and go to university and become a teacher. I worked diligently in high school and continued to get good grades. My biology teacher, recognizing my talents in the biological sciences and my somewhat rebellious attitude toward authority, suggested that becoming a dentist might be a better career choice. This would mean even more competitive grades, and in our talks, he indicated that he believed that I had the capability to succeed if I continued to apply myself to my studies. I had to study very diligently to achieve my grades, while some of my colleagues could party and have time for sport and still frequently beat me on exams. It left me with certain doubts.

190

In university, the study habits that I developed worked well, although the first year was tough. Several of my friends from high school had to drop out as the high school lifestyle didn't make the grade. I had to take speed-reading courses to be able to study sufficiently to make the grade. PreDent/PreMed programs are highly competitive programs, and at the time class sizes of 350 or more were not uncommon. As I was unsuccessful on my first application, I reapplied and in midsummer got a notice that I was on the alternate list of (fifty applicants) and that any drop outs would be filled from the alternate list. In late August I got notice that I had been accepted into the Class of '78 starting on September 1.

Dental school was the right choice for me, and it was a surprise to everyone when— having gotten in as the fiftieth of fifty students—my grades put me in the top few students in the class. I attribute good grades to learning how to organize knowledge from one of my classmates. Without that, I would still probably know as much but would not have done as well on exams. We had many excellent instructors in the dental program, and one in particular encouraged me to consider specialty training, which reinforces the recognition of success and fosters the confidence.

After several years in private practice, I found it necessary to further expand my knowledge and decided to get a master's degree. I encountered a former professor that agreed to be a mentor, and with his diligent care and attention, I was successful in completing the degree.

The burden of our success is partly carried by others, and in my case my wife carried the extra burden of caring for our children and managing the household while I took two days per week and countless evenings doing my research and writing. Without her caring encouragement and love, this would not have been completed.

Following the completion of my master's of science in Oral Biology, I had the opportunity to teach at the University of Alberta Dental School, eventually as a full-time clinical instructor. I recognized a need for certain changes in the existing curriculum, researched what changes were needed and how to implement them, and got approval from the requisite committees to implement the changes. The heavy lifting was done by the teaching team. Recognition from my peers and students, in the form of a national teaching award was an unexpected and pleasant surprise.

As I think back on all my other successes, I realize that at almost every critical junction, there was someone who had a positive influence on the outcome. I believe it is important to recognize the importance of these people in our lives and take the time to recognize them and thank them.

Ivano Ongaro BSc, DDD, MSc, now retired from his forty-year career of dental practice and teaching at the dental school, is pursuing his passion for creative expression through sculpture. Ivano has lived a life of service to his community with passion that has earned him the love and respect of his patients as well as teaching awards. He has an insatiable curiosity and passion for art and science and has striven for excellence in all of his endeavors. Ivano and Marlene are celebrating their forty-first wedding anniversary. They have three grown children, Aurora, Orion, and Aaron, one grandson, and three granddaughters.

www.OngaroSculpture.com

The Secret to Business Success

George Partsalidis

Yes, I admit it! I am addicted to anything that has to do with personal development. I love learning about the tremendous potential we humans possess. I have been on the journey of self-discovery for decades. It has been a rewarding path full of excitement and life-changing experiences.

That's why, a couple of weeks ago, as soon as I found out that Tony Robbins' Unleash the Power Within, "the firewalk seminar," was coming up in Dallas, Texas, I bought the ticket and booked my hotel right away. I had taken the seminar before; I did walk on fire, and I couldn't wait to do it again. I also thought that would be a great place to write my chapter for the *RockStars* book.

Of course the seminar was fantastic. As always, Anthony Robbins gave nothing but his best to deliver an extraordinary seminar in front of over 8,000 people. I experienced his passion for what he does one more time. And the appreciation and love the audience had for him was mind blowing. Being in that atmosphere of perfectly chaotic, but harmoniously creative, constructive, revolutionary environment, covered by screams, laughter, dreams, hopes, believe and trust, I too surrendered and became one with the collective consciousness that empowers us to break through limited beliefs and old destructive habits and to see our true potential that builds new pathways and core beliefs so we can shape our future and make goals and dreams reality—and the impossible, possible.

Even though it was my second time attending the event, there was an abundance of new information and experiences, even at a deep personal level, that marked the event forever in my heart. For any UPW attendees, Yes! Yes! Yes! You know what I mean: Now You Are the Voice! . . . Step Up! Step Up!

There I realized that Tony and I share the same reasons for being successful in our business!

Coming back to Toronto, I reflected on the reason that my business has been successful. It has to do with the love and respect I have for my customers. I service them with sincerity and passion. With me, offering great service goes back when I was working in the food industry. In the restaurant business, you experience the value of service instantly, as you work so closely with the customers and interact with them all day long.

When it comes to retail sales, it becomes a lot harder for many people to maintain a high level of service and truly focus on their customer's needs. I thought I would never get into sales. I had the perception that to be a salesperson, one definitely had to be a liar or a thief! Most sales books I had read and much of the training I had attended talked about how to overvalue your product, how to up-sell your customer, and how to close the deal. Once I started my floorcovering and window covering business, I did not follow that school of thought. I did not follow any book. Actually, I threw the books away!

My approach was to treat my customer as I would like to be treated, as I would treat my best friend, and as I would treat my brother.

For over twenty-three years, my team and I focused on understanding the needs of the customer, finding the right product that fulfills those needs, and making sure they are totally satisfied at the end.

But that was not easy, especially in the beginning! Things would go wrong sometimes either because the product was defective or because of the installation or other reasons outside of our control. But no matter what, we would always make sure that we would rectify everything a soon as possible.

Of course, we have had customers that we could not please. Even though everything was done right, they would find reasons to be unsatisfied and complain. And no matter what we would do to help them and even redo the whole job perfectly, they were still unsatisfied and kept complaining. I realized that some people are happier when they're miserable; they just are so used to that state. They have the need to complain as they believe that nothing goes right in their life.

Slowly but steadily through the years, our attention to detail and the customer service experience we offered helped our business grow— mostly through referrals and word of mouth. And that is even more important now at the age where social media channels dominate everybody's smartphone and everyone's life. To start a successful business, among many other things you will need:

- Capital
- Planning (your business map)
- Networking skills
- Marketing and advertising
- Product knowledge
- Clear understanding of your industry
- A purpose and meaning for your business

But most importantly, the Secret to Business Success is to:

- Truly care about your customers.
- Always service them with sincerity and passion.
- Be obsessed with customer service.

Then you will create not just satisfied customers, but raving fans!

In his book *The Celestine Prophecy,* James Redfield mentions that one should look at one's business as a place where souls gather! Taking this approach gives a totally different meaning to the word *service*. It gives your business a higher purpose.

I wish everyone reading this chapter success in their business endeavors. Remember, what you put in, you will get back tenfold.

Meet you at the top—or as Zig Ziglar said, OVER THE TOP!

George Partsalidis lives happily with his family in Toronto, Canada. He is a successful entrepreneur, realtor, and still owns his award-winning flooring and window covering business, Kingsway Carpets & Blinds. His goal is to teach his children by example to love life, conquer their fears, and create their dreams.

www.GeorgePartsalidis.com

WELCOME TO FINISHING SCHOOL

Roberta Perry

Welcome to finishing school . . . which is really the end of the story, so let's start at the beginning. All good stories have a start, and this is mine.

It happened that on a cloudy Seattle day the "steaks were high" (pun) when I got my foot in the door at Stuart Anderson's Steak Restaurants. My goal was some lofty rung on the corporate ladder, and I had high hopes. Months later, as a secretary for the entertainment director, I was getting nowhere. Where was the first rung and how was I going to climb it? Meanwhile I was being schooled, in a more or less humorous way, by some of my female coworkers. "You can't wear nylons with support toes." "No slacks in the office for us women." "Where did you get that mini-skirt outfit?"

I wish I could say that a lightbulb went off, but in fact I was finally embarrassed enough to enroll in a nine-week John Robert Powers Modeling Agency etiquette class for businesswomen. Every week for nine weeks, I had to wear a different outfit from my closet to show my style. And every week I flunked and had to walk the proverbial plank in front of the others. It was like failing recess. Did I even have a personal style?

What I desperately needed was a mentor, and during week nine, I found one. Sheila was our hairstylist consultant. She said, "Get $500 together—we're going shopping." It was the shopping trip that changed my future. I went into the dressing room looking like a college grad wannabe and walked out looking every bit the executive. An exquisitely tailored navy-blue suit, two blouses, pumps, and a London Fog raincoat. To my surprise, the outfit was commanding, not stuffy. Following John T. Malloy's advice in his bestselling book Dress for Success, I decided then and there to dress as though I already had the job. Then I started watching not only my boss but my boss' boss—his clothes, his attitude when he walked into a room, his gestures and deportment, his general personal presentation. And from that I awoke to a broader awareness. It all boiled down to one word: impact. He was creating an impact without saying a thing, opening a door to eventual success before the first word was spoken.

By now I was on the right track. There was so much more behind success in business than a "de facto dress code."

In time I worked out two simple rules that enable the chance of success when dealing with people in any business setting:

1.   If you're presenting to Coca Cola, don't go in wearing Pepsi "blue and red."
2.   Act like you mean it—and mean it!

Naturally, the key to my own success along this line was working out—at the detail level—my own presentation in any and all types of business relations (and may I point out here that you can remove the word business from this sentence and expand your success in all areas of life).

What was the image I wanted to communicate visually as well as verbally? What did I want to project in that critical three seconds after I entered a room or shook a hand or smiled hello to someone? Was I nervous or feeling pressured? Was I asking in my style and manner for a license to survive? Or was I creating the impact that would generate the exact response I wanted? I listed dozens of scenarios and created appropriate personal presentation factors for each one. I started defining the exact impact I wanted to make in business situations and then owning the level of personal commitment and action necessary to achieve that impact. It's a process that continues to this day.

If you get the two rules above dialed in and fine-tuned for yourself, what is possible? For me it was the "ten-minute, multimillion-dollar deal." Early in the 2000s I was working with an international entertainment investment company based in Los Angeles. A Tennessee client wanted to discuss particulars and arranged to fly us to their offices for a meeting. On the scheduled day we got together promptly at 9:00 a.m., and within ten minutes they had agreed to the terms previously outlined and we immediately signed a letter of intent. Later in the evening we were all having dinner, and I asked the female senior executive how she had come to the decision so readily. I will never forget her response: "It was easy. You walked in wearing a Chanel suit and Ferragamo shoes and carrying a Gucci briefcase. And your partner was dressed in the same high-end style. Both of you had a positive air of success! I knew then you were successful and exactly what we wanted."

A great philosopher once said that life is art. Some women are born works of art with style and grace. Not me. I had to learn to pick up a brush and paint my own way to Tiffany's and diamond stud earrings. So take a minute here for yourself. Try this little drill. On a piece of paper, describe your own personal presentation. Does it say executive? Or temp worker? What is your attitude? Does it create an effect even before you say anything? And make sure it creates the appropriate impact; you could wear jeans with shredded knees, but is that for a barbecue fest or the boardroom?

Have a good time with this . . . and "WELCOME to FINISHING SCHOOL"!

Roberta Perry is the senior vice-president of Edwards Technologies, Inc., and president of Roberta Perry & Associates. She has served as chairman of the Nightclub and Bar Association; was president of the Themed Entertainment Association; sat on the Seattle Fair Campaign and Practices Commission; has been the international board director for Toastmasters International; and currently serves on the board for Lawrence Anthony's Earth Organization.

WHY NOT CHOOSE LIFE?

Cinda Roffman, C.Ht.

My heart was beating very fast as I got on the freeway to go to work. I'd been having breakfast with a friend and was telling her about my daughter's upcoming wedding when my heart started to race. *No problem*, I thought, *I'll just go about my day, and it will get better.* It did not. After about four miles, I decided that it would be wise to go to the ER at our local hospital. It took me about fifteen minutes to get there. I calmly parked the car and walked in.

The intake nurse said my heart was beating at 230 beats per minute (normal is between 60 and 100). They took me right in to a treatment room—no waiting for heart problems. My diagnosis was Supraventricular Tachycardia or SVT. The treatment is to stop the heart and hope that it resumes beating on its own at a regular rate. It worked, but I had several more episodes of SVT, including one where I passed out as I was being wheeled into the ER.

I went to a cardiologist who prescribed a drug to control SVT. I did not tolerate the drug well. I felt like I was underwater, and everything I was doing took incredible effort. I did not want to live my life like that. I looked for an alternative and learned they could ablate (burn) the heart where it was misfiring, and that would prevent it from happening again. It took three procedures, but I finally was cured. Some people might have stayed on the drug, but I wanted a cure that would let me live the rest of my life as a healthy person. Why not?

I found it ironic that my heart was the part of my body that had a problem. My parents did not tell me they loved me until I was an older adult and I told them first. My mother's reaction when I told her I loved her was to say, "Of course, I love you too." (She just hadn't bothered to say it for forty-five years.) Hugging and sharing emotions were not part of their culture. Alcohol, however, was. My father was an alcoholic, and my mother had an undiagnosed bipolar disorder that she self-treated with alcohol.

By day, they were conservative, upstanding, high school teachers. By night they were serious drinkers. Every night they drank cheap red wine from a gallon jug under the sink poured into water glasses. That's how they drank their bourbon, too—in a water glass over ice. I grew up believing this was normal, but there were a few things that were different. I was never allowed to have friends over for dinner or for a sleepover—that would interfere with their drinking. I was never allowed to talk about what went on in the evenings. It was a shameful secret.

Sometimes I tried to talk to them about their drinking, but these conversations always escalated into arguments. One time I got so mad that I poured all the alcohol I could find down the sink. My parents were really angry! I know now that they did the best they could. I don't think they realized the negative effect their drinking had on me. My mother was very cold and distant. My father was a little more caring, but he followed my mother's lead in most things.

As soon as possible, I went away to college and never lived at home again. I was ashamed of my parents. Nobody listened to me, and I felt that no one cared about what happened to me. None of my relatives or friends of our family offered to help. A sympathetic ear from an adult, any adult, would have been welcome. I have to believe that some of their family and friends knew what was happening at our house. I was ready and determined to choose a different life. Why not?

I found a partner who is kind, caring and protective. We consciously choose to create a warm and caring home that does not revolve around alcohol. We tell each other and our three children on a daily basis, "I love you." Many years later, after a family intervention, my parents stopped drinking, and we were able to develop a better relationship.

When my youngest child was about to graduate from high school, I started back to school. I completed the two-year Wagner Program in Human Services Paraprofessional Training to learn about counseling and how to listen to people and their problems and concerns. Wanting to find a way to combine my life experiences and my education, I explored hypnotherapy, enrolled at the Hypnosis Motivation Institute, graduated in 2008, and opened my practice.

I became a hypnotherapist so that no one else will have to feel ashamed of whatever is happening in their lives; everyone will have someone to listen—really listen to them—and no one will feel that no one cares about them. I give each client my undivided attention, helping them to know they are heard. From my negative upbringing and medical problems, I have learned to embrace life. I share that each day with my family, my friends, and my clients.

Every day we all have choices to make. When we get up in the morning, what will be our attitude? Will we expect rain? Will we expect sunshine? What has happened to us in our lives affects our view each day. We have the option of choosing our focus. I could have focused on my difficult childhood and my medical problems. Instead I chose to see how I could help others. Why not choose life?

———————————

Cinda Roffman is a certified hypnotherapist trained in Therapeutic Guided Imagery, Neuro-Linguistic Programming (NLP), Weight Management, Emotional Freedom Technique (EFT), Smoking Cessation, Sports Performance, and more. She uses her gifts, wisdom, training, and life experience in a heartfelt manner, creating an individualized experience for each client, helping them to make desired changes in their lives. A published author, many of her clients use her book *The Power in Affirmations: A Hypnotherapy-Guided Affirmations Journal for Personal Transformation* to record and reinforce their personalized affirmations. Cinda has offices in Westlake Village and Tarzana, California. She is available for distance sessions worldwide.

www.cindaroffman.com

POWER OF WISDOM

Cali T. Rossen

How wise are we about the effects our thoughts have in our lives? While ruminating on that question, overwhelming waves of emotion surge through my body, bringing them to the surface. A heap of memories crest and begin flooding my mind. The trappings of those thoughts and words were so powerful. Now the acknowledgement of how they shaped my life washes over me. I observe how thoughts and words quite literally hold the power to create and destroy. Creating appreciative, cheerful, and benevolent thoughts and words are welcome, but when one's thoughts and words are intended to destroy the bright spirit of another—that is heartless.

Watch your thoughts for they become words,
watch your words for they become actions,
watch your actions, for they become habits,
watch your habits for they become your character,
watch your character for it becomes your destiny.
—Ralph Waldo Emerson

Can you remember a specific time when you experienced being profoundly valued, loved, and adored? YOU ARE valued, loved, and adored, aren't you? Our first experience of being valued and loved happens most often than not *before* learning the language of words.

As infants we instinctively recognize the language of energy. As tiny tots we reach out through body language, sound, and spirit. Thought is energy connected to our feelings. Feelings mirror our thoughts in any given situation, which is something we innately have in common. We establish images, letters, words, language, and things. As language is learned, it is joined with our innate energy, and a dynamic creation happens. High energy words raise our health as well as the health of those around us, and the opposite may be created too.

Next, I'm going to expose how a pattern of thoughts were created in my life and the words that I formulated, what unfolded to become my fate, and how this vicious cycle ended so I could manifest the incredible destiny that is unfolding. The outcome of these invalidating words that sabotaged my world for years began as a toddler when words had just begun to connect neurologically to meanings, images, and language. I lived with my high-spirited mom after my parents divorced, and when my father showed up for visits, he was routinely in a drunken state. At these moments I sensed extreme unease, dread, and even panic exude from my mother. In the course of this experience, I was energetically pained with an inner icky feeling and constructed the words: "Something is wrong."

Meanwhile I was being treated for a series of grand mal seizures, but I have no recollection of the seizures. I vividly recall a number of EEGs with gooey sticky electrodes pressed against my scalp, then left alone in a dark room. A young child left alone in an unknown dark room is going to have brain impulses off the chart! Because of this undertaking these words began to take shape: "Something is wrong . . . with me."

On my first day back at school after the summer break, I sat gazing out the door of the classroom wondering why my classmates from kindergarten were walking up the hall into a different room. Then I was told, "You've been held back," and I begin to slowly come to terms with: "Something is definitely wrong with me to be held back." These words became solid in my thinking. After that point, my grades were consistently low over the coming years in the Massachusetts school district.

Fast-forward to my teens. My mom married the best dad ever, and we move to Texas. It's my first week in the new school, and I'm about to finish up a meeting with Mrs. Wheeler, Dean of Girls. Before I head out the door to my next class, she stands up and points directly at me, declaring, "You're going to be somebody one day—I just know it!" The potential of her words repositioned my entire future. My grades swung around in a flash, and for the rest of my high school years, I was on the honor roll. My top grades garnered me an audition for the school dance troupe, I was selected, and I performed at halftime shows. In college I graduated magna cum laude and became a member of the Phi Theta Kappa International Honor Society.

Since childhood, performing has always been a love of mine. Guitar improvisation and singing for my mom's entertainment is an endearing memory I cherish. Over the years I performed in talent shows, commercials, and musicals, and when the chance to move to Hollywood presented itself, I took it. I'm immensely grateful for the incredible opportunities that came from taking that chance; from being cast in roles opposite award-winning talent, learning to produce, edit, and write songs to becoming Ms. North Hollywood Elite, a bestselling author, an Ambassador for Save the Children of Tibet, and holding hands with His Holiness the Dali Lama on Earth Day.

Challenges happen, especially when least expected. When they do, how will I pick myself up after I fail, feel like a loser, or act like a complete fool? I will prompt myself to think of a positive thought. The Power of Wisdom can shape and alter our life in miraculous ways. Beyond any doubt, thoughts become words, and words become actions, and ultimately come to light.

I'd like to add that "you can be anything you want" were *a*mong my mom's last words to me before passing June 14, 2019. Like her, I want to be loving, optimistic, generous, grateful, forgiving, joyful, creative, discerning, true, and successful. Success is vast, its meaning different for each of us. Success to me is creating what I want, discovering and increasing my strengths, and letting go of discord and unkind thoughts.

What are your most recurring thoughts? What do you speak about most? Is it empowering? *POW!* Align your thought seeds with what you want, and as you plant your word seeds, watch what flourishes and then tune accordingly! *I Love You XO*

Cali T. Rossen is a bestselling author, keynote speaker, and Rock Fashion Art docu-series creator. *"First, and foremost, she is an Artist, but with a capital A. As an actress, singer, fashion model, painter, she is on a roll now having won the title Ms. North Hollywood among a formidable group of stunning contestants. I should know. I was there. She was born to play an extensive range of roles from the femme fatale, the sensual seductress, the sweet mom, the lost soul, not to mention the neurotic wife. The role has not been written that could contain her talents"* (James Metropole).

www.ThePowGirl.com

Hey You, Life Is Calling: Chasing Happiness from Mediocrity to Extraordinary

Nicole Russell

Have you ever been called eccentric, "the artist," a rebel, or colorful? Those descriptive words are often used for those of us who've deviated from one of many life scripts. Life script example:

> Go to school. Get a good job. Have kids. Take care of family.
> Save for retirement. Travel. Die.
> —Life Scriptwriter 101

People generally navigate life in linear fashion. We'll call them "linears." For the most part, "linears" love and want the best for you, but they just don't understand us "eccentrics" very well. In their favor, the sample life script is actually a very honorable and promising path to follow. It's worked repeatedly. But like any script, deviations and challenges are inevitable, while your right to happiness and total fulfillment looms. And those on the sidelines are waiting to say, "I told you that wouldn't work. You should've stuck to the script."

The problem: Pre-written, generic scripts aren't for eccentrics.

It doesn't mean reinventing blue jeans, either. It means that it's our duty to harness what others may not understand as our greatest strengths and powers. Strength and power to stand proud, be boldly you. Strength and power to feel, love, and be free. To guide. To be a mover and shaker. To command acceptance and equality. To explore the limitless opportunities that divine life vividly offers. To contribute to the world your ever-so-colorful gifts. To be "Extraordinarily Happy."

During childhood we've all been asked the same question: "What do you want to be when you grow up?" I've always admired those with single, definitive answers, the one thing that drives their life's purpose and focus their efforts. My answer was, "I want to be a doctor, lawyer, model, artist, fashion designer, dancer, actress, and entrepreneur." I still remember having that conversation in the back of my mom's yellow Chevrolet Citation with my childhood friend. My answer was honest. I believed I could do it all.

Although it may be difficult for some to take me seriously in my blue unitard with stirrups, light pink mini-skirt, paint-splattered sweatshirt, leg warmers, and pink high-top Converse® sneakers, my parents were always supportive. Maybe it was the good grades, spelling bee trophies, or their love. Albeit, I was destined for major ad-lib from the linear script; however, I hadn't studied the art of improv nor scriptwriting. Would I ever find my way?

As an adult, I entered several entrepreneurial races. Entrepreneurship always topped my career list and I pursued it emphatically. Winning this race would mean everything. The prize for first place was Happiness, but it was elusive. So the chase was on.

In Grasp: The $300,000 note-brokering deal

What happened: My trainer stole the deal, separated from the company, and then bought a house in another state.

Place: Dead last

That loss was a spirit-breaker. It meant it was back to the workplace to pay the bills. In hindsight, it was the start of understanding my power—the power to learn and quickly find hidden gems that were desirable enough to steal. It was my first taste of what happens when you veer from the script.

In Grasp: Major book publishing deal

What happened: Told my story on a major TV show, shared my book, was offered a publishing deal, turned it down to self-publish

Place: Fourth

Writers are cringing at this moment because publishing deals are minimal. I was naive and desired to keep creative control. Successes: 1) secured self-love; 2) major entity acknowledgment; and 3) follow-through. Nevertheless, it wasn't on bookshelves across America.

In Grasp: Success in the traditional workplace

What happened: Achieved success at every level from entry to executive

Place: Third

While hierarchically successful, I chased happiness most often here. Mediocre at best, some of my darkest moments loomed. "Why am I here?" The traditional workplace was life's placeholder when entrepreneurship wasn't flourishing. The emphatic pursuit of meaningful work eluded me. Always out of necessity. Salary dependency. Someone's view of my worth. The limitations. The influx of *linears* chanting all the reasons I should stay.

Getting a better grasp on the concept of happiness opened the window to win the desk job game.

In Grasp: Success in entrepreneurship

What happened: Created a forward-thinking plan, executed it, fought through apprehension, and became the number-one most-innovative custom roller skate company in the world.

Place: Second

There's a lot more in store along with new business deals. Creating something from scratch and watching it grow is nothing short of spectacular. Resolving the impossible is tremendously gratifying. Extraordinarily happy arrives repeatedly, but it's short-term.

In Grasp: Happiness
What happened: The moment when I finally heard, "Hey You, Life Is Calling!"
Place: First

I'd been chasing the wrong script!

The moment I knew how to harness the power of who I truly am was the moment I learned I was happy with each achievement.

Achieve even the most mundane tasks extraordinarily. How do you answer the phone? Deliver a package? Embrace the presence of children? Embrace the wisdom of seniors? Embrace how you make people feel when assisting with any nugget in their life.

New script:

> *Learn and give your best positive self. Do it BIG. Live. Grow. Happily, fulfill.*
> *Repeat. Your gift to the world matters!*
> *—Nicole Russell*

I am an eccentric who loves making those around me feel important. I live extraordinarily happy when I try new things and move from achievement to achievement with no apologies. Now I'm taking those achievements to the highest levels by helping others on a larger scale. I love life and take time to feel and enjoy every moment. My gift to the world matters.

I am happy. And now I'm unstoppable.

The Top Secret: **"That Moment Is Always Where You Are Right Now."** That's when you know that where you are right now is the right place to be—the right place to start—the right place to grow—the right place to be extraordinarily happy.

What's your extraordinary? Life called; did you answer?

Nicole Russell, MBA, is the co-founder and chief strategist for SK8 Fanatics, a custom roller skate and lifestyle company. SK8 Fanatics has been featured across the world including in the *New York Times, Vanity Fair, Barcelona, Spectrum News,* HBO via the documentary *United Skates,* music videos, branding campaigns, celebrities, and skate celebrities. Having developed Cali-Slide, a four-day annual skate event hosting two thousand skaters from over fifteen states, Nicole is sought after to develop industry movement events and idea-moving campaigns. Her upcoming projects include the soon-to-be bestseller *Your Amazing Itty Bitty® Guide to Winning the Desk Job Game* and the campaign America's Idea-to-Action Pledge.

www.nicolesumbrella.com

THINGS DON'T ALWAYS GO AS PLANNED . . . AND THAT'S A GREAT THING

Scott Schneider

Do you remember as a kid how you answered the question: "What do you want to be when you grow up?"

For me, from the time I was seven years old, the answer was "a doctor." That answer got refined a bit at nine years old when, on December 3, 1967, Dr. Christiaan Barnard performed the first successful human heart transplant. A couple of weeks later while in the grocery store checkout line, Dr. Barnard, a nurse, and the recent organ recipient were smiling at me from the cover of Life magazine, enticing me to read about their fantastic story. I decided to spend the princely sum of thirty-five cents to purchase a copy of the magazine, and I read and reread their account many times over. That event clinched it for me—when I grew up, I was still going to be a doctor, only now I was going to be a thoracic surgeon.

For the next eight years, the topic of school projects and papers was the human heart. I learned about the four chambers of the heart: their function and physiology, the major blood vessels and valves, and the effects of smoking, lack of exercise, injury, disease, and cholesterol. My childhood occurred during the Apollo space program, and while most boys my age had Revell models of the mighty Saturn V rocket or the Apollo command module gracing their bedrooms, my dresser displayed the Invisible Man—a see-through anatomic model of the human body showing the skeleton and organs . . . and a break-away model of the human heart.

I was also involved in the Boy Scouts, where I made the motto "Be Prepared" my mantra (and yes, learning how to tie knots was probably a good skill for a surgeon to acquire). Throughout junior high school and high school, I took the tough courses—algebra, calculus, biology, physics, chemistry—that would prepare me for my vocation and courses such as Spanish and German that would qualify me to meet the requirements of university-level institutions. I took my PSAT and SAT tests with my college-bound friends.

As the first person in my family to attend college, I wasn't exactly sure of the process to submit applications, and I ended up missing a lot of the deadlines. Even though I worked and saved all I could, tuition and books were going to require careful budgeting. I decided to attend a community college for the first two years to save some money. But even in community college, the costs caught up with me. Toward the end of my second semester, it was clear that the remainder of college—let alone medical school—were probably beyond the reach of my finances. At nineteen years old, my lifelong dream was shattered on the shoals of reality. There was no "Plan B"—because I was going to be a thoracic surgeon. It was all I ever knew or wanted in my short experience on earth. This was what I prepared for my whole childhood. Life had sucker-punched me. I was devastated. What now?

Being practical, I knew I had to get a job to replenish my savings. There were two things I knew how to do well: laboratory work (from my classes) and computer programming. One required a degree and a state license; and the other didn't even require a degree (at that time)—you just had to get your foot in the door. I set about a new course in life. I found a job in the mailroom of a major company in Southern California (the crack in the door), introduced myself to the data processing director, and offered to work for free during my lunch hours and weekends (the foot in the door). I was offered a full-time computer programming position within six months; and although I was making more money than I ever thought possible, it was still my goal to get a college degree.

I changed my major to Business Administration and went to classes at night after my nine-to-five job. As a programmer, I mostly worked on financial systems—Accounts Receivable, Accounts Payable, Payroll, General Ledger—and came to learn a new language: the language of business, Accounting. Although I could have easily passed courses in Information Systems, I decided to become an accounting major. It was hard.

Upon graduation, accounting majors naturally apply for positions at accounting firms, and although I had no desire to become a CPA, I followed suit and discovered a niche I had unintentionally made myself proficient in—auditing computer systems. It required a bit of accounting and a lot of programming, and with computers becoming more attainable for small and medium-sized companies, there was a shortage of skilled IT auditors. Despite a less than 4.0 grade point average, I was offered a position at a prestigious "Big 8" firm and went on to establish and build an IT audit practice in their Orange County office.

My education and experience have served me well. I have been very fortunate to have been able to navigate the uncertainties of life in my career. My audit and compliance skills were in high demand when technology was not (remember the dot-com bust?). My technology skills allowed me to explore new career opportunities in cutting-edge industries that didn't even exist when I was in college, such as cellular and satellite communications and satellite television. Excesses in business led to the Sarbanes-Oxley Act, which made my compliance skills desirable. And all of this led me to my current vocation: cybersecurity.

I have been blessed to travel, live, and work all over the world. My skills have always been in demand, and they were not only satisfying, but also financially rewarding. While I'll never know the accomplishment of watching a heart beat in the chest of a transplant recipient, I have met people, made friends, seen interesting places, had wonderful experiences, and enjoyed a rich and satisfying life. I guess I've learned that while things may not always go as planned, there is a lot of possibility out there. So when things don't go as planned for you, don't be discouraged; be open to—no, EMBRACE—the possibilities. You never know where the journey will take you.

Scott Schneider is the Chief Information Security Officer at a community bank in Southern California, where he is responsible for protecting the bank's information systems and their customer's privacy. In his spare time, Scott shares important cybersecurity experience with business leaders and entrepreneurs in a practical and understandable way through speaking engagements and seminars.

www.scottschneiderspeaker.com

NOTHING IS IMPOSSIBLE! EXPECT MIRACLES!

Robert Sidell

What would it be like if when you woke up each morning, you declared "I celebrate the vast possibilities of my life"? Can you imagine how it would start to change your life? You would surge with energy and excitement. You would smile more, laugh more, and make decisions more quickly. In short, your life would begin to soar.

If so, spend a few minutes with me as we journey to an entirely different way to experience life. Every day we are bombarded with messages of limitation, of negativity. People are quick to speak gloom and doom. Why is this? It is because we have been programmed by the world around us. The news, and even our entertainment, frequently focuses on the negative.

What is really true about this world? What should you feel, and how can you take charge of your mind and feelings? Did you know that no scientist has ever found a limit on the ideas your mind can conceive?

Today we have abilities to live in this world that go beyond even the most amazing dreams of a hundred years go. When my father was born in 1913, airplanes were primitive devices, with no cabins, no airlines, and practically no use for them. Only daredevils were willing to fly them. There were no computers, no radios, no televisions, no internet, no antibiotics. Phones were just getting started. Electrification and lighting were just getting started.

Yet in his single lifetime, we went from the Wright brothers to supersonic jets, and man actually landed on the moon. All things that appeared impossible when my father was born.

We live in a miraculous world!

If we have learned nothing else from all of this change, it's that our individual future, and humanity's future, is only limited by our ability to conceive new ideas. By virtually every standard this world is virtually limitless in its ability to progress.

No scientist has ever found a limit on the human mind's ability to conceive of new ideas. The mind is a virtually unlimited resource and has boundless potential to continually bring new ideas, new possibilities.

Reach for the Stars!

The only real crisis that exists is our belief in ourselves and in life. If we really want to celebrate and live a miraculous life, we must get in the habit of allowing ourselves to cultivate wonderful, inspiring, hope-filled dreams.

When we dream, we activate our own inner miracle-working power. The very act of dreaming stretches the mind and stimulates all kinds of wonderful effects in the body and mind. When we dream, we unleash creative powers. We create a powerful cascade of thoughts that greatly enhances our success potential.

Virtuous Cycle. Your body is flooded with endorphins that enhance your happiness. This in turn causes your ideas to become better, leading to more success. We often hear about vicious cycles, where things spiral downward. But this is the exact opposite. As you reach for the stars, as your dreams begin to take form, an upward cascade of positivity will occur. You will start to look healthier, be happier, and in turn better ideas get generated. Martin Seligman, bestselling author, professor, and psychologist has studied this idea extensively. He has concluded:

Optimists do much better in school and college, at work and on the playing field. They regularly exceed predictions of aptitude tests. . . . Their health is unusually good. They age well, much freer than most of us from the physical ills of middle age. —*Learned Optimism* (Knopf, 1991)

This strongly supports and proves why we each should be exercising our mental power to believe, to dream, to expect miracles. It is like having a magic wand to dramatically improve the quality of life. Simply by changing our mindset, we gain a competitive advantage and become much more successful.

There is more opportunity than ever before!

You see, it really comes down to this: within you is a great power, free to use, as it is for every human being. Your power to see opportunity, to dream of opportunity, to create opportunity in your life.

Truly, this is the only condition in life you are actually in control of. None of us are in control of the world around us. We are all faced with a world of change. Yet in the midst of this change, we can all learn to see opportunity and cultivate our expectation of miraculous good.

The great miracle available to all of us is that by changing our mindset, we literally set ourselves up for a much more successful life. We then begin to discover opportunities that we could never see before.

The internet, along with all of its possibilities, gives us the ability to leverage our success to levels never before imagined. People are growing in success at a faster rate than ever before. Hans Rosling has written a book called Factfulness: *Ten Reasons We're Wrong about the World—and Why Things Are Better Than You Think.* In that book he points out that for almost every major criteria, the quality of life for human beings is greatly accelerating. World poverty is declining, and world health is improving.

What it comes down to is that we must be careful to preserve our attitude that life has "vast possibilities."

Make Bold Decisions—it's in moments of decision that your destiny is shaped.

If we are armed with an optimistic, opportunity-filled point of view, we must make inspired decisions as well. It's only when we translate our mindset into decisions that true magic begins to unfold. As Tony Robbins puts it: "It's in moments of decision that your destiny is shaped."

In closing I challenge you: start each day with this simple truth: I celebrate the vast possibilities of my life! If you do this, and take bold action, you will indeed walk into a miraculous life!

———————————

Robert Sidell is a nationally published author, motivational speaker, attorney, and radio host. He hosts the weekly radio show, *The Gateway Show*, on KXNT, the number-one talk station in Las Vegas, on Sunday nights at 6:00 p.m. His book *The Gateway: Discover the Power to Live an Outrageously Prosperous and Happy Life* was nationally published. He has practiced law for forty-two years and has been in Las Vegas for over thirty-five years. He graduated with honors from Boalt Hall, the Law School at the University of California, Berkeley, in 1977. He is a member of the bar in Nevada, California, and Arizona.

www.RobertSidell.com

A Very Proud But Humbling Experience

Frank Stichter

A few months ago my wife and I experienced something we never expected. After over a year and a half of preparation and testing, our son did a very noble deed—he donated a kidney to a friend. Yikes!

I know this occurs frequently these days, but as a father I was extremely nervous, as you can imagine. More nervous than my son even appeared to be on the day of the surgery.

Let's go back a year and a half or more. Our son Drew has an old high school buddy (we'll keep his name anonymous and call him Buddy) who was in his wedding that had a genetic familial kidney condition called polycystic kidney disease, which ultimately leads to kidney failure and death.

Buddy reached out to Drew back in mid-to-late 2017 about the need for a kidney transplant. His two siblings have had transplants, and Buddy's father died of kidney failure. Drew agreed to go through the testing needed to see if he was a match. When he told us what he was going to do, you can only imagine the feelings a parent would go through: disbelief, nervousness, uncertainty, fear—you name it, we had it.

Drew is an athlete—skier, hunter, golfer, softball player—and has no medical conditions. I guess we never thought he'd be a match. I mean, how often does that occur? He had to travel to the local hospital and then to Denver (almost five hours away) to be tested over and over. As it turns out, Drew and another guy were perfect matches, but apparently there were some health issues with the other guy.

In the spring of 2018, Drew informed us that he would be traveling from Crested Butte, Colorado to Indianapolis for the surgery. He didn't know exactly when, but it was being scheduled. Weeks and weeks went by without a confirmed date, only to be told that Buddy's condition wasn't bad enough to have the surgery.

This was an inevitable surgical procedure. It was going to occur. Why would this be dragged out longer than needed because Buddy's condition wasn't bad enough? His kidneys were only functioning at about 20 percent at that time. How bad did they need to be?

As it turns out, Buddy's insurance company wanted to wait until Buddy's condition was on the verge of dialysis before paying for the surgery. Oh, by the way, what if Drew got hit by a bus? Where would the next donor come from, and how long would the surgery be delayed then because another perfect match had to be found? Would Buddy's condition go "south" in the meantime? Why would they want Buddy's condition to be so bad before they would pay? You would think they would want his condition to be better, not worse, when they performed the surgery so that recovery would be easier.

To make matters even more frustrating, we couldn't get any information from the insurance company about what they were going to pay for Drew's expenses—the DONOR!

His flight, his meals, his rooms while he recuperated—it was as if it was their first rodeo. We couldn't get any information from Anthem, from the hospital, from Buddy's employer's insurance policy, from the social worker—no one! In fact, a week before the surgery in Indy, our questions about the expenses resulted in one of the nurses stating that Drew could have the surgery in Denver so he would be closer to home and didn't need to worry about any high costs. WHAT? Where did this curve ball come from? What hospital? What surgeon? What's their track record? We hardly knew anything about the doctor and hospital in Indianapolis, and now this?

My wife and I flew to Indianapolis the day before the surgery, rented an Airbnb for a week (the doctor insisted that Drew stay in Indy for that period of time just in case of complications) and tried to get mentally prepared.

We were at the hospital at 5:00 a.m. the next day, and I remember my son saying as we walked through the doors, "Let's get this done." Shortly thereafter, we saw Buddy, his mother, and his girlfriend, and there were hugs, tears, and a boatload of thanks and gratitude.

At the end of the day, everything turned out fine for Drew and Buddy. In fact, Buddy told me within hours after the surgery that he could already feel the difference. He had felt so bad for so long that now he felt like his body was running at ninety miles an hour. WOW!

I'm humbled and yet very, very proud of the selfless and noble act my son did to a help friend. I get tearful just talking about it. He's recovering and doing well, and Buddy has a new life.

———————————

Frank Stichter serves the employee-benefit needs of employers nationally, consulting, designing, and implementing innovative health plans for self-funded employers. He has nearly forty years' experience working with public and private sector employers. Frank speaks about Self-Funding and Healthcare Risk Management programs at national conferences and seminars throughout the country and has written numerous articles and position papers on these topics as well. The author of *You Don't Know What You Don't Know*, Frank has served as president of the Chamber of Commerce and is a member and past president of the Crested Butte Rotary Club.

www.strategichpc.com

THE SILVER LINING OF CANCER: IT REALLY DOES TAKE A VILLAGE

Karen Strauss

Barely glancing at me, the technician told me to go back to the waiting room as they needed to get more pictures of me. When you've had as many mammograms as I have, I knew what that meant. I was petrified, anguished, paralyzed. I kept going up to the front desk and asking when they would call me back. I waited another thirty minutes, and finally I could not breathe—I thought I was going to faint.

So I ran! Out of the double doors—out into the street where the sun was shining that warm July day. I ran to the bus to take me home so I could put my head under the covers, irrationally thinking that if the words weren't spoken, I wouldn't have the dreaded "c" word.

When I got home, I had several messages from the lab telling me it was urgent I go back. I finally called them and scheduled my appointment for the next morning at 8:00 a.m. I called my best friend, and she insisted that she go with me. It didn't hurt that she is a women's health provider and knows her way around an x-ray.

They confirmed that I had breast cancer. The bad news was that it had already started to spread outside the duct, but the cancer was really small and it had been caught early.

The biopsy, endless meetings with surgeons, oncologists, my primary doctor . . . Susan was with me through all of it. I was so grateful to her; she was my advocate. She took notes; she could hear what the doctors were saying, while I could barely listen.

It would be a long, dreadful year, but that's when I realized how many amazing friends and supporters I had. This was the beginning of my transformation, but I didn't know it yet.

You see, I had always been a very independent woman. Even when I was very young, I could always "do it myself." I didn't need anyone to help me; *I* was the one who people turned to when they needed to talk about their problems. I always saw needing help from someone as weak. I was the strong one. I was not going to be vulnerable—I would manage just fine!

I could take care of managing my business, my clients, my employees, my co-op, my house in the country, my dog—and now my cancer. This was just one more thing . . . right?

Well, I could not have been more wrong! I didn't realize what a big deal this was, and I needed to focus every bit of attention on getting well. From choosing the surgeon, the oncologist, getting second and third opinions to finally undergoing the surgery, enduring more endless tests, and setting up the chemo treatment. And then living with the effects of the chemo itself—the nausea, the fatigue, the memory loss . . .

Throughout this process, I don't know how I would have made it through without my family, good friends—surprisingly even those that weren't such good friends.

For instance, one person (now an Oscar winner for the movie *Birdland*!) who I knew from the dog park called me and offered to take my dog, Izzy, to the park anytime I wanted. I did not know him very well at that point, and his generous offer floored me.

Similar offers came. A woman in my building is a makeup artist, and when I had a swanky holiday party to attend, she offered to do my makeup—complete with false eyelashes!

And one night, when I decided it was time to cut the remaining hair on my head (a very emotional decision for me), my friend (whose husband works on Broadway) brought over one of her friends who cuts hair professionally for Broadway productions. They made it fun—we had champagne and hors d'oeuvres.

One neighbor, who I knew just to say hello to, came to my apartment every night while I was going through chemo to check on me, see if I needed anything, and offer to walk Izzy. This was a lifesaver, since by then I was pretty wiped out and sometimes couldn't even make it off the couch, let alone get dressed in five layers, dress Izzy, and walk out in 10 degree weather so Izzy could do his business.

I could go on and on about the generosity and support offered to me by friends, family, and acquaintances who were ready and willing to do something, anything, to help me.

And for the first time in my life, I let them! Wow! What a feeling—I went from feeling guilty to feeling grateful and appreciative of the fact that so many people wanted to support and help me. All I had to do was say yes and give them a task.

So many people came to sit with me during the four hours each week I had my chemo treatment. My friends who thought they were stand-up comedians practiced on me, their captive audience. Some of my friends came to gossip, or spill their problems, or just discuss world events. I was SO grateful not to have to talk about "how I was feeling," or about my illness in general. It made the time fly by.

I have never forgotten this lesson. I no longer want to be a loner, to have to make decisions by myself, to not allow myself to be vulnerable. This has stood me in good stead to grow my business as well as become more intimate in my personal relationships.

I've learned that life is more fun when I let people in. I no longer feel the weight of the world on my shoulders. I know I have mentors, friends, advisors, and loved ones who will keep me grounded, supported, and constantly aware that I do not have to go through life alone.

It really does take a village—and I am deeply and profoundly grateful!

———————

Karen Strauss has worked in publishing for more than thirty years and has held management and marketing positions at major publishing houses, including The Free Press, Crown, Random House, and Avon. Karen founded Hybrid Global Publishing in 2011 to help authors, speakers, and entrepreneurs get their message out by writing and publishing a book. She offers publishing, distribution, and marketing services for organizations and individual authors.

www.hybridglobalpublishing.com

BUILDING YOUR DREAM LIFE

Stacey Stuart

D o you want to build your own dream life—or do you want to help others build theirs?

I am blessed to live an amazing life with my wonderful husband and loving family. We own several successful businesses and are continually adding to our list of multiple income streams. However, it hasn't always been this way.

Throughout life I've endured several hardships and challenges both personally and professionally. I've been through two divorces, forcing me to leave companies I helped successfully build. Each time I had to go back to working for somebody else until I could get back on my feet. This was always challenging for me as I knew I was built for much more. I hated feeling like I was trapped under an income ceiling and limited when it came to using my creative talents, and I dreaded having to be on someone else's nine-to-five schedule.

I come from a family of entrepreneurs and have been an entrepreneur myself, owning multiple companies over the past twenty-five years. I've found there are three common elements that have definitely added to not only my success but also to the success of others I've helped and coached.

Success largely comes down to having the "WILLINGNESS" to take risks, the courage to continually take blind leaps of faith. It's saying "yes" to opportunities and then learning and figuring it out as you go! Not waiting until you're confident, or you've researched the subject to death, because by then the opportunity will have usually passed. I learned from the Success Resources Quantum Leap program that it's Ready—Fire—Aim, and that has been a life-changing tool for my husband and me.

Hire at least one coach and mentor and join a mastermind group. Most successful entrepreneurs go by the formula of hiring three coaches, two mentors, and take part in at least one mastermind group. That's the formula I followed and definitely recommend.

Your mindset is CRITICAL. Continually working on keeping a positive attitude and mindset is EVERYTHING when it comes to your level of success in business and living a life of abundance.

My husband and I followed and continue to follow the steps above, and it has been life-changing for us, our family, and our business. I believe it's also important to expose our children to the opportunity of becoming an entrepreneur and instill these same habits in them. That's what we did, and I'm proud to say that our adult children have made the decision to create and build their dream lives and are on their own entrepreneurial path.

Our daughter, Lexi, is twenty-two years old and owns Cascade Consultations, which is a home staging consulting company. She helps real estate agents and home sellers of occupied homes learn what needs to be done to showcase their home and maximize their best ROI.

Our daughter, Mikayla, is twenty years old, and she is an Independent Home Staging Designer who is frequently hired by our home staging company to help stage homes. She is also the founder of the Y.E.S.S Lifestyle (Young Entrepreneurs Seeking Success), which provides tools and resources for young adults seeking to find out if becoming an entrepreneur is right for them. Her YESSlifestyle.com site provides information and resources on how to start a business and offers a resource guide for finding the right vendors.

Our son, Neale, is sixteen years old and still in high school; however, he is already an author of a book that will be released this fall called *Win Your Team—Win Your Game*. It's about the importance of coaches teaching players the power of a positive mindset and how that alone will affect their overall performance and ultimately win more games.

I believe it's important—whether you're a young adult, just getting out of high school, or someone who just doesn't feel like they're on the right path to financial freedom—to consciously draw a mental line in the sand and make a critical life decision of how you ultimately want to spend your life. Do you want to spend your life building your dreams—or spend it helping others build theirs?

Whether you're a new entrepreneur seeking guidance or a seasoned entrepreneur whose business may just need remodeling, take action and find the help you need by investing in coaches and mentors that will help catapult your business to the next level. Get involved in a mastermind group where you can continually surround yourself with like-minded individuals who will show you new and different perspectives while keeping you focused. These practices are crucial in keeping yourself and your business current, cutting-edge, and STANDING-OUT from the competition.

We're all here to ultimately make a positive difference in the world. I don't believe we're meant to just live life on auto-pilot each day; we are meant to actually LIVE. Prepare to leave your legacy and help others to do the same!

Stacey Stuart is a creative and seasoned entrepreneur, owning multiple companies over the past twenty-five years. She is the creator of the 6S-Toolbox™ Business System, Remodeled Agent & Entrepreneur Coaching Program, and founder of Pacific NW Home Staging, which specializes in staging vacant homes to sell quickly and for top dollar in the Seattle/South Puget Sound area. Stacey is passionate about helping real estate agents and entrepreneurs with kick-starting and elevating their business to the next level. She is a proud mother of three children who are all on their entrepreneurial path to success.

www.StaceyStuartGlobal.com

CATAPULTED INTO BUSINESS

Bonnie Taub

After nineteen years of marriage, my whole world as I knew it turned upside down. My husband came home from a two-week Rotary International trip in Ecuador. At the time he was teaching Spanish in a middle school. This was a perfect opportunity for him to see another culture and visit the local schools there. He arranged for the local school children to become pen pals with his students. Our marriage, although not perfect, was on pretty solid ground—or so I thought. I had a part-time job managing a local bagel store, we had no kids, and he had a full-time career in education.

When he returned from his trip, he started asking me, "What are you going to do with all the body work trainings you've taken?" You see, for the past several years, I had been studying Lomi Lomi (Hawaiian massage) by taking ten-day residential trainings in Hawaii, Canada, and upstate New York. I just followed my teacher around. None of the trainings were affiliated with any school or led to any kind of certification. Since we lived in New York, one needed a license to be able to work on people and be compensated. His argument was that I was spending all this money and getting nothing in return. He told me I should go to massage school, get licensed, and start having a career. So I did.

What I didn't know was his motivation behind wanting me to go to massage school. I just thought he had my best interest at heart. After enrolling in massage school, I figured out that he was having an affair with a woman who had been on the Rotary trip. She was a flamenco dancer in a dance troupe on Long Island. I guess this seemed exotic to him and more exciting than our relationship. He told me that he found the love of his life; he wanted to divorce me and marry her. If he divorced me, he wanted me to have a career and be able to support myself.

He moved out and took an apartment near where she lived. It may not seem logical, but I helped him move and set up his apartment. I had entered psychotherapy and wanted to keep the lines of communication open in the hopes of saving my marriage. He agreed to marriage counseling after realizing that this woman was not interested in anything permanent and ended the affair. He reevaluated what he had, and we agreed to continue our marriage with lots of changes. I am thankful to say that we are still together, and after fifty-two years, we still relish each other's company.

Had it not been for this hiccup in our marriage, I would not have been thrust into seeking a career. When I went to massage school, I found that I really liked it and was actually quite good at it. I graduated with a 4.0, passed the state exam, and became a licensed massage therapist. I never worked for anyone. I opened my own practice in my home for a few years and then rented space in a yoga and wellness studio.

My career has continued to take many twists and turns. After graduating, I joined the faculty at the same school and taught both oriental theory and technique classes. I became a clinic supervisor in the student massage clinic. I taught Lomi Lomi technique classes in the continuing education department, putting all those trainings to practical use.

During that time, I found the Upledger Institute and started studying Lymph Drainage Therapy with Dr. Bruno Chikly, an osteopath from France. After completing several levels of that program, I became a certified teaching assistant, which I continue to this day with the Chikly Health Institute.

My massage school training included looking at how nutrition plays a role in the physical body. A natural progression into a more in-depth training of nutrition led me to the Institute of Integrated Nutrition. After ten months and another year in their Immersion Program, I graduated as an Integrated Nutrition Health Coach. While this program gave me good coaching and listening skills, I still felt there was something missing. Two graduates of this school started their own programs. Each program looked at nutrition from a functional medicine perspective. I studied Full Body Systems with Andrea Nakayama first and then entered the School of Applied Functional Medicine with Tracy Harrison. I am currently in the second year of this program, learning the interconnectedness in the body.

In between these two programs, I discovered the Nutritional Therapy Association and enrolled in their Nutritional Therapy Practitioner program. This finally married both nutrition and bodywork. Through the hands-on assessment tool called Functional Evaluation, one gets in touch with the body's innate intelligence. Since everyone is unique, there is no one protocol that fits all. This functional evaluation, called the FE, allows for the tailoring a protocol for each individual and facilitates healing.

Since graduating as an NTP, I have become a group leader in the program. I love participating in the education of future graduates and providing individualized programs for my clients.My latest massage therapy education has led me to the John Barnes Myofascial Release Approach in Sedona, Arizona. By working the fascia, connective tissue, in the body, old traumas, whether physical or emotional, are released. This allows for healing of the mind, body and spirit.

I have since moved to Arizona and have obtained my massage license here. My business is now incorporated to include both massage and nutritional counseling. It has evolved into a career that I absolutely love. This would not have happened without what I call "the hiccup" in my marriage. Though adversity comes, something wonderful emerges.

Bonnie Taub, NTP, INHC, LMT, BS, is a well-respected Nutritional Therapy Practitioner and Licensed Massage Therapist. She is passionate about guiding her clients in their journey toward optimal health. Her treatments and programs are highly individualized. Specialties include Lymph Drainage Therapy, John Barnes Myofascial Release Approach, Crohn's Disease, and Digestive Wellness. Bonnie is a certified teaching assistant with the Chikly Health Institute in the Lymph Drainage Therapy program.

www.yourharmonizedhealth.com

THE FEAR OF PUBLIC SPEAKING

Mellissa Tong

People always say public speaking is their second biggest fear behind the fear of dying. As much as I would love to agree, that just wasn't the case for me.

I grew up in the British Colony of Hong Kong and learned to read and write in kindergarten. After primary school, my parents sent me to an English secondary school where all the classes were taught in English, except Chinese Literature and Chinese History. Although English was my second language, I was always very comfortable speaking it.

When I moved to the United States in 1991, I still spoke with a British accent. After I finished my MFA degree, I found a job at The International Channel, one of the first satellite TV stations in the U.S., working as a TV News Anchor/Reporter and Producer. At the time, I thought if I could sound more American, people would not assume that I was a new immigrant. So I enrolled myself in an *accent reduction class*, taught by the famous Hollywood dialect and accent coach, Robert Easton.

As I was slowly picking up American idioms and slangs, I started dating someone I met at school. Soon after, we got married. I knew he was particular with words, but I had no idea he was actually a wordsmith! Eager to make myself sound less foreign, I welcomed him to correct every mistake that I had, big or small. At one point, I felt so fortunate to have married someone who could teach me words like *spatula* in English, something I could not have learned in Hong Kong, no matter how good my English was, because I simply did not need to say that in English.

But as time went on, the correcting began taking a toll on me. I became completely self-conscious. It got to a point where I could not speak in front of more than four people without having to memorize what I had to say the night before.

At one point, I was pitching a TV idea to the executives at Miramax Studios. I had memorized six pages of notes the night before. After my presentation, they thought I did such a great job without messing up. I said thank you and smiled, still feeling the cold sweat on my palms.

A few more years went by. My fear of speaking in front of people got even worse. There was a time when I had to do a client presentation. Again I stayed up all night and memorized the material. I was nervous, something I had become very used to by that point. The reality was, however, that *I wasn't able to say anything freely*. I felt completely paralyzed. My creativity was suppressed. No doubt, this limited the potential for both myself and my business.

For years, when watching people speak on stage, I always wondered if they had memorized their words too, like me. Yet they seemed to be speaking so *freely*. My thought was *If only I could do that someday (without having to memorize)*.

Fast-forward to 2013. I was in the middle of something one day and thought, *What the hell happened to me?* I was handpicked by a teacher at four years old to give a speech to congratulate the graduation class in kindergarten. They tested everyone in class, and I was among the very few that didn't mess up. I still remember very vividly the moment I was on stage. They had a huge spotlight on me. I was looking out to the audience, trying to find a familiar face, but it was pitch black. All I could see were dust particles, floating in the air. When I was done, I remember very loud clapping, and as I walked backstage, my mom was standing by the curtain. I didn't have one ounce of fear in me. So how did I go from being completely fearless to terrified?

As soon as I had that realization, I vowed to do whatever it took to get back to my four-year-old fearless self. The first thing I did was to tell my husband at the time to stop correcting me. He was reluctant at first, thinking that would hurt me because my English would no longer be perfect. But I insisted, saying that if I made any mistakes, so be it! They would be my mistakes; I'd have to learn it my way. Bit by bit, I noticed myself speaking more freely at meetings and presentations.

By August 2014, I was ready for my ultimate test. I was giving a three-hour seminar at SBA, the Small Business Administration. Since I was only volunteering, I thought that even if I messed up, the worst-case scenario would be they would not bring me back. I made a PowerPoint presentation, but I did not have a script. I took a break during the presentation and checked in with myself, I was feeling OK. By the time I finished my presentation, I was certain my fear had parted ways with me for good. Since then, I have done many presentations and a lot more public speaking, and I've been completely at ease every single time. If you asked me seven or eight years ago if I would ever see myself being a public speaker, I would have said, "No freaking way!"

I remember Oprah Winfrey once said, "The longest journey we have is the journey from our head to our heart." Now that I've experienced this myself, I can help others speak from their hearts so they can tell their stories and make a bigger impact in people's lives.

If you feel fear about any aspect in your life, I would encourage you to make a decision and go back to the place where you were fearless and felt triumphant. Use that feeling to propel you to move forward. You may be surprised at how quickly you can turn your life around and take your power back!

Mellissa Tong is the founder and CCO of an award-winning video marketing and content production company, DuckPunk Productions, Inc. DuckPunk works with Fortune 500 companies such as Nissan, Verizon, and Wells Fargo. DuckPunk has won many awards, including the Clio, Addy, Telly, and many others from various film festivals. Prior to founding DuckPunk, Ms. Tong was a news anchor/reporter/producer at the International Channel in Los Angeles. She interviewed thousands of people from all walks of life and covered over 1,200 stories during her four years at the station. Ms. Tong is an MFA graduate from the California Institute of the Arts.

www.duckpunk.net

THE DREAM THAT CAME TRUE

Carol Ann Wagner

In recollecting the first time that the dream was apparent to me, I must go back to the beginning of the memory, with my dad leaving for work dressed in a suit and white shirt and carrying a briefcase. That picture sits in the front of my mind decades later and has motivated and mesmerized me to this day.

My dad was a *colporteur,* a French word meaning "peddler," which in 19th-century America came to be used for the door-to-door peddlers of religious books and tracts. Every Monday morning, he would leave us to travel to Western Kansas, his assigned territory, to do his "canvassing." His product was *Uncle Arthur's Bedtime Stories,* a collection of stories that were true and written to assist parents in teaching their young ones how to be happier using an example of another young one being tempted to lie, steal, or cheat and how they overcame the temptation or paid the price for not listening. Another of his products, *The Bible Story* by Arthur S. Maxwell, contained stories from the Bible written in a way to teach children in a non-legalistic form and were beautifully illustrated.

He became the top salesperson in the United States, fueled by his strong German work ethic and his determination to support his family. He was self-funded and self-motivated and did all his bookwork and collections. Often while we were on vacation, we would take a side trip to either collect a set of books that a customer was delinquent on or pick up a payment and a promise to pay their monthly payment timelier. We lived a charmed life from his hard work and I grew up wanting to emulate him.

It was in my sixth year of being on Planet Earth that I can remember making up my mind that I too would be a business person and work for myself just like my dad did, and the journey began.

Starting at six years of age, my mom would take my brother and me to town every week, and we would go door-to-door and sell Golden Crumbles, Butter Toffee, and Katydids to the office people in the businesses there. We also took the candy on any vacation we went on and sold it to fellow campers and travelers. This went on through eighth grade, and my dad put a third of the money in a savings account that I was given access to when I graduated from college.

Starting in the sales business at such a young age sure was a great start to fulfilling my dream. In my teens I worked in multiple jobs—from a plastics factory making sleeves for plants to janitorial work and kitchen duties in a school—but my favorite job was in a mom-and-pop nursing home in Enterprise, Kansas. What a great time I had on the evening shift, cooking dinner, passing out medications, doing the laundry and putting up to eighteen people to bed. Little did I know that this work would frame the rest of my life.

The nursing home theme ran through my college years, where I was the lead a.m.

cook on weekends at a 170-bed nursing home. When I graduated with a degree in business management and accounting, I had the opportunity to train in management in the nursing home business, and my background and love for the elderly was key. Sam, who gave me the chance to be in administration, was touched by my story of my dad carrying his briefcase and my always wanting to be a businessperson like him, and that pushed me through my interview process with him.

Many years were given to my career in the nursing home industry. One of the qualifications for a nursing home administrator to keep licensed with the state was to complete Continuing Education Credits (CEUs). These CEU courses were approved by the Department of Health and then offered to licensed administrators for their requirements to stay qualified to run nursing homes.

I heard of a way to get my CEUs from a women who had written and certified many courses and made them available by mail versus having to sit in classrooms for forty hours. She was highly recommended, and little did I know that this would lead to my dream coming true.

The courses were well written, and instead of just getting the certification for my license over with, I very much enjoyed the coursework and the learning. Soon after, I called Gisela and let her know that if she ever wanted to sell her business, she should call me.

Years passed, and one day that call came. Gisela was ready to sell and had decided to let me have first chance on buying the business from her.

The phrase "the rest is history" fits well here. The business has been a wonderful way to serve my industry and grow in business. I'm now in a position to expand my continuing education business and offer others a way to use their professional intellectual property to educate and train in their respective industries with continuing education requirements.

Stay tuned—the best is yet to come! I'm excited about fulfilling others' dreams of sharing their knowledge and creating a potential legacy. If you have an interest in creating a course in your industry, please be in touch at www.BuildaCeuBusiness.com.

Carol Ann Wagner, NHA, MS, is dedicated to quality care and fun in sub-acute, rehabilitation, skilled, and long-term care nursing facilities. With over thirty years of experience in the industry, she does consulting and interim work with businesses that need refined leadership skills, an ability to prioritize with successful outcomes, and readily develop rapport with residents, families, staff, and other health care professionals. She uses humor and resilience to create a best outcome for all involved in a very difficult and yet necessary phase of life and work environment. You can find her at Best Source Learning Center.

www.BestSourceLC.com

THE 90 PERCENT

Pat Walley

In the fall of 1970, bloodcurdling screams pierced the Virginia night and snapped my mother awake. There I was, her four-year-old precious boy, standing next to the bed—fully engulfed in flames! My skin was literally melting right in front of her eyes. She quickly pulled off her blankets and smothered out the fire. I don't know which was worse for Mom during that agonizing sixty-minute car ride to the hospital—the crackling sound of burned skin as it cooled or the putrid flesh stench of the smoke. Likely it was the helpless feeling of watching me fade in and out of consciousness and wondering if I had just died in her arms.

The doctors told her, "I'm sorry, Mrs. Walley, your son has major third-degree burns on most of his right leg, and it is damaged so badly, there's a 90 percent chance he will never be able to use it again." Ninety percent. That is almost a guarantee.

I spent the next two months in the hospital, enduring countless surgeries to rebuild my mangled leg. It looked like a chicken wing after being left on the grill way too long. One day, as I lay in the hospital ward, watching other kids in wheelchairs, I decided that I was not going to be crippled. No way. The fight was on.

Some memories are etched so deeply they can be recalled in an instant. I can still vividly remember changing the dressings on my leg. The pain was indescribable. They always got stuck. I only now realize how difficult it must have been for Mom as she peeled my skin away every time the bandages were removed. I would squirm to escape the inevitable searing pain and tearfully beg her to please, PLEASE stop. She did this every day for over a year. Mom nursed me back to health while raising my twin sister and younger brother. She did this mostly solo since my dad was deployed overseas in the Navy for eleven months. She encouraged me daily, and she never, ever quit. Don't tell her about 90 percent!

I was laid up for months, and that's when I discovered my superpower. It was READING! I read everything within reach. Canned food, cereal boxes, medicine tubes, and more! By the time I was five, I was consuming newspapers, magazines, dictionaries, encyclopedias, and anything else Mom could find. We were way beyond Dr. Seuss! Reading was great, but my goal was clear: I had to learn to walk again.

After nearly two years of therapy and countless failed attempts, I finally took my first tentative steps. Hooray! I beat the 90 percent! But I wasn't out of the woods yet.

A couple years later, as most boys do, I had a growth spurt, and it was a doozie! It started at 4 feet 11 inches and didn't stop until I reached 6 feet 5 inches tall! That was quite a spurt! My leg—skin graft, surgically reconstructed tendons, scarred muscles, burned bones and all—had to grow right along with the rest of me at the rate of almost four inches a year for five long, painful years. Painfully, my feet also grew a shoe-size every year.

There were some side effects. My burned leg ended up shorter than my left leg, which caused me to walk on the outside of my right foot. In my twenties, I permanently damaged my weakened right ankle—a Stage 4 Talar Dome fracture, very serious. I was told I would lose 90 percent of my foot motion after surgery. A couple years later, I tripped and broke the scaphoid bone in my wrist—not the bone you want to break. Again, 90 percent of my flexibility was supposed to be gone as the bone died. It seemed that the doctors always used 90 percent. Instead of just accepting their diagnosis, I embarked on a journey of pain. Each injury took several months of rehab. Months of sweat, tears, excruciating pain, and demoralizing failures. If the therapist told me do one set, I did three. Fifteen minutes of flexing turned into thirty. I struggled to keep my focus and looked for answers, but I never would accept being crippled. I pushed through the pain and mental anguish. The wrist bone did not die, and I still have nearly full range of motion. My surgically repaired ankle has some arthritis, but I only have a slight limp. Ninety percent? No Way.

Fifty years ago, most of my right leg was turned to charcoal and the doctors had to scrape tendons, muscles, and bone and rebuild everything under my kneecap. They told me I wouldn't walk. My ankle was not supposed to work right, and my wrist was supposed to be locked into one position for the rest of my life. The odds were 90 percent that I would miss out on so much in life—football, soccer, skiing, mountain climbing, fly fishing, and bouncing my children on my knee. Instead God spared my life when I was four and stretched me as I grew. He healed my bones when I broke them. I have been blessed to enjoy all those things and so many more.

God was by my side when I faced overwhelming physical odds—not once but three separate times. I believe since I was willing to do the work, He was willing to do the rest. He also instilled in me something I just can't explain: an ability and will to overcome any adversity. I did not create this part of me. Maybe it's stubbornness, maybe it's a desire to succeed, or maybe I just don't like failing. I'm not completely sure. What I DO know is that God has been with me through the years and guides my way daily. My superpower (reading) has allowed me to really understand and interpret the story of Jesus (the Bible). God has plans for me—and it's not the 90 percent.

Pat Walley is passionate about helping others succeed. For over twenty-five years, he has worked with 350+ businesses in forty-eight states, training owners and employees in point-of-sale systems, basic accounting, and successful business practices. His specialty is simplifying complex things. Pat is also a gifted speaker and writer. Audiences immediately connect with his stories and have fun while learning. He founded Dignity Credit Solutions to equip consumers and businesses with the tools to win. Most consumer credit reports have errors and nearly 90 percent of businesses fail. Pat's mission is to help them overcome the 90 percent.

www.dignitycreditsolutions.com

HOPE FOR CHANGE

Paul Wenner

When people ask me when I was born, I always tell them the same thing: "I was born under the foul ball of Joe DiMaggio." My father was professional baseball player Dick Wenner and played for the San Francisco Seals. On June 5th, 1947, my mother and grandmother were seated in the bleachers watching my father's team play the Yankees when Joe stepped up to bat.

As expected, Joe got a piece of the ball, and it hurled out into the stands . . . right at my pregnant mother. Luckily, she and my grandmother were able to dive out of the foul ball's path and into the aisle. Not so luckily, my mom lost her balance and tumbled down the steps. Minutes later she went into premature labor.

Racing to the hospital, my father was greeted with several surprises. First, he now had a healthy baby girl. Next, the biggest surprise: he had twins! Five minutes after my sister Peggy was born, my mother gave birth to me as well. Now the least welcome surprise: I was born with underdeveloped lungs and heart valves, leading to pulmonary and respiratory problems as well as tuberculosis. They would last my entire childhood.

School was a whirlwind of bullies, asthma attacks, and horrifying gym classes. Even my best friend started making fun of my wheezing. That was when I realized I had to do something different. I had to BE something different. Fortunately, that was also when I saw the commercial.

It came on during a break for *The Lone Ranger*: a middle-aged man appeared onscreen and asked: "Are you tired of being tired, and sick of being sick? Check out of poor health, and check into DIET!" It was advertising a health food store in downtown Portland, the city's first and only. My family waited with impatience for the commercial to end, but I was enthralled. It was as if the man was looking deep into my soul and speaking only to ME.

I could barely walk twenty feet without getting winded, but somehow I made it to the bus stop the next day and all the way downtown to the building I had seen on our black-and-white TV set. It was even more majestic in color. I will never forget the tingle of the bells as I entered for the first time and started my journey toward health and finding myself.

I wandered the store alone for hours, seeing things I had never seen before and reading every label I came across. Yet though I was invigorated, by the end I felt no closer to "healing" than when I stepped inside. On the verge of defeat, I made my way back toward the front door to leave. And that's when it happened: a book fell off the shelf and landed at my feet. I picked it up and looked at the cover: *The Miracle of Fasting* by Paul C. Bragg.

I opened the front cover and began to read, and each subsequent page struck my young mind like a bolt of lightning. This was IT. This was what I had been waiting for. I took my find to the register and emptied the contents of my pockets: every coin in my shattered piggy bank. When I got on the bus back toward home, I was carrying the treasure with me.

They say a mother knows her son better than anybody, and perhaps that explains why my mom noticed the change in me long before the rest of my family. We had an old red-and-white *Betty Crocker Cookbook* in the cupboard, and I immediately commandeered it and set about following the endless recipes for myself, careful to only use fresh and healthy ingredients.

Two things happened next: first, I got stronger physically. Second, I began to get stronger MENTALLY (which was when people really started to pay attention). I was more extroverted, more outgoing, more ready to take on the world. Soon I was cooking for my entire family. I even cooked the best Thanksgiving turkey we'd ever had. This made my father very happy. I followed this up with an announcement: I was going to be a chef. A GARDEN chef. I would be a cook for life, and everything would be plant-based. This did NOT make my father very happy.

So not-very-happy was he, in fact, that just after my eighteenth birthday, I found myself dragged to a military recruitment station with instructions to not come out again until I enlisted in a division. I picked the Air Force (the line was shorter). Though I tested positive for TB, I was now healthy enough to volunteer and support the war efforts in Vietnam.

Though getting shipped off to war is perhaps not the ideal ending to that anecdote, the profound effect healthy eating has had on my life (INCLUDING being in physical condition to enlist) is proof of the power of setting goals for yourself, however small. This would later allow me to parlay my modest invention of the Gardenburger° into a literal food revolution and the highest performing public American stock for a time.

I often think back on the trip I took that day to the health food store and what it has meant for me in my life. I was just a boy getting on a bus, not sure of what the end goal was and armed only with hope. Yet that hope was enough to change my life forever. With hope, you can change yourself, and through that, you can change the WORLD.

What do these words and dates have in common? 1947, premature, San Francisco, Joe DiMaggio, foul ball, TB, 1965, Catholic, Paul Bragg, vegetarian, Air Force, 1969, shoe shines, Mt. Hood College, radio and television production, 1973–1994, food and nutrition instructor,1974, first electric car dealer, 1980, Gardenhouse Restaurant™, 1982, Gardenburger°, Jazz Festival, Homeless, 1985, Wholesome and Hearty Foods, 1986, one thousand locations, eleven years later, thirty thousand locations, 1992, #1 growth stock in the nation, 1985–1998, 150 TV shows, 250 magazines and newspapers, Brad Pit, *GardenCuisine*, Simon and Schuster, *Power of Our Forks,* Kellogg's, Next Gardenchicken° . . . **Gardenchef Paul°** is the answer!

www.GardenChefPaul.com

FORGIVE LIKE A ROCKSTAR

Kelly White

I received a note from my son's third-grade science teacher. "He is a potential leader and *should* be doing better."

His teacher had the power to encourage him and instead tore him down by her "should." This letter about my beautiful son really rocked me to my core.

I had a teacher, Mrs. Noshlon, who colored how I see myself. I was told I was stupid, I was dumb, I couldn't read, I couldn't do math, I talked too much, and I didn't pay enough attention in class. She kept me after school so often that my car pool kicked me out.

I looked her up online. I read her obituary. I stared at her picture, the one with her black beehive hair and joyless face.

Her husband had died the year before she became my teacher, I read. She was a new widow and a new teacher when she was teaching me to read and doubt myself. She had two young children at home. The days she kept me after school, she did not get to go home early to be with her own kids.

Her daughter lived in Bakersfield and had died of pancreatic cancer a year before Mrs. Noshlon died of Alzheimer's. She had a son named Greg who lived in Colorado. He was in his sixties and looked like a nice man.

I have unknowingly given this woman full access to how I feel about myself. Did all of my self-doubt come from her? No, but what could I do to free myself from this visceral reaction I had when I read that letter from my son's science teacher?

Forgiveness. There is a Hawaiian method of forgiveness called Ho'Oponopono taught by Dr. Hew Len. The word *Ho* means "to make" and *Pono* means "right"—hence "to make right."

Ho'Oponopono was made famous by the Hawaiian therapist who helped heal an entire hospital of the criminally insane without ever seeing one of the patients. Dr. Hew Len reviewed each of the patient's files, and then he healed them by forgiving himself. He healed himself *and* the criminally insane by using the Ho'Oponopono forgiveness prayer.

I would like to "make right" my first-grade experience for the beautiful girl I was— who was and is so lovable. I had not only endured a year of Mrs. Noshlon's criticism—I have endured years of speaking those lies to myself.

I closed my eyes and took three centering breaths. I looked inside for the first-grade version of myself. I see my six-year-old self, lost in a first grade classroom with a teacher who hates me. My teacher tells me how stupid I am. My last school where I attended kindergarten was named Lamplighter, and there we sang and cooked French food. "A child is not a vessel to be filled but a lamp to be lit," a Hebrew proverb states. They liked me there at Lamplighter.

In my mind's eye I see how beautiful, sweet, and scared I am. I see how uncomfortable I am in class and how afraid I am to raise my hand.

I walk over and put my hand on her shoulder. I look in her eyes and say to her: "I am sorry. Please forgive me. I love you. Thank you."

I bend down and start to do the math worksheet with her patiently and lovingly. 'You've got this," I whisper. "You are so brave. I believe in you. Together we can do anything."

Again, I say to her: "I am sorry. Please forgive me. I love you. Thank you."

Slowly and surely my little first-grader turns toward me, her magnificent face smiling. She reaches out to comfort me. She is glorious. She reminds me to forgive myself also.

I put my hand on my heart and say the Ho'Oponopono prayer to my adult self: "I am sorry. Please forgive me. I love you. Thank you."

Can I offer my forgiveness to Mrs. Noshlon? No. I don't care that she was a recent widow. She hated children. She hated me. I feel hooked in my self-righteousness and anger.

I look at my younger self sitting there doing her work, trying her best. I look up at Mrs. Noshlon. As an adult I can see how hard she struggles. I believe she is doing the best she can in this moment. I need to forgive her. I want to forgive her.

I place my hand on my heart; I say, looking at my teacher, "I am sorry. Please forgive me. I love you. Thank you."

My first-grader lays her hand on my arm. I reach down and hold her hand, and we both forgive Mrs. Noshlon. "I am sorry. Please forgive me. I love you. Thank you."

I now look at my teacher, not with hate, but with love. Slowly Mrs. Noshlon's face softens, and she says to me, "I never hated you. I know how smart you are. I was frustrated, sad, scared, and intolerant, but my upset was not about you. It is time for you to move on so I can rest in peace."

She fades into the distance. I had carried her so long in my heart. I made tapes of her voice into my own voice. These tapes repeated false beliefs about myself to myself. It was time to redo these tapes.

The truth is: I am lovable, I am worthy, I am good, I have something to say, and I am worth listening to. My shoulders relax. Standing in that classroom, I see now how I wanted my first-grade experience to be: my younger self is happy, clear, and contributing in class. Mrs. Noshlon looks at me with kind and loving eyes. As I move leave the classroom, I look back and smile at my younger self, proud of her.

"To make right by forgiving"—perhaps I can extend this forgiveness to my son's science teacher. Forgiving like a RockStar is where my freedom is found.

Kelly White, MA, is a licensed marriage and family therapist and also a licensed professional clinical counselor. She holds a master's degree in both Clinical Psychology and Spiritual Psychology. She is an adjunct faculty member at Pepperdine University. She teaches Practicum in their Master's of Psychology Program. A direct and compassionate, solutions-oriented therapist, Kelly helps clients to live their best life. She offers workshops in person and online on a multitude of subjects, and she is a sought-after speaker and seminar leader. She has appeared on several hit television shows as herself.

www. KellyWhiteMFT. com

Rescuing Panda

Jennifer Williams

It's been said that cats have nine lives, but an American bulldog-pit bull mix that I know has had at least two lives. I met Panda in December 2013. I had received a phone call about a pit bull living in a field that looked like she had just given birth.

I got a description of the location, and my co-rescuer, Kristi, and I went there, not knowing what to expect. We found the location of the mama and her puppies by playing YouTube videos of puppies crying very loudly. Then we spotted the mom and followed her back to where she had built a nest in a drain behind some bushes and under a tree.

Kristi climbed right in and started taking the puppies out of the drain and handing them to me. I put them in a soft-sided crate. We managed to leash the mom and walk out to the car. Once we had the crate in the car, Panda jumped right in with her puppies.

Based on what our vet told us plus the date that we rescued them, we figured the puppies were going to be exactly eight weeks old on Christmas Day. We found all five of them great homes, and the following week, we gave Panda a spa day before getting her spayed.

That following Saturday, we took her to the local PetSmart, where we held our adoption event. One of the managers adopted her and we thought that would be the end of her story. Fast-forward a whole year to Christmas week 2014: we found out that Panda had gone missing.

The family that had adopted her had split up, and the dad was living in a car with her. He decided that she would be better off with someone else. Instead of asking us for help, he put her on Craigslist and found her a home. The day he delivered her, the adopter's wife didn't know that a dog was coming to the house. When she got home and opened the gate to come in the yard, Panda got out! It was raining and also freezing cold!

The minute I found out that she was missing, I drove to San Bernardino and started looking for her. I visited a homeless encampment and knocked on doors. I went to businesses up and down the road. We posted flyers, mailed out postcards to every home in the neighborhood, and hoped against hope that someone knew where she was.

I contacted a person known for locating dogs by using a dowsing rod. I phoned an animal communicator, who told me Panda was alive and safe and with people that thought she would make some beautiful puppies. The communicator gave me a general area for where I might find her.

My other rescue work had to continue, though. On May 8, my team and I were out trapping a Border Collie in Corona, California, when we got a call that there had been a Panda sighting. I asked for a picture, and as soon as I realized it was her, we immediately drove to San Bernardino. We couldn't get there fast enough!

I kept the girl who saw her on the phone the entire time, because if Panda left the area, I wanted to know exactly where she was. When I got there, I was saddened to discover that Panda didn't recognize me. She barked at me, but I used an old trick. I took off my sweatshirt and threw it over the fence to her and then walked around to where I thought I could get in the backyard. By the time I got to where she was, she had smelled my sweatshirt. I was able to leash her and bring her to safety.

We had recently moved, and Panda had never been to our new place. I did know that she was really good with puppies, and for three or four months, she fostered litters of puppies for us! Because of her sweet nature, we didn't really want her to be adopted by anyone because we had already been through so much to keep her safe, but after a while, I started thinking that she would be much happier in a home. If I found somebody who understood what she had been through, maybe I could let her go.

At one of our adoption events, a lady asked us if she could adopt her. I encouraged her to come meet her one-on-one at another time. I had been talking to some of my volunteers, and I let them know that there was a possibility of her being adopted. One volunteer, Jack, looked at me and said he didn't realize that she was available for adoption. I told him that for the right family, she was.

He went to his car, got a leash, put it on Panda, and took her home. She's been very lovingly cared for by Jack and his wife, Pam, ever since!

A California native mom, pet matchmaking expert, miracle creator, and dog- parenting consultant, **Jennifer Williams** has over thirty years' experience helping people and animals. Whether it's been business-to-business sales or community involvement, Jennifer has the ability to get great results. As a local business person, she has a volunteer force of approximately fifty people who have rescued and rehomed over two thousand dogs. She has also opened a resale boutique in Norco to support the medical, housing, and veterinary needs of her business, 2nd Chances Rescue. As seen on Facebook and other social media outlets, Jennifer is passionate about her work with humans and about saving their companion animals.

www.2ndchancesrescuenorco.com

JUST GET ON WITH LIFE

Chuck Woodson

Once upon a time. . . . That's how I grew up, and the stories were wonderful, positive, uplifting, and (apparently) motivating. Maybe it's my mother saying (following some disaster), "Don't cry over spilled milk. Just clean it up and get on with life." At least that's the gist of what I remember.

Over the years of growing up and getting older, that comes back to me as a basic value I've used to get through life. Another maxim I like comes from Satchel Paige: "Don't look back. Something might be gaining on you."

As it turns out, these many decades later, life is what has helped me become what I am today. I'm reasonably healthy, older than I look (to most people), and still looking forward to tomorrow. I can also attribute my current positive outlook to my faith, which I'm sure is largely responsible for most of my successes in business as well as in life.

I freely admit to an absolutely unquenchable belief in a savior: Jesus Christ. I came to believe the truth of the gospel message as part of my teenage Sunday school lessons. It's taken a lot of years to realize that believing is only the beginning—acceptance of the gospel message is the real start to a spiritually satisfying life.

OK, so a spiritual belief system isn't the only thing you need. You also need a team of folks who help develop the standards and work ethic to be successful. My real team building began when my wife (we've been married fifty years now) disrupted my life in college by interrupting a private conversation, catching me unawares (and unprepared), which resulted in me agreeing to a date. Mind you, at this point in my life, I was recently out of the Navy and working diligently to repair my disastrous pre-Navy college experience, working full-time, going to school full-time, with no time for romance.

Well, it has obviously worked out. *Worked out* is the operative phrase because, as my wife and I have both learned, marriage is a work in progress. And progress it has been. With Elaine's unwavering support in good times and bad, I'm a better man for the experience.

Ups and downs were not what we looked forward to after returning from our honeymoon in 1969. But the roller-coaster ride has always been manageable. I can assure you that what goes up must come down but then very likely will go up again. Sort of like *two steps forward, one step back*. The hard part is remembering that there is an upside just around the corner. The challenge is the journey it takes to get to the corner.

There are a lot of self-help books and programs to help with this lifelong turmoil. However, if you keep focused on the "next" rather than the "last," you will find strength and courage to continue. Your faith is important because it's what helps you see (and perhaps around) that next corner.

Early marriage found us both still in school, but we made a decision that I would quit full-time work to finish my college engineering degree. Although I didn't know it at the time, I learned that Elaine was very fearful of this step because she grew up with stories of wives who supported their husband's college degree pursuit only to be served with divorce papers. I'm thankful that she had the faith to let this part of our life story play out.

I had no sooner graduated from college, expecting to get a good job to pay back the student loans (and other debts that arrived during the academic pursuits), that the first of the next generation appeared on the horizon. That was to be expected, although not so soon. Then the real challenge arrived: a son with a bilateral cleft lip and palate. What a shock—a new baby that couldn't come home right away due to the birth defect. I think our son has occasionally struggled with his problem, especially after multiple surgeries to work on repairs. But the bottom line is that we did survive the shock, and our son has grown up to be a responsible adult (not always an easy challenge in today's world).

Two daughters later, we managed to discover the solution for our expanding family. This came in part because Elaine finally decided that, unlike her initial enthusiasm for a large brood, she was ready to work on what we already had rather than what might be.

Somewhere along the way we started our small business. That came about because we were still working through challenges of number-one son and a new home with a mortgage while Elaine was a stay-at-home mom out of necessity.

For several weeks I read (and reread) an ad in our local, twice-a-week newspaper for part-time tax preparers. I am naturally a do-it-yourself (DYI) type, and I finally called. The first challenge: They wanted the vast sum of seventy-five dollars to take the tax preparer course.

Fortunately, they were quite willing to let me make two payments to get started. The rest, as they say, is history. I took the course and knew, without a doubt, that being a tax preparer is what I wanted to do with my professional life. It was slow at first, more of a hobby than a business. But I was enthralled with the process. You name it, I read it. I disrupted more conversations by explaining my recent education and found that many people really wanted help with their taxes, and that fanned the flame.

Now, forty-two tax seasons later (and counting), I consider myself very fortunate to have found a career that I love as well as rely on for an income. I'm sure there will be a time that I'll have to set the career aside. But right now, you'd have a hard time tearing me away.

I love this job!

———————————

It all started in 1976 when **Chuck Woodson** enrolled in a basic training class for tax preparers sponsored by Tax Corporation of America (TCA). Thus began a saga spanning four decades. His office is centrally located in San Diego. Chuck served as the 1991 president of the San Diego Chapter of the California Society of Tax Consultants (CSTC). He specializes in trust and estate tax income tax returns (the infamous 1041) and has taught beginning and intermediate-level tax preparation workshops. Chuck's family consists of his wife, Elaine, one son, two daughters, a grandson, and multiple grandchildren and great-grand-children.

www.HorizonPlanning.com

I Beat Sugar

Donald Wright

In the African-American community, diabetes is often called sugar diabetes or just sugar. A person may say "he has sugar," meaning the person has diabetes. "Having sugar" is often a slow boat to a life of debilitating illness and often death from diabetes-related issues. Complications along the way may include and are not limited to limb amputations; blindness; kidney problems and dialysis; high blood pressure; obesity; heart disease; impotency and stroke. To beat sugar is to win your health back and reverse diabetes! YES, I beat sugar!

When my doctor announced that I had diabetes, the dreaded sugar, my wife sat grim-faced. The words hit me like a hard belly punch, nearly knocking the wind out of me. My mind screamed "Oh no, not sugar!"

Horrified thoughts and memories rushed in and swirled through my mind. Just months before my beloved mother had died from diabetes complications. The year before my brother had died from diabetes complications. While in high school, my grandmother died from diabetes complications. The black-and-white photograph of my sweet, bedridden Mama Dear popped into my head. She is a brown obese, bacon slab of a woman barely fitting into her bed. Her face is contorted into a painful grimace.

My eighty-four year-old father is slim and has diabetes. A few years ago, he was erratic and talking out of his head and had to be physically subdued. He was transported to the emergency room. In a grave voice, the doctor said to my wife, Brenda, "His glucose levels are very high. His blood chemistry is out of normal range. He will be lucky if he makes it."

LUCKY IF HE MAKES IT! The words echoed in my head. Six of us nine siblings have diabetes. My eighty-four-year-old father-in-law died of diabetes complications. This once-proud, six foot, four inch dark-skinned, extremely strong, hardworking and vital father of twelve lay in a home hospital bed suffering from diabetes and a paralyzing stroke. As Brenda washed-up her father, he sadly said, "I used to be a man." My father-in-law got diabetes when he was seventy-nine years old. My mom had diabetes since she was thirty-five years old. I was fifty-nine years old. Was it my turn to experience, like my mother, forty years of declining health and ever-increasing debilitating medical issues?

Like coming out of a fog, my consciousness returned to the doctor's office. I heard my wife and doctor mumbling something about attending a weight loss class. My doctor issued a pill prescription to help my body use glucose better. I remembered that at first, my mother took one pill and then ended up injecting insulin at least three times a day.

True, for a while my doctor had been saying that I was prediabetic, borderline diabetic. She said my BMI was too high and my A1C was increasing, but I didn't really know what that meant or how to get those numbers to decrease.

After we walked out my wife said, "You know you can reverse sugar."

"Reverse sugar?" I questioned.

I decided that I would reverse sugar. I did not want to die from diabetic complications. I did not want to die obese and disease-weakened like my mom and grandmother. I am highly motivated to make the lifestyle changes to beat sugar.

I wholeheartedly began the journey of lifestyle change. My mind was made up.

Lifestyle changes included sleeping more than three hours; to exercise; to relish the joys in my life; to pray and to express gratitude to God for his blessings.

I let go of the bad foods. No fried food. Meats were baked, boiled, or stewed. No burnt animal fat. No sugars. I changed from relaxing with a half-gallon of ice cream and a spoon while enjoying my favorite DVD movie. Goodbye moon pies; goodbye candy. Goodbye sodas and sweet sugary drinks. Goodbye deli meat—bologna, salami, pastrami; these meats have a lot of nitrates and nitrites. Goodbye oils and salad dressings. Goodbye gluten: wheat, rye, barely, and oats.

Gluten interferes with absorption and is inflammatory. It significantly raises blood sugar. It effects the endocrine and hormonal systems. It causes intestinal sludge and blockage.

I developed new healthy food favorite recipes: delicious tomato salsa with tomatoes, onions, and garlic and other vegetables. My sisters eat it by the spoonful. I cook a five-greens mix which my wife calls "greenie greens." As I incorporated good foods into my diet, my taste changed and now, I appreciate flavors that I didn't like or eat before.

A key thing I learned is that one must properly supplement with minerals, vitamins, and essential fatty acids, for life, regardless of eating plan. Nutritional deficiencies are the root causes of many diseases Also, you cannot routinely eat bad foods and then take enough supplements to compensate. Doctors have known since the 1950s that diabetes develops when two specific minerals are lacking. Could it be that your doctor is withholding or telling you information which is not true? The Bible says the truth will set you free. The truth allowed me to beat sugar.

In 2017 I lost forty pounds and have kept it off for two years. I lost ten more pounds from 2018 to 2019. In 2017, my doctor told me that my blood work showed I was no longer diabetic! Yes! My wife and I were all smiles. I beat sugar! No more sugar pills. No more finger pricks. I found that I can add in some old favorites from time to time. Yes, ice cream—but not a whole half-gallon at one sitting. Bad eating and bad lifestyle can bring back sugar.

To find information and recipes on line how I beat sugar, visit www.Ibeatit.life. You can call Donald at 424.206.3232 or 1.800.567.7847. My email is donsgotit4u@yahoo.com.

Donald Wright is passionate about sharing how to prevent and reverse diabetes. A student of health and wellness and medical missionary-trained, he has a BS in biology from Loma Linda University, Loma Linda, California. He is an organic gardener and accomplished natural food chief. As a coach, Wright mentored inner city youth for twenty-six years using sports as the vehicle. He also does residential construction. Married nearly forty years to the former Brenda Taylor, they have four adult children and four young terrific grandchildren. They reside in Altadena, California.

WHEN LIFE GETS BLURRY, ADJUST YOUR FOCUS

Lori Zapata

Funny, one of my favorite quotes is: "If I could tell my story in words, I wouldn't lug around this camera" (Lewis Hines). Yet, here I am again, a photographer, writing my story in words.

Writing is healing. It compels you to look deep into your soul, you learn things about yourself, and you grow. Hopefully we all are constantly learning and growing; it is an important part of our journey through life. If you try to look at your most difficult moments as a lesson you need to learn, sometimes that can help you through it. I learn and grow by writing about my life experiences. However, I also learn and grow through taking photographs. Sometimes I learn more from the bad photographs I take than the good. That reminds me of another favorite quote: "Never regret a day in your life. Good days give you happiness and bad days give you experience." So true, and I've had a lot of experience!

I became a professional photographer during a difficult time in my life. I had to leave a lucrative job that I loved, and then my mom passed away suddenly. If that wasn't enough, I had also been dealing with an extremely debilitating and rare chronic pain condition for years. Then it all came to a screeching halt with the news that I was diagnosed with ovarian cancer. What is it they say? "When it rains, it pours." Well it was pouring buckets, and it was hard to remember that this must be another life lesson—and it just can't rain all the time, can it?

We can't always control what life throws at us, but we do have control over how we react to it. When bad things happen, we often feel FEAR. Well think about the word F-E-A-R as "You can Forget Everything And Run" or "You can Face Everything And Recover." It's your choice. Feel free to take a day, or two, to cry and take it all in. Crying is healing. Even science tells us that tears remove toxins from our bodies. So by all means cry and cry and cry. "Never underestimate the healing power of a good pity party" (Lori Zapata). I don't remember how many days I cried. I just knew that I wasn't finished with this life and I had to fight hard and just believe. I would tell myself, "I'll be okay, just not today!" (I'm sure it's obvious by now that I love quotes.) Another favorite of mine is "Rain falls because the clouds can no longer handle the weight. Tears fall because the heart can no longer handle the pain." We all need to release that pain when we feel it. After all, "Life is like photography; we develop from the negatives." Give yourself permission to feel bad for a bit, then get up and get back to it.

There had been so much happening without the cancer, but none of that was life-threatening. Had I not faced the fear of dying, I don't know if I would have chosen photography as my next career. I had always been a photographer. I had been taking photographs since I was old enough to hold a camera, though I never thought about doing it for a living. When I left my big corporate job, I initially thought about applying for a similar opportunity with another corporation, another office job. However, when faced with life being cut short, I realized I needed to do something that I loved, something I was passionate about. In all my previous careers, I had dedicated my time, my hard work, and my life to someone else's dream—what about my dreams?

What do you dream about doing? Is your voice telling you that you can't? What about the voices around you? Many of the people in our lives tell us we can't. Sometimes subconsciously they don't want us to live our dreams because then they may have to look back at why they didn't follow their's. I've heard it all, and you will too. Don't listen, face your fears and do something you love. Ralph Waldo Emerson said, "What we fear doing most is usually what we most need to do." I needed to be a photographer. I needed to be my own boss this time and work for my dreams.

Now I did choose photography, but in many ways, photography chose me. I have always been moved deeply by photographs; they fill me with so many emotions. I feel as though I see life through a lens. Everywhere I go, I look around and try to find something that would make a great photograph. I also try to find things that others would overlook and never see at all. I've been on many photography outings with other photographers, and I am always amazed at the difference in our photographs, all taken at the exact same place and time. We all see different things, and we all see things differently. That is the beauty of life.

We take photos so we can return to moments otherwise gone. "A photograph is the pause button of life." Don't let all your photos live in your phone or computer. Print them, enjoy them, share them. Hire me to take them! "Life is a journey, not a destination," so highlight the beautiful moments of your journey with photographs printed and displayed around you. I practice what I preach—my problem is that I don't have enough wall space to display all I would love to display. I think I may start a "rotating art for the seasons" thing, so I can display and enjoy more photographs. Surround yourself with photographs of your best memories; they will help you through those moments when it rains again. "For without rain nothing grows, so learn to embrace the storms in your life." Then, "when life gives you rainy days, wear cute boots and jump in the puddles."

If you haven't already guessed, I also learn through quotes. Quotes have gotten me through a lot, and I am happy to say that today I am cancer-free! Quotes are a great way of refocusing us when we get off track. So focus on the lessons to be learned, focus on the beauty in your life, and focus on your dreams, because "today is the perfect day to start living your dreams." So go live your dreams and "when life gets blurry, adjust your focus"!

Lori Zapata says that photography is who she is and the thing that she's sure will drive her insane one day, as she forever searches for candid moments happening in perfect natural light. Writing and speaking about her journey keeps her sane. Her photography work can been seen in the *Chicago Tribune, New York Hockey Journal,* Linda Eder's CDs, and other publications. Her writing can be found in the bestselling books *Women Who Rock* and *Rock Your Life.* Being Mom to two amazing young men is her greatest joy in life.

www.LoriZapata.com